The Roma

A 174-mile triangular walk following Roman roads through Oxfordshire, Gloucestershire, Wiltshire, Hampshire and Berkshire using public rights of way.

Elaine Steane

Illustrated by
John Steane

2010

For my parents, who led me to delight in the natural world

REARDON PUBLISHING
PO Box 919,
Cheltenham, GL50 9AN
Website: www.reardon.co.uk
Email: reardon@bigfoot.com
Tel: 01242 231800

ISBN 9781874192022

Written by Elaine Steane

Illustrations by John Steane

Book production by Marion Stockton
Publishing Services

Printed on 50% recycled paper by
Information Press, Oxford

Acknowledgements

The theme of Roman Roads has been the inspiration for this project and my thanks go to my core team of walkers, all of us members of the Ramblers, who have provided the 'footmen'. We have made new discoveries, walked across ancient landscapes and enjoyed the camaraderie won from days out together on the open road.

It was Robin Harrison's idea for the team to tackle this triangular route following Roman roads. He, John & Connie Beasley, John Eyre, Brian & Jean Hackett and Judy Westgate contributed mapping skills and historical research, and together we completed the first circuit.

The initial walk of the 174 miles called for careful checking by fresh eyes. Bruce Howard, Irene Davison, Mike Hotchkiss, Sonia Nash, Russell Summers, Phoebe Chandler, Jean Hall, Tony & Pam Dale, Shaun & Liz O'Sullivan, Tony & Lesley Lewis and Ann Truesdale have all walked parts of the route to provide quality control.

In addition, we have benefited from the expertise of Paul Booth, Ebehard Sauer, Mogs Boon and Bernard Phillips (archaeology); Philip Powell and Alan Cobb (geology); David Viner and Robina Rand (history); Ian Gourlay, Vic Austin and Mike Willson (natural history). Museum staff, Rights of Way representatives, Sites and Monuments officers and the MoD have answered queries, whilst local people 'en route' have all enriched the detail and accuracy of the description.

Back at home, Melanie Fyson and Lizzie Ruffell typed the first drafts. My mother Nancy Fullard, Brian Dix, David Godfrey, Jean Hackett, Ros Muston, Janet Redfern, Penelope Ward, Stella Welford, the late Trevor Welham, Jenny Knight and Holly Welham have all read the text and have made valuable comments. Judy Dendy together with Jane Ivimey and Christine Sekulla have undertaken the final editing.

Thanks are due to Marion Stockton for her skilled project management and book production, Gerard Little for the maps, and publisher, Nicholas Reardon.

A special tribute to my husband, John Steane, for capturing the idiosyncrasies, historical detail and humour in his illustrations.

Elaine Steane – December 2009

Care for the Countryside

Please respect the Country Code in the following ways:

- Enjoy the route, but keep to the rights of way.
- Close all gates and avoid damage to crops. Please keep away from farm animals.
- To avoid disturbance to wildlife or farm animals, keep your dog under close control at all times, preferably on a lead through fields with animals in. (**N.B.** if you are being harassed by cattle, it may be safer only in this circumstance to let the dog off the lead).
- Please take all your litter home. It looks unsightly and can be dangerous to wildlife and farm animals.
- Take extra care on country roads. Walk on the right side except round blind corners.
- If travelling by car to rendezvous points, please park carefully in order not to obstruct gateways or cause a danger to other road users. (Access points are places along the route where facilities and car parking space is available for the option of a shorter walk.)
- **Be prepared!** Carry a compass (all the map sections in the guide are north orientated). A pair of binoculars is useful to 'spy out' distant waymark signs. Always carry a rucksack with some warm and waterproof clothing, plenty of water, a flask of hot liquid in winter, and sun protection in the form of a hat, long-sleeved shirt and sun-screen for summer.

Key to the OS maps

Route of the Roman road

Route of the walk

Presumed route of the Roman road

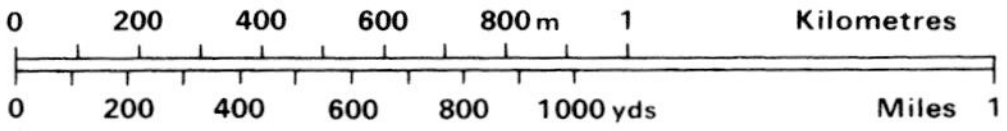

Scale 1:25 000 or $2\frac{1}{2}$ inches to 1 mile

Contents

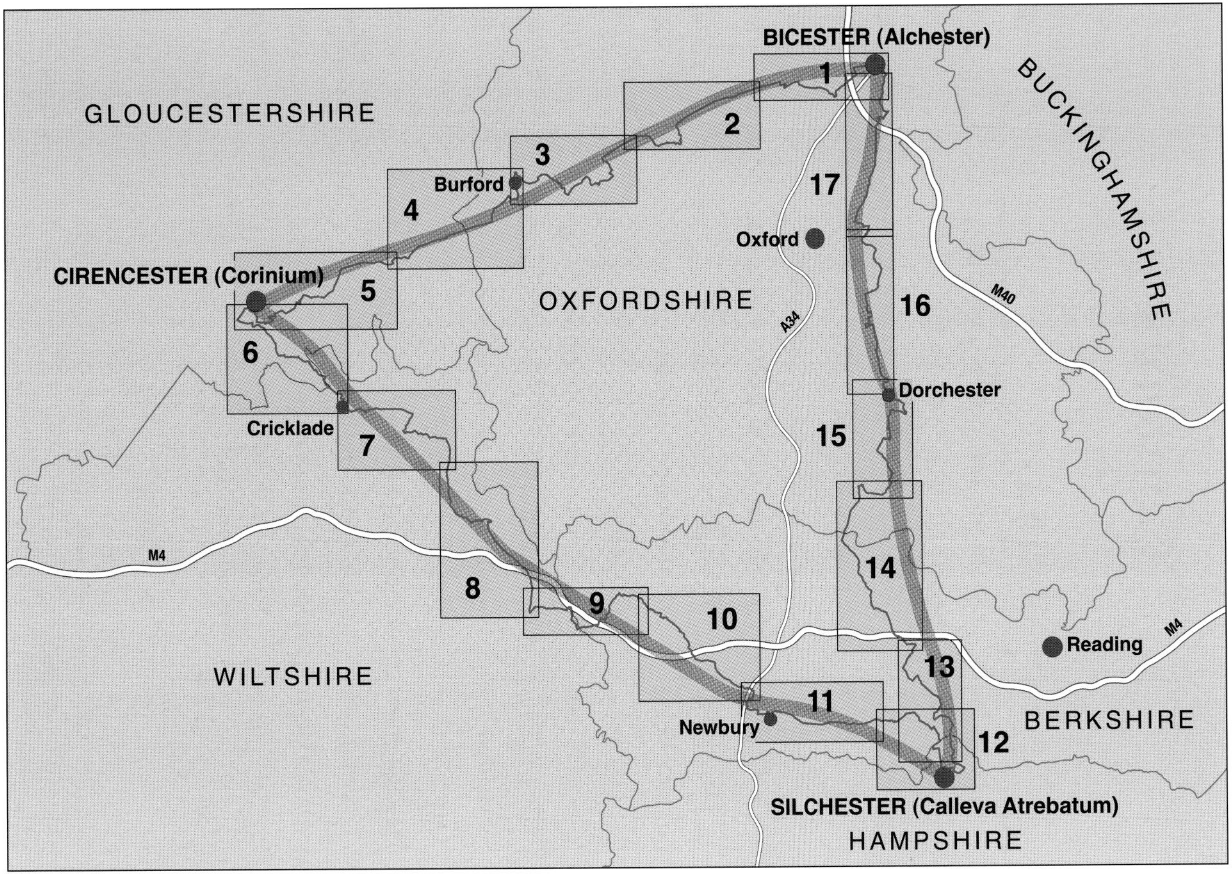
BICESTER (Alchester)
BUCKINGHAMSHIRE
GLOUCESTERSHIRE
Burford
Oxford
CIRENCESTER (Corinium)
OXFORDSHIRE
M40
A34
Dorchester
Cricklade
M4
Reading
WILTSHIRE
Newbury
BERKSHIRE
SILCHESTER (Calleva Atrebatum)
HAMPSHIRE
1
2
3
4
5
6
7
8
9
10
11
12
13
14
15
16
17

Roman Roads

The Romans have left many traces of their presence and activities in the countryside of Britain. These include the sites of farms and (in the highland zone particularly) forts. But it is their roads for which they are justly famed that still attract most attention in the modern landscape.

Roman roads were military in origin, having been pioneered in the early years of conquest to further the penetration of the province by the legions. They served to facilitate reinforcements, patrolling, observation and they gave the island a new unity by breaking through previously impenetrable belts of forest, marsh and mountain. They would have been laid out by legionary surveyors, but actually constructed either by troops or prisoners of war or by labour from conquered tribes.

The maintenance of these routes was the responsibility of the provincial government who provided rest houses (mansiones – places to stay overnight) and posting stations (mutationes – places for changing horses) for the use of travelling imperial officers. As the province settled down to stable periods of peace they served as communications for commercial purposes, each regional capital being linked to the rest, part of a national network.

The Romans started building the roads soon after their invasion in AD 43 and quickly advanced to the Fosse Way in Gloucestershire, which became the frontier running between Exeter and Lincoln in about AD 47. The use of Alchester (OE ald-caester) as a legionary camp dates from roughly this period, and ended before AD 71. This camp was strategically placed at the junction of five Roman roads that connected three of the most important towns in Roman Britain, Londinium, Verulamium (St. Albans) and Aquae Sulis (literally the waters of the goddess Sulis) or Bath which is its modern name. The name Akeman Street meant the road to Bath, and is derived from the Anglo-Saxon for Bath, Acemannesceastre.

It is doubtful whether there were many maps in existence, though during the Roman occupation, 'road books' of Britain were created. The village of Speen (Spinis, see page 117) was included in the Antonine Itinerary, the first to be written. Hugh Davis, in his book *Roads in Roman Britain*, describes the basic techniques used by the legionary surveyors to build the roads. They set up markers on high or open ground, aligning poles with an instrument called a groma. The men first dug a drainage ditch at either side of the route, then piled the spoil in between to create an embankment or agger. On top of this linear embankment, a foundation of large stones was laid, then a layer of compacted smaller stones, gravel and flint (see Day 2, page 13). Heavily travelled roads and town streets had a topping of paving stones with kerbstones. A cambered surface for good drainage finished the road to provide a carriage way sufficiently wide for carts and other vehicles to pass each other (about 15–20 feet across). Milestones were erected and sometimes carved with the names of the emperor or road builders.

A day's march for a Roman legion was seven hours at 100 steps a minute, and usually covered 15 to 20 Roman miles. This Roman mile was calculated in passus (paces). A pace was the length of five pedes (feet) and was in fact a double pace measured from left foot to left foot (5.3 feet in length). The word mile comes from a thousand paces, mille passus and was therefore shorter (1,611 yards) than the modern statute mile (1,760 yards). At the end of the day there were no cosy teashops, pubs or B&Bs; instead, Roman soldiers set about digging latrines and a defensive ditch around their camp, then using the two stakes (pila muralia), each 7 foot long, that they had carried all day to form a fence. Life was not too comfortable: vivid accounts from Hadrian's Wall include the request to "send more socks", and many other examples can be found on various websites.

John Steane
Elaine Steane
David Godfrey

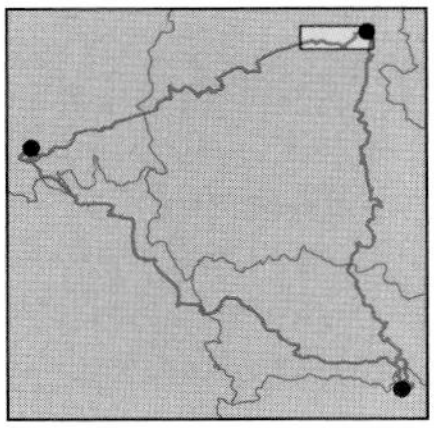

Day 1

Chesterton to Sturdy's Castle

Chesterton GR SP 560213 to Sturdy's Castle Inn, near Kidlington GR SP 463193

We start the walk at Chesterton. This is likely to have been a Roman station nearby to the military fort at Alchester and we begin marching along one of the main Roman roads, Akeman Street. Now, the motorised traffic takes advantage of the straightness of the road, so we take a footpath route south-west across the quiet agricultural land to Weston-on-the-Green. The route-finding needs careful attention, so we recommend allowing extra time for this. Once on the distinctive agger of Akeman Street, it is an easy way to Sturdy's Castle.

Distance: 8.5 miles (13.6 km).

Maps: Explorer 191 – Banbury, Bicester and Chipping Norton.
Explorer 180 – Oxford, Witney and Woodstock.
Landranger 164 – Oxford.

Transport:

Trains
- Bicester and Tackley – www.nationalrail.co.uk

Buses
- Bicester/Wendlebury/Chesterton/Kirtlington/Bletchingdon/Oxford, 25/25A.
- Oxford/Tackley, 59/59A.
- Tackley/Sturdy's Castle, 201.
Traveline – Tel: 0871 200 2233. www.traveline.org.uk

Taxis:

Bicester
- Alpha Cars. Tel: 01869 252552.
- Union Cars. Tel: 01869 325325/248248.

Kidlington
- Sunny Cars. Tel: 01865 373300 or 07900 125321.

Woodstock
- Travel Taxis. Tel: 01993 891888.

Car Parking: Chesterton – Chestnut Close, Fortescue Drive or residential side roads 120 yards west of The Red Cow pub along Green Lane.
Tackley – Sturdy's Castle Inn. Car parking (with prior permission – Tel: 01869 331328) in the car park north of the inn beside A4260 road.

Accommodation/Public Houses/Refreshments:

Bicester
- Bicester Visitor Centre. Tel: 01869 369055. www.visit-northoxfordshire.co.uk

Chesterton
- The Bicester Country Club. Tel: 01869 241204.
- Bignell Park Hotel. Tel: 01869 326550.
- The Red Cow PH. Tel: 01869 241337.
- The Garden House B&B. Tel: 01869 250271.

Weston-on-the Green – www.wotg.org.uk
- The Ben Jonson PH. Tel: 01869 351153.
- Weston Grounds Farm B&B. Tel: 01869 351168.
- Westfield Court House, North Lane. Tel: 01869 350777.
- Village Stores. Tel: 01869 350230.

Kirtlington
- Vicarage Farm B&B. Tel: 01869 350254.
- The Oxford Arms PH and Restaurant. Tel: 01869 350208. www.oxford-arms.co.uk
- The Dashwood Hotel and Restaurant. Tel: 01869 352707. www.thedashwood.co.uk
- Mill Lane Farm at Pigeon's Lock sells ice-creams, cakes, cream teas and coffee on Sundays only, 12–6pm. (Advance booking required for groups). Tel: 07837 362683 or 01869 350501.

Tackley
- Gardiner Arms PH. Tel: 01869 331266.
- Sturdy's Castle Inn, Banbury Road. Tel: 01869 331328. www.sturdyscastle.com

Woodstock
- Woodstock Visitor Information Centre and teashop. (Situated in the museum, 2.5 miles off route, GR 444167). Tel: 01993 813276.
- www.oxfordshirecotswolds.org for information on B&Bs and pubs.

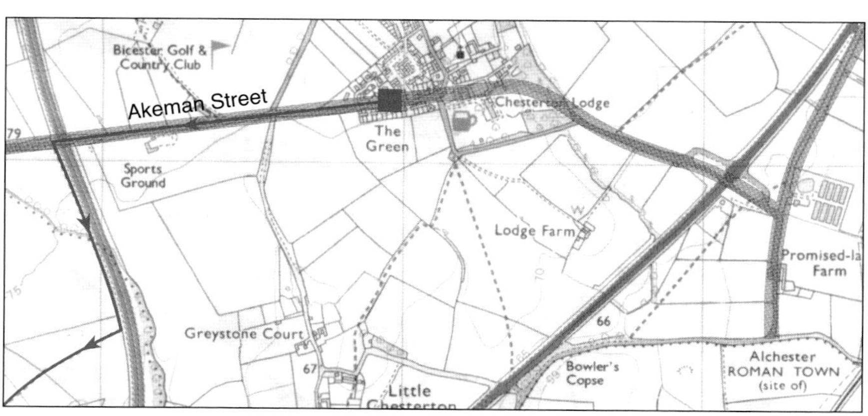

Chesterton is named from the Old English for Chester, as Ceaster means a Roman station or settlement alongside the Roman road, the 'ton' part of the word means farm.
Margary, in his vivid and detailed 1973 account, describes this stretch of Akeman Street as "a fine specimen raised 2–4 feet on an agger generally 30 feet wide". Agger is Latin for a raised linear mound or bank made of earth and stones on which Roman roads were built.

Construction of a Roman road

Turn right (W) out of Fortescue Drive away from the Red Cow pub to begin walking along Akeman Street (now Green Lane). Beware of fast traffic on the straight road.

As the cars sped by, we enjoyed spotting the diversity of butterflies and flowers in the hedgerows in July.

Cross the minor road and keep walking (W) to cross the M40, then turn immediately left (S) onto a footpath signed 'Weston 2'. Descend the steps and follow the fence on the west side of the motorway. The original timber fence has been increased in height to prevent deer from jumping onto the motorway.

Walk along beside the motorway (S) to the end of the second field where there is a waymark sign. Here, bear right (242°). At the far side, only 60 yards from the north-west corner, there is a concealed bridge and stile in the hedgerow (much nearer the northern field corner than shown on the map).

Butterflies and arable weeds

When we walked along beside Akeman Street, then along the hedgerows, there was a great variety of butterflies: gatekeepers feeding on the bramble flowers, hedge browns and ringlets on the grasses and red admirals on the teasel flowerheads. Black and white marbled whites were on the scabious flowers, large whites on the arable weeds and red admirals feeding on the thistles. The vivid black and yellow striped caterpillars of the cinnabar moth were feeding on the flowers of the ragwort. The agricultural weeds included flowers such as scarlet pimpernel, fumitory, shepherd's purse, field pansies, speedwell, chamomile, fat hen, groundsel and the striking yellow and orange toadflax.

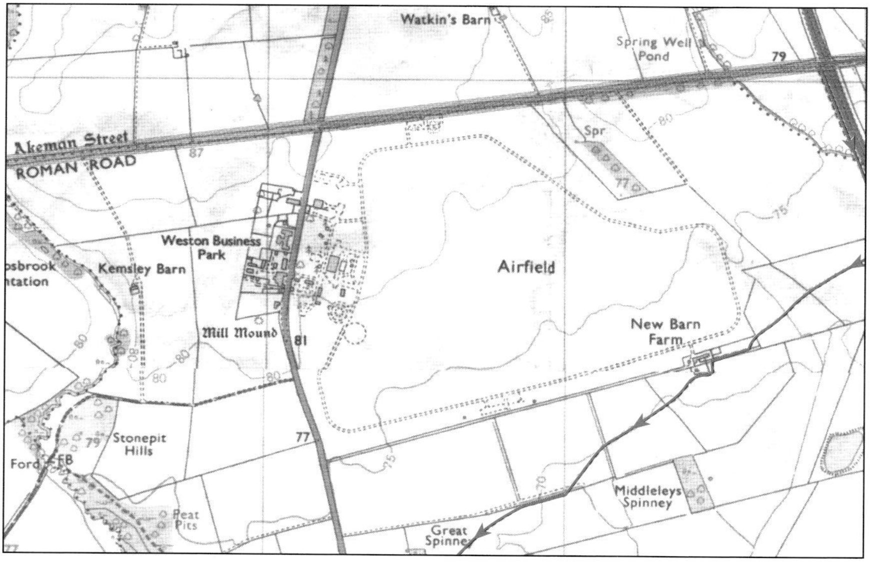

Cross the next small field in nearly the same direction (228°) to go over a stile and bridge into the third field from the motorway. Bear slightly more left (210°) to the stile at the left (S) end of the hedgerow on the far side. The stile is about 20 yards right of a metal field gate in the corner of the field (just right of a pole supporting overhead electric wires).

Cross the stile and the paddocks lengthways (SW), to go through the central gate to the far left corner before the farm buildings. Cross two stiles and into the garden of New Barn Farm.

Weston-on-the-Green airfield
While crossing the field, the Weston-on-the-Green airfield comes into view to the right. The orange windsock flying from the top of a pole gives not only the direction of the wind, but also an indication of the strength by the angle it makes to the ground. If it is horizontal, the wind speed is more than 15 knots. This airfield, built for World War I, with its perimeter track is now mainly used for aerial sporting activities: mostly gliding and free-fall parachuting.

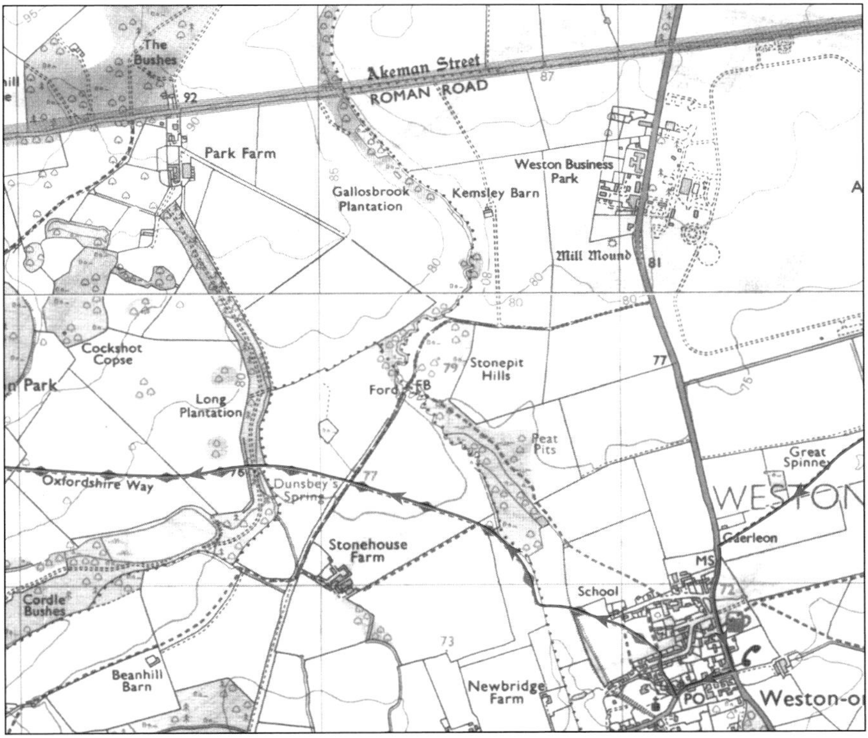

Follow the gravel drive left and cross the stile in the fence (S) of the drive. Bear right (225°) across the corner of the field, and over a stile and bridge. Cross the next field (215°) aiming for a bridge and stile half way along the opposite hedge.

Continue in nearly the same direction (225°) cutting across the left corner of the field (SW) aiming right of a group of poplar trees in the hedge. Cross a bridge through the hedgerow, turn sharp right and follow the edge of the field (SW) keeping the hedge on the right. 100 yards before a large gap in the hedge, a path bears diagonally left away from the hedge (227°).

Cross the field to aim for a gap in the far hedge. Keep left of Great Spinney, the clump of trees in the centre of the field. Go through the gap, turn right, and bear right (235°), again cutting across the corner of the field to a gap in the far hedge to meet the B430 road at a fingerpost.

The house name 'Caerleon' on the map marks the Roman associations here, since Caerleon means 'camp of the legions' in Old Welsh.

Turn left (S), to **Weston-on-the-Green**, passing a restored milestone 'Brackley 12, Oxford 9' on the right.

If the busy traffic allows on this dangerous road, it is worth examining a leaf of one of the reeds of the village pond, to see how the leaf is attached. Reed leaves grow from one ligule (flap between the stem and leaf) down, so that they can swivel in the wind, thus reducing resistance and therefore damage to the leaf.

At the old oak tree, turn right (W) into North Lane, then left (S) in front of Prospect House, where there were house martins nesting under the eaves and masonry bees in the soft lime plaster between the stones. Pass the Ben Jonson pub on the right (Ben Jonson worked at the Oxford court as a judge). There is a farmhouse on the right with its original dovecote in the gable wall. Pass a bus stop. Then, at the village green with the village stocks, turn right (SW) into Church Road, past the Old Forge and the village stores.

Stocks, Weston-on-the-Green

Access Point: Weston-on-the-Green church, 3.0 miles. Shop, B&Bs, telephone. GR 531186.

St. Mary's Church dates from the eleventh century, though there could have been a wattle and daub church on the site before that. The church was given to one of the richest abbeys; Oseney Abbey, and Weston Manor was purchased by the Abbey in 1227. In January, the whole churchyard was covered in drifts of snowdrops.

On approaching the church, bear right into Mill Lane and immediately turn sharp right before the village hall (N) along the Oxfordshire Way footpath that we follow all the way to Sturdy's Castle. Enter the drive to Walnut Tree Cottage, then at the road servicing the bungalows, dog-leg right and left along the side of number 22.

Go through the kissing gate, then diagonally left between the wooden posts. Some of the original thatched cottages on the north side of the village can be seen. At the branch of the paths, keep left to go across a hay meadow, where there are remains of medieval ridge and furrow cultivation on the left.

It is sometimes possible to see the different vegetation on the dry ridges (thistles) and the damp furrows (sedge).

At the hedge, go through another kissing gate beside a metal gate and left over a concrete bridge. This is Gallos Brook, a tributary of the River Ray. Go diagonally right over the next narrow field.

All this land is low-lying and is not drained, so it provides a wet habitat for plants such as sedge.

Cross the plank bridge through a small metal gate to turn right alongside the wood on the right. Go through a metal gate and a small wood where there are good examples of hazel coppicing. Cross the corner of the next field to the hedge gap.

Go diagonally left (290°) to meet a crossing bridleway. Dog-leg right and left across the bridleway after the hedge gap. Cross the field diagonally left (280°) to go through a wood and over a stream from Dunsbey's Spring, then ahead (W) beside a wire netting fence on the left.

In the rough pasture in July, the purple of the creeping thistle flowers, and mauve of the great and rosebay willowherb flowers glowed in the sunshine.

Go through a gap in the fence to cross the next field in the same direction. Kirtlington Park house, in Palladian style, can be seen to the right, with its balustraded staircase and stable blocks with cupolas.

Palladian architecture is a classical style drawn from the buildings of ancient Rome. The house has a fine unobscured view (SE) to the lake.

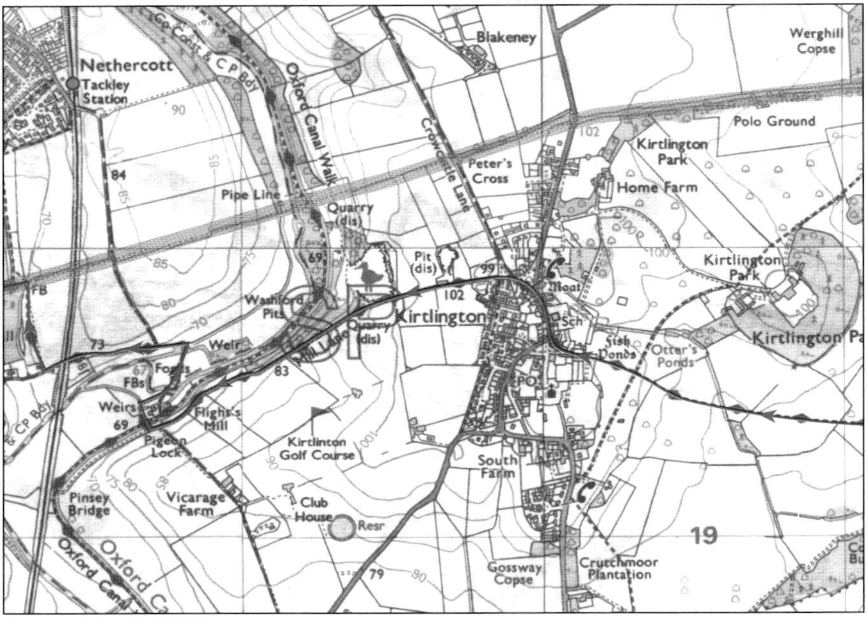

Continue in the same direction (256°) left (W) of two circular copses.

This footpath is part of a conservation walk managed by the Countryside Service with the aim of enhancing the wildlife interest. The grasslands are managed by traditional sheep grazing and there is restoration of the stone walls. The antlered oak trees here are part of the original parkland landscaped by Capability Brown in 1760.

Antlered oak, Kirtlington Park

Go across the park in the same direction (280°), over a plank bridge between a pair of gates to bear right (290°) to walk up the slope towards the village of **Kirtlington**, aiming for the gabled house. Go through the kissing gate and the village hall car park is to the left.

Access Point: Kirtlington Village Hall car park, 5.1 miles. Pubs, shop, post office, telephone. GR 501196.

Go along the tarmac road to bear right beside the triangular green. (The Oxford Arms and shop are 100 yards to the left.) Turn right (N) along the main road at the Dashwood Hotel.

This is a reminder that the Dashwood family, a branch of the famous family at West Wycombe Park, were the former owners of Kirtlington Park and the estate village.

At another triangular green, bear left at the telephone box and follow the track (W) along Mill Lane (the Oxfordshire Way).

This lane passes Kirtlington Quarry where the limestone beds, 168 million years old, have yielded a wealth of fossils including bones of a giant dinosaur. The stone provided the raw material for cement, and would have been transported by barge from the wharf beside the lock.

Continue along Mill Lane until reaching the bridge of the Oxford Canal and Pigeon's Lock. Cross the bridge, join the footpath (N) away from the canal, turn right to cross the weir bridge, and follow the footpath (N) crossing two channels of the River Cherwell.

There were water forget-me-nots and azure damsel flies here in July.

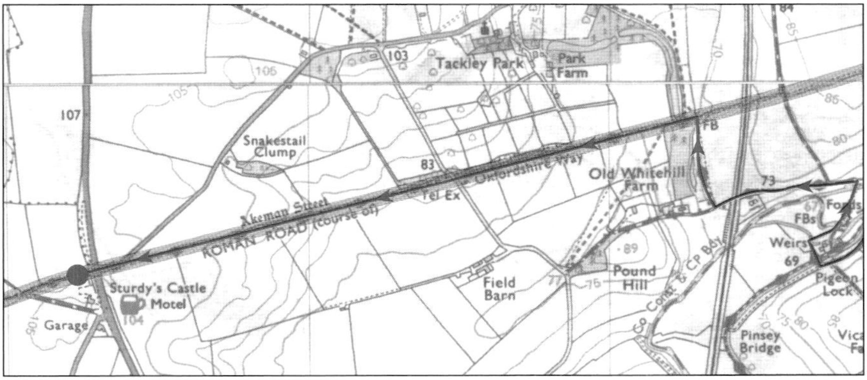

Turn sharp left (W) along the path. Ignore the bridleway (NW) with signs to **Tackley** village shop to continue following the route of the Oxfordshire Way under the railway. Just past the railway bridge, turn right onto the footpath (N) before Old Whitehill Farm (a deserted medieval village).

In the field to the right is a habitat creation project, Operation Bumblebee, designed to increase the numbers of bumblebees by 600 times within two years. This can be achieved by making a patchwork of pollen and nectar areas on low yielding farmland or hedge banks. Red clover and white dead-nettle are particularly rich food sources for bumblebees.

Go through a hedge gap over a bank. This is Akeman Street running east/west. It is worth looking back at the distinct agger (bank). Turn immediately left (W) over a small brook, up a slope, over a stile and along the agger. The route now follows the raised agger of the Roman road with ancient laid ash trees and Cotswold stone walls.

The composition of the agger

It was here that Margary describes how "a small piece of the agger was examined and found to be 12 feet wide, composed of a top layer of small pieces of yellow limestone packed in clay, 3–4 inches thick at the sides, but almost lacking in the centre, upon a layer of 6-inch thick slabs of the same limestone, under which was a foundation layer of white limestone much mixed with clay and brushwood".

Cross a minor road to walk in the same direction for nearly 0.75 miles to join a minor road that meets the A4260.

The agger is wide and low and on it was a delightful mixture of wild flowers. We saw mauve scabious and nodding thistle, white yarrow, hedge bedstraw and bladder campion, yellow lady's bedstraw, purple knapweed, flowering plantain, the green fruit of wild hop and cow parsley covered with bright orange beetles.

At the road, turn left to the busy A4260 and cross it with care to Sturdy's Castle car park. The bridleway waymark for the start of Day 2 can be seen. The inn's sign shows a wrestling pair as it was a fight over land that gave the pub its name: it was Sturdy who won!

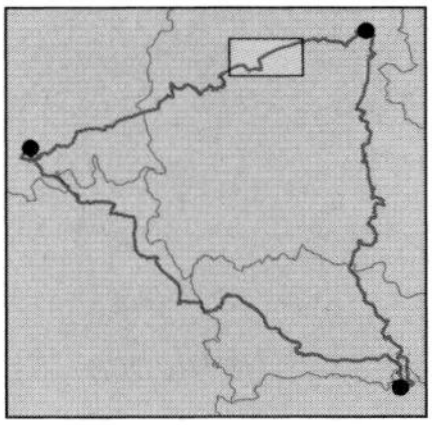

Day 2

Sturdy's Castle to Ramsden

Sturdy's Castle Inn GR SP 463193 to Ramsden GR SP 357152

We follow the agger to pass Sansom's Platt, a settlement within easy marching distance from Alchester. We then cross the great park of Blenheim Palace to Stonesfield. Stonesfield was the site where the very first description of a dinosaur was made. We travel on to the North Leigh Roman villa and pass through a Roman roadside trading centre at Wilcote to reach the village of Ramsden.

Distance: 9 miles (14.4 km).

Maps: Explorer 180 – Oxford, Witney & Woodstock.
Landranger 164 – Oxford & surrounding area.

Transport: Buses
- Ramsden/Witney, 69.
  Traveline – Tel: 0871 200 2233. www.traveline.org.uk

Taxis:
- Kidlington • Sunny Cars. Tel: 01865 373300 or 07900 125321.
- Woodstock • Travel Taxis. Tel: 01993 891888.
- Ramsden • Safe-ride. Tel: 01993 868226.

Car Parking: Tackley – Sturdy's Castle Inn. Car parking (with prior permission – Tel: 01869 331328) in the car park north of the inn beside A4260 road.
Ramsden (north of Witney) – Restricted parking near church if no service, or along High Street leading NW out of village.

Accommodation/Public Houses/Refreshments:

Stonesfield
- The White Horse PH. Tel: 01993 891063.
- The Black Head PH. Tel: 01993 891616.

East End:
- Elbie House B&B. Tel: 01993 880166.
  www.cotswoldbreak.co.uk
- Leather Bottel Guest House B&B. Tel: 01993 882174.

Ramsden
- Royal Oak PH, restaurant, B&B. Tel: 01993 868213.
- Ann's Cottage B&B. Tel: 01993 868592.

Ramsden Heath
- Hilltop Garden Centre Café. Tel: 01993 868403.
  (0.75 miles from Ramsden village centre – GR 346157)

Whiteoak Green • The Bird in Hand Inn, B&B. Tel 01993 868321. www.birdinhandinn.co.uk (600 yards from the route, on the B4022, SW of Ramsden – GR 343139)

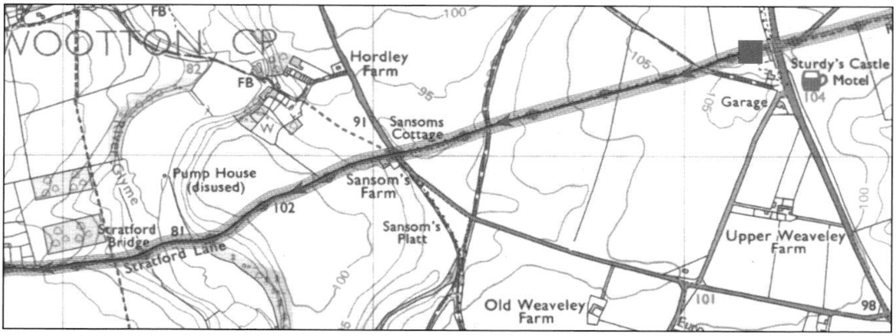

Turn left (N) out of the car park for 75 yards beside the main road to turn left (SW) at the footpath sign onto the Oxfordshire Way. This is Akeman Street and is an ancient tree-lined path. Cross an intercepting bridleway, through a wooden gate to walk (SW) across the field on the raised bank (the agger of Akeman Street) which rises to at least a metre high at the western end.

In July, among the rough grass, there was a glorious mixture of poppies, thistles, scabious and the large white trumpet-like flowers of columbine with red-tailed bumble bees, red admiral and painted lady butterflies feeding on them. Skylarks and yellowhammers provided bird song.

Cross two fields and a surfaced track, Sansom's Lane.

Sansom's Lane and Sansom's Platt

The lane is a former saltway dating from the days of transportation of salt from Droitwich in the north-west to the south. From Iron Age and Roman times, salt was a vital commodity for food preservation and the Anglo-Saxons developed an extensive, well organised network of saltways.

At 12 kilometres marching distance from Alchester is Sansom's Platt to the south, a Roman roadside settlement with evidence of a Romano-Celtic temple.

Cross the road at Sansom's Farm (now the Oxford School of Drama). Continue walking (SW) along a narrow, minor road (still Akeman Street) taking care of the traffic. It is worth noting how the parish boundaries follow the Roman road because it was a convenient physical landmark. Descend the lane to cross the River Glyme at Stratford Bridge. Here there is a group of alder trees which 'like their feet in water'.

After climbing out of the valley, and from the brow of the next hill, the road verges are part of the Oxfordshire County Council's Nature Reserve project, and are mown only twice a year in order to encourage the bio-diversity of wild flowers. There are remains of a limestone wall on both banks of the road.

At the road junction signposted 'Woodstock 2', turn left to walk for 50 yards towards the busy A44. Cross it with care, bear slightly right, then go through the high wooden gate in the boundary wall of Blenheim Park. A few yards on, dog-leg right onto the track, then left through a wooden gate continuing south-west (266°). Across this next field it is just possible to see the line of the raised agger again, left of the path. Aim for a wooden gate to the right of some farm buildings, go through a small wood to pass right (N) of Furze Platt's farm. Beyond here the agger is very clear on the slope up from the double gates.

The structure of a Roman road

Codrington writing in 1903 describes that "a section cut in Woodstock Park showed that the foundation of the road was of flags of the local stone called Stonesfield Slate, about an inch thick, and from 14 by 12 inches to half that wide. They were laid sloping in the direction of the road at an angle of 20° to 25° and upon this foundation was a layer of six inches of gravel under the sod. The width was 17 feet".

Go through a gate and follow the track to cross the avenue of the formal park with the Column of Victory to the left (SE).

This column commemorates Marlborough's victory in 1704 over the forces of Louis XIV of France, at the Battle of Blenheim in Austria.

The golden balls on the roof of Blenheim Palace can also be seen to the left.

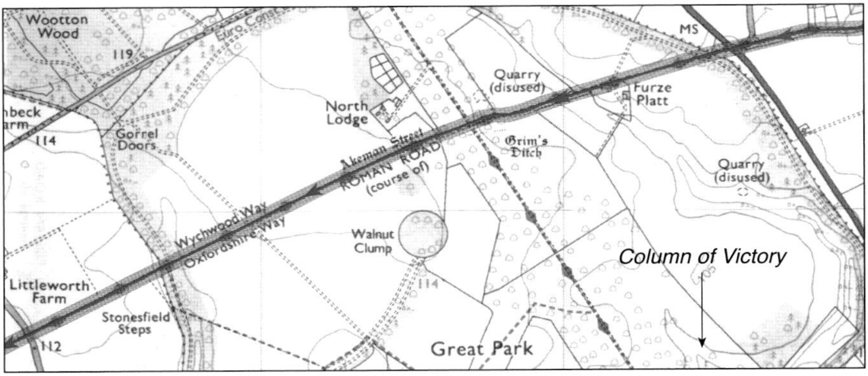

Grim's Ditch
On the left are the prehistoric earthworks of Grim's Ditch. The name originates from Saxon times, since the Saxons thought that anything unusual was the work of their pagan god Grim, or Woden as he was also called. (See Day 12).

Access Point: Woodstock, 1.5 miles. Shops, post office, accommodation, pubs, cafés, telephones, bus service, car parks. GR 444167 (County Museum). Blenheim Palace open 10.30am–4.45pm. The Palace only, closes in December and January.

Follow the track past more of Grim's Ditch to go through a wooden gate, and along beside a small wood on the right. Start on the stony Blenheim footpath (SW, 245°), still on the raised bank of the agger.

There were skylarks singing here in January.

Go through a linear wood and over the steep Stonesfield ladder stile to leave the Blenheim estate.

We have joined the Wychwood Way, a circular walk of 36 miles around the original boundary of Wychwood Forest, and Shakespeare's Way, from Stratford-upon-Avon to the Globe Theatre in London.

Continue in the same direction to cross a minor road (N/S) confusingly also called Akeman Street.

Along this part of the Roman road there are several oak and beech 'standards' (a forestry term for solitary trees grown for timber) with wild flowers on either side of the agger, including scabious, yarrow, wild thyme, marjoram, knapweed and restharrow, all favouring the limestone soil.

Continue on (SW) past the site of the Stonesfield Roman villa to the right (N) although there is nothing to see now.

It was here that we felt what it may have been like to be a Roman marching across this part of the countryside.

Cross a minor road to pass the disused Stonesfield slate mines to the right; the spoil-heaps of the unwanted waste limestone are still noticeable.

The valley of Bagg's Bottom on the left is a piece of undisturbed woodland, and is one of the best places in Oxfordshire to see tree pipits.

Stonesfield Slates

The production of Stonesfield slates has a curious history. The stone was mined, put on the surface in clamps (heaps), and covered with soil in order to keep the slates moist. Then, in the winter when frost was expected, the church bells were tolled and, even if it were night-time, the quarrymen would be roused from their beds. They would gather to uncover the stones. After exposure to the frost, the blocks of stone could be split readily into thin roof tiles.

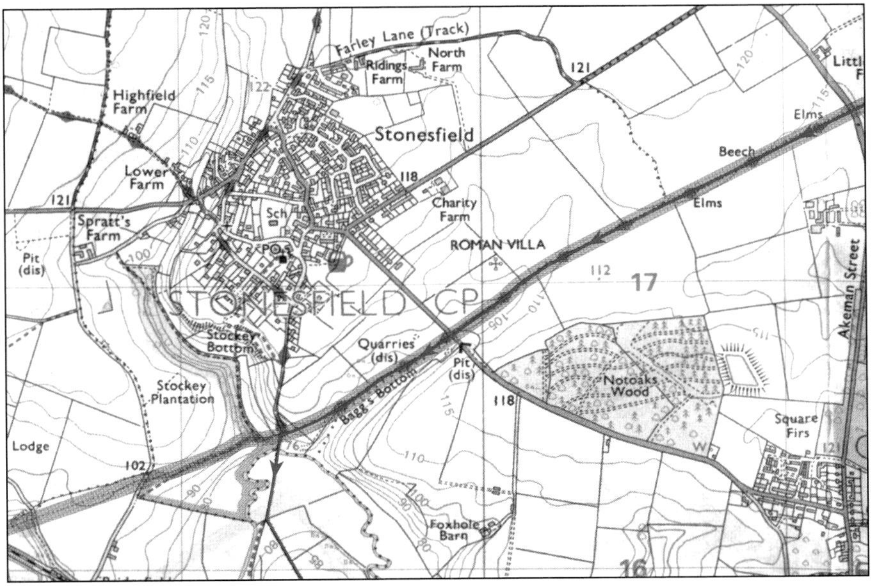

The very first dinosaur

In 1824, the lower jaw bone of a Megalosaurus, a carnivorous dinosaur about 8 metres long, was the subject of the very first scientific description of a dinosaur by Dr Buckland. This jaw bone and other bones were found in this area and are on display at the Oxford University Museum of Natural History.

Megalosaurus, Stonesfield

Go through the metal kissing gate descending along the river cliff down to the River Evenlode, the next river valley after the River Glyme. Go through another kissing gate where there is a footpath uphill to Stonesfield village.

Access Point: Stonesfield church, 600 yards from route, 4.8 miles. Telephone, shop, post office. GR 393171.

The route of Akeman Street continues directly (SW) towards Wilcote, but to keep on public rights of way we need to make a loop southwards, so turn sharp left (S) to cross the river. Continue south on the bridleway across the field (188°). Go through a small wooden gate beside a field gate and follow a track uphill (152°), ignoring a path that goes into the wood on the right. Go through a pair of double gates passing a track that goes left to Lower Ridings Farm. Bear right and follow the lane to go over the railway from Oxford to Moreton-in-Marsh. 225 yards from the railway bridge, turn left downhill on the footpath to the small cottage at the entrance of the North Leigh Roman villa.

North Leigh Roman Villa

The earliest evidence of occupation of this site is a bell-shaped hearth from the Iron Age (1st century BC to 1st century AD), which is under the south-west range of the villa. Little is known about the Roman occupants of the villa, but their livelihood probably depended on farming. They were likely to have been Romanised Britons and perhaps people of some importance within the native tribe of local Dobunni. They lived here in the most prosperous period of the Roman occupation, but deserted it early in the 5th century. In this site of palatial proportions, there are tessellated pavements and hypocausts, which are the Roman version of under-floor heating.

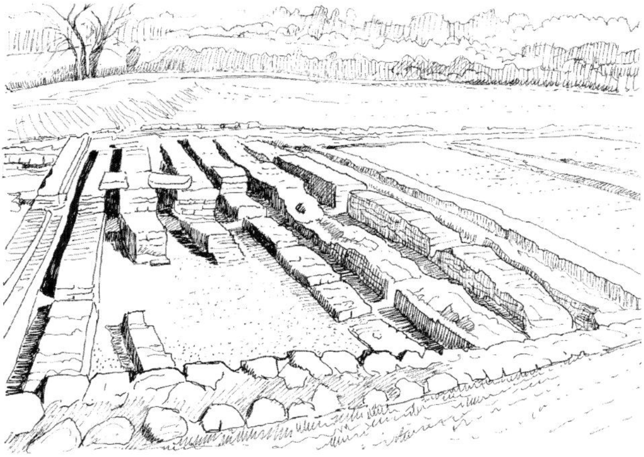

Hypocaust, North Leigh Roman Villa

The site is managed by English Heritage and is open all the year, and although access to the Roman mosaics is only possible on some summer weekends, they can be seen through the glass window of the low wooden building in the south-west corner of the site.

Roman mosaic, North Leigh

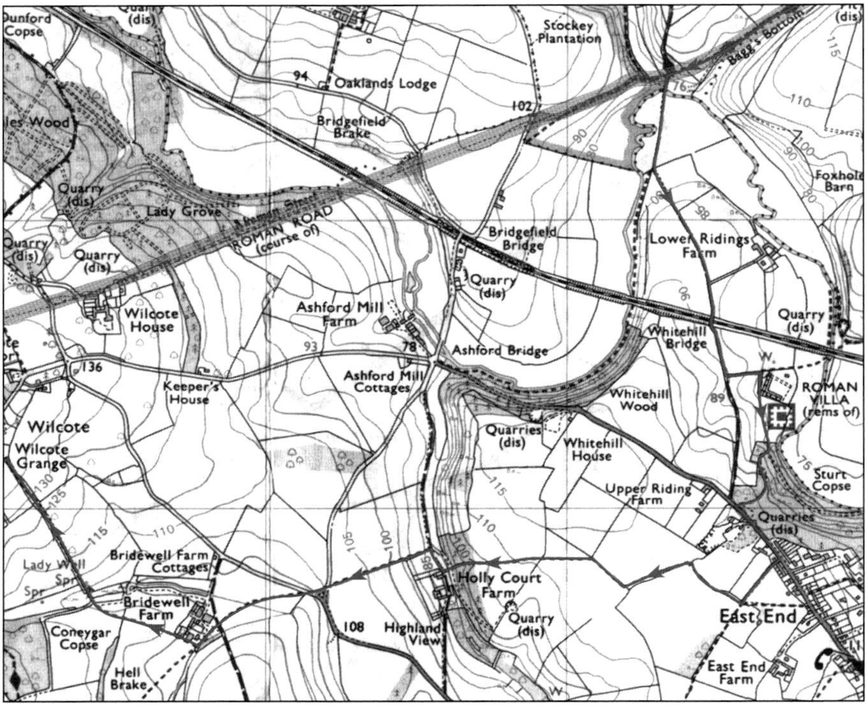

On leaving the villa, instead of retracing steps back to the track, turn left (S) along the perimeter fence of the site. At the wall corner, go half left (175°), to cross the field towards a wood. Go over the stile and, after a few yards, keep to the right and ascend through the wood, always keeping to the right at any fork.

This is Sturt Copse, with several plant species, such as dog's mercury, wild garlic, sanicle and spurge laurel, which all indicate its antiquity. We saw the uncommon blue clustered bellflowers here in July.

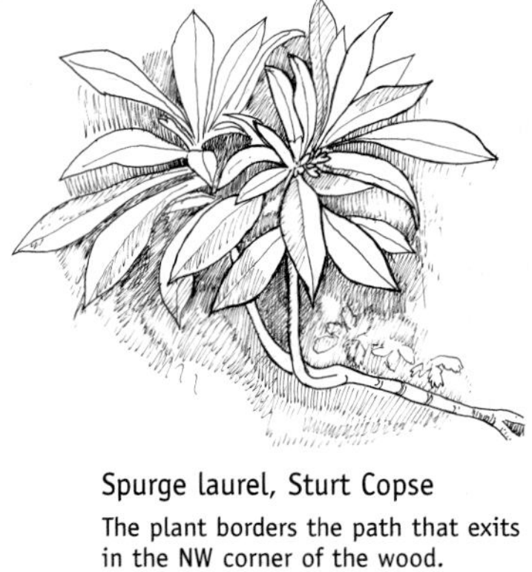

Spurge laurel, Sturt Copse

The plant borders the path that exits in the NW corner of the wood.

Roman Snails

On the trunk of a beech tree in the wood we saw an enormous Roman snail (Helix pomatia). Its pale brown shell was nearly 5cm across. These snails are thought to have been introduced by the Romans as a source of food, hence the name. They are sedentary, meaning that they do not move far, and others have been found in the woods near Chedworth Roman Villa in Gloucestershire. This species is so rare that it is illegal to disturb or move them.

Leave the wood to turn left (SE) and go 250 yards along the road into the village of **East End**, where there are B&Bs. At the repeater 30 mph sign on the right, turn right over a stile at the sign, 'North Leigh', into an enclosed footpath between houses and go along beside the first field. Go through the hedge gap to turn immediately right, alongside the hedgerow (NW, 300°).

This hedgerow, with its old oak standard trees, has a winding course indicating its antiquity.

Follow the edge of the field, then at the corner of this field, go through the gap into the next field to turn left and go along SW with the hedge on the left. At the next corner go through the hedge gap and immediately turn right at the signpost (NW, 312°). Follow the hedge on the right to another hedge gap. Do *not* go through this, but bear left across the corner of the field to go through a hedge gap by an old oak tree.

Bear left to go across the next field (W, 270°) towards a shelter belt of pine trees. On descending the field, the Cotswold brash (limestone rubble) is visible on the surface of the soil. Go down the track to Holly Court Farm, which has a fine Stonesfield slate roof, a chapel and dovecote.

Turn right along the track. Here there are two alternative ways of crossing the stream (a tributary of the River Evenlode). Either cross the wooden bridge 20 yards further on to turn right on a bridleway along the bottom of the field, or after 100 yards, go left by a metal gate onto the footpath and cross the stream. Turn left to climb the hill (SW, 253°) keeping to the right side of the hedge. Go by the double steel gates onto the road to turn left to a small triangular green.

The grassy bank nearby was full of marjoram and basil thyme plants.

Bear right (NW) on the road to **Wilcote**, but after only 50 yards, bear left onto the footpath to cross a field (SW, 260°). Cross the field ditch via a footbridge, and keep in the same direction aiming left of the farm buildings ahead.

Bridewell Farm is a fine three-storied eighteenth century house (1767) originally with large windows, each with fanned keystones, and a porch.

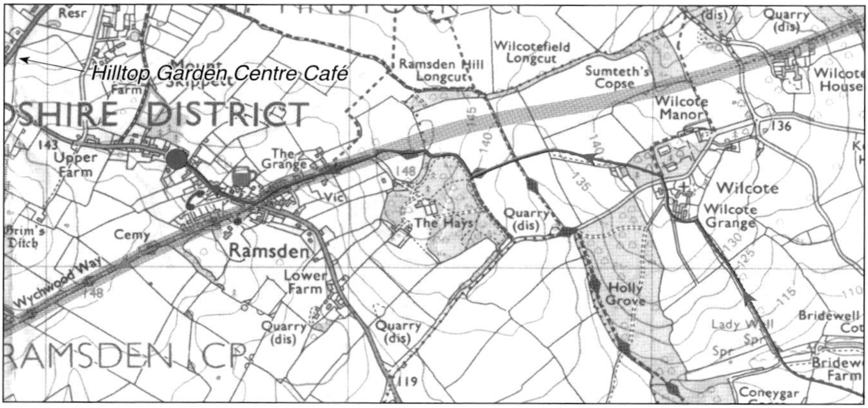

Intaglios

In 1910, three tiny intaglios (seal stones), each the size of a fingernail, and made of Roman gem-stones with incised designs, were found in a field near Bridewell Farm. An oval enamelled seal-box and a denarius (a silver coin) of Faustina were also found: they are almost 2,000 years old. They were donated by Miss Blake and can be seen on display in the Ark gallery at the Woodstock Museum. Wilcote, the hamlet 0.8 miles north-west, was the probable site of a Roman roadside settlement on nearby Akeman Street: the Roman equivalent of a motorway service station, with traders' stalls perhaps selling high-class goods.

Ceres Intaglio ring, Wilcote
(Actual size: 20 x 23mm)

Turn left to pass in front of the buildings and the pond, to the left, then turn right uphill at a waymark sign, with the hedge on the right (NW, 288°). Where the hedge turns right, bear left across the field to go through a gap in the hedge at the top of the slope, then bear slightly right downhill (292°) to the hedge ahead. Go through a wooden kissing gate where there is a colony of giant hogweed (beware, do not touch it). Go up the slope passing Lady Well Spring to the right with steps leading down to it.

Limestone Springs

It is in this area that the springs emerge hence some of the place names indicate the sources of water (Bridewell). Lady Well was known as an ancient fertility spring, and local people used to visit it on Lady Day (25th March).

Ancient pollarded ash avenue, Wilcote

Walk up through an avenue of 300-year-old pollarded ash trees to reach Wilcote Grange. Turn left along the fenced path in front of the house, and along the drive (N) to a minor road. Cross it and go into a small wood. Take the left-hand path (W), not the one straight ahead, to pass some old willow trees and ponds.

Leave the wood via a stile, and turn left along the field hedge on the left. Cross a farm track. At the field corner, take the third hedge gap, just past an oak tree, to turn left towards another wood crossing the Wychwood Way. Turn right along the edge of the wood and turn left at the staggered wooden railings to follow a path along the right side of a mixed woodland.

There was white honeysuckle growing here: the flowers only turn yellow when they have been fertilised.

Go over a stile by a pond, then cross the corner of a field to a gate. Turn right down a minor road (Akeman Street) in the village of **Ramsden** passing the Grange with its high walls, and go towards the church with its spire and the ancient Royal Oak Pub.

Ramsden means in Old English 'the valley of ramsons (wild garlic)'. St. James' Church is a relatively recent church, built in 1842, until which time to that the parish church was at Shipton-under-Wychwood 5.5 miles away.

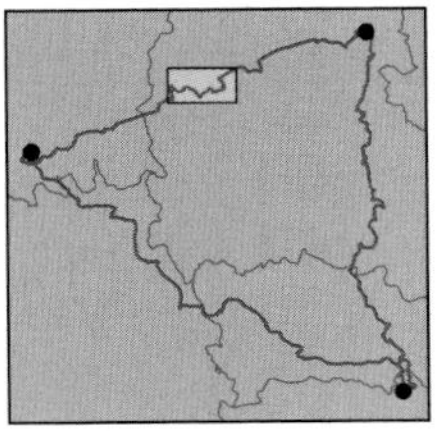

Day 3

Ramsden to Burford

Ramsden GR SP 357152 to Burford GR SP 254123

We follow the same south-westerly direction of Akeman Street, partly on the route of the Roman road, though most of it beside the meandering course of the River Windrush. This is a quiet place with evidence of the woollen mills that produced the material for the former Witney blanket factory nearby. There are Minster Lovell Hall and ancient churches to visit but also an opportunity to walk through protected water-meadows where redshank call in winter.

Distance: 10.75 miles (17.2 km).

Maps: Explorer 180 – Oxford, Witney & Woodstock.
Outdoor Leisure 45 – The Cotswolds.
Landranger 164 – Oxford.
Landranger 163 – Cheltenham & Cirencester area.

Transport: Buses
- Ramsden/Witney, 69.
- Witney/Minster Lovell/Burford, 853.
  Traveline – Tel: 0871 200 2233. www.traveline.org.uk

Taxis:
Ramsden
- Safe-ride. Tel: 01993 868226.

Minster Lovell
- Angela's Taxis. Tel: 01993 771122/771072.
- Excel Cars. Tel: 01993 775198.

Burford
- Fairways. Tel: 01993 823152 or 07751 472125.

Car Parking: Ramsden (north of Witney) – Restricted parking near church if no service, or along High Street leading NW out of village.
Burford – Town car park south-east of the church (no charge). Toilets.

Accommodation/Public Houses/Refreshments:
Whiteoak Green
- The Bird in Hand Inn, B&B. Tel 01993 868321.
  www.birdinhandinn.co.uk
  (600 yards from the route, on the B4022, SW of Ramsden – GR 343139)

Crawley	• Lamb Inn. Tel: 01993 703753. (550 yards from route)
Minster Lovell	• The Mill and Old Swan Inn. Tel: 01993 774441. www.deverevenues.co.uk/find-venue/the-mill-and-old-swan.html
Asthall	• The Maytime Inn, B&B. Tel: 01993 822068. www.themaytime.com
Swinbrook	• The Swan. Tel: 01993 823339.
Burford	• Burford Visitor Information Centre, Sheep Street. Tel: 01993 823558. www.oxfordshirecotswolds.org for comprehensive list of accommodation.

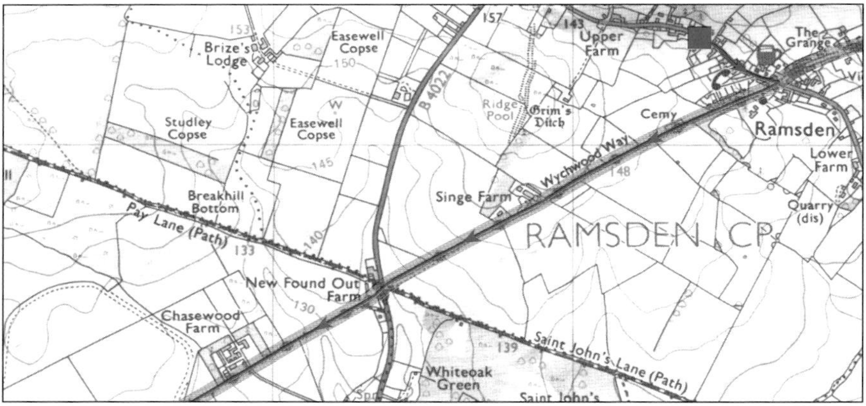

Pass the ancient Royal Oak pub to take the road past the church (SW) to climb the long straight road, Akeman Street. To the left (S) there can be a good view across the valley of the River Thames as far as the Berkshire Downs, 17.5 miles away. At the road junction, go left for 100 yards, to turn right (SW) before a bungalow to take a byway (also part of the Wychwood Way).

The track is still Akeman Street, and the agger is described by Margary as being between two and three feet high and following the line of the old ash trees. In Roman times, this road would originally have been 17 feet (5 metres) wide, with small ditches at either side.

Follow the bridleway (SW) to cross the driveway to Chasewood Farm, a 19th century Victorian model farm built by the Duke of Marlborough. Continue along the lime tree avenue to where the stone spire of Leafield church can be seen to the right (NW).

Chasewood Model Farm
Model farms incorporated the most advanced technology of the time in order to provide examples of progressive farming

Akeman Street, Whiteoak Green

Continue in the same direction across a former World War II airfield (known as R.A.F. Akeman Street) with grass runways, crossing the concrete perimeter tracks marked by the double dotted lines on the Explorer map.

When we walked across it in May, the air was full of skylark song above the rough grass. The birds establish their territory by singing over an area of land, in contrast to many birds that have a tree as a singing post.

Continue on the same route to reach the signpost to Field Assarts. Then turn left at this minor road. Walk along Riding Lane (SE) for nearly a mile taking great care to avoid the fast traffic.

'Riding' was a commonly used name for a lane through woodland. The nearby settlement name, 'Field Assarts' is also an indication that the ancient woodland was cleared for farming here.

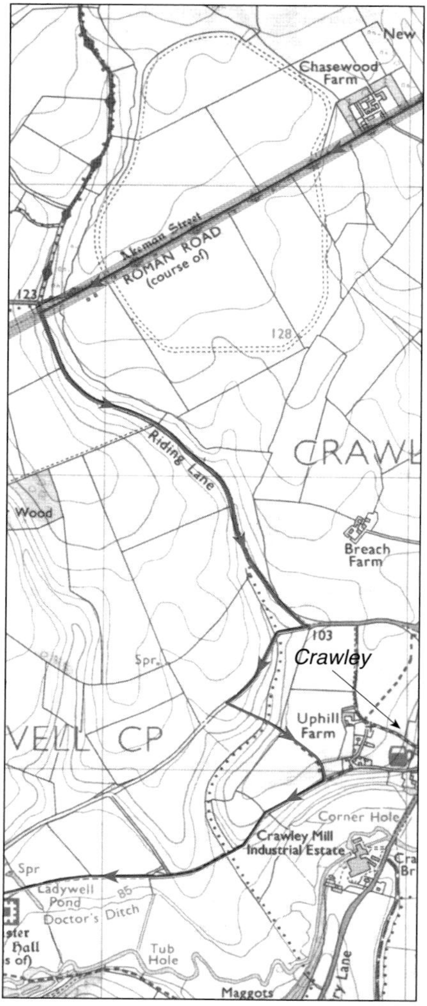

A multi-specied hedge

We amused ourselves along this lane by identifying both the newly planted and older native and non-native species in the eastern hedge. Our score was elder, guelder rose, hazel, yew, holly, dogwood, leylandii, laurel, spindleberry, hawthorn, field maple, oak, apple, ash. There are some midland hawthorn bushes, which are the 'wild wood' species, showing that this hedgerow was originally part of an ancient woodland. The flowers on the bank to the left indicate a limestone base: yellow rock roses, knapweed, toadflax and scabious.

Turn right along the road (SW) towards Minster Lovell and Burford. After only 400 yards, just over the brow of the hill, turn left over a stone stile in the hedge and descend the field bearing slightly left (118°). Go over another stone stile and uphill on the right side of the hedge, and then over a wooden stile. Continue through a level field to another wooden stile by a kissing gate.

We saw red-legged partridge (French partridge) running here; they are easily distinguishable by their barred flanks, black and white face pattern and red legs. For those interested in old farm machinery, there is a rusting Fordson tractor (made in the 1940s) nearby that used to run mainly on paraffin, using petrol only to start it. The chimney of Crawley Mill (a former corn and fulling mill), the stone packhorse bridge, the pollarded willows and the steep river cliffs that the River Windrush has created are visible. This is part of the Upper Thames ESA (see box below). Signs of otters have been seen along this quiet river valley.

Red-legged partridge

The Upper Thames Environmentally Sensitive Area

As the notice explains, this is an area where the government is working with farmers to conserve and enhance this characteristic landscape of the Upper Thames tributaries. In the past they were grassland and wetland habitats created by traditionally-managed hay meadows and wet pastures that support populations of now rare wild flowers and breeding birds. These valleys also contain networks of ancient tracks and historic field systems. Now the farmers limit the use of fertilisers and pesticides, and maintain landscape features by methods such as pollarding the willows and hedge laying.

Descend on the left side of the hedgerow to cross another stile onto a footpath in a green lane. Turn right (SW) here. Follow this path through kissing gates and stiles in the limestone walls and into the first large river meadow. Go through another kissing gate next to a spring called Ladywell Pond. Go through this gate, to where the path divides. Bear left (220°) towards Minster Lovell Hall on the permissive path across the water meadows to the manorial ruins. Turn right through the high, now roofless, great hall, and further on if you wish to visit the dovecote.

Minster Lovell Hall

Minster Lovell is a fine example of an unfortified baronial mansion of the Wars of the Roses period when it belonged to the Lovell family. It has a great hall, with vaults, stair turrets and service buildings including a kitchen, buttery, pantry and a domed dovecote where the pigeons would have provided a fresh source of meat and eggs throughout the year. To the south, near the river, are the medieval fish ponds which were a source of fresh fish. Built in 1440, the house was dismantled in 1747 by the last resident, Thomas Coke. He then moved to Holkham Hall in Norfolk where he revolutionised farming practice.

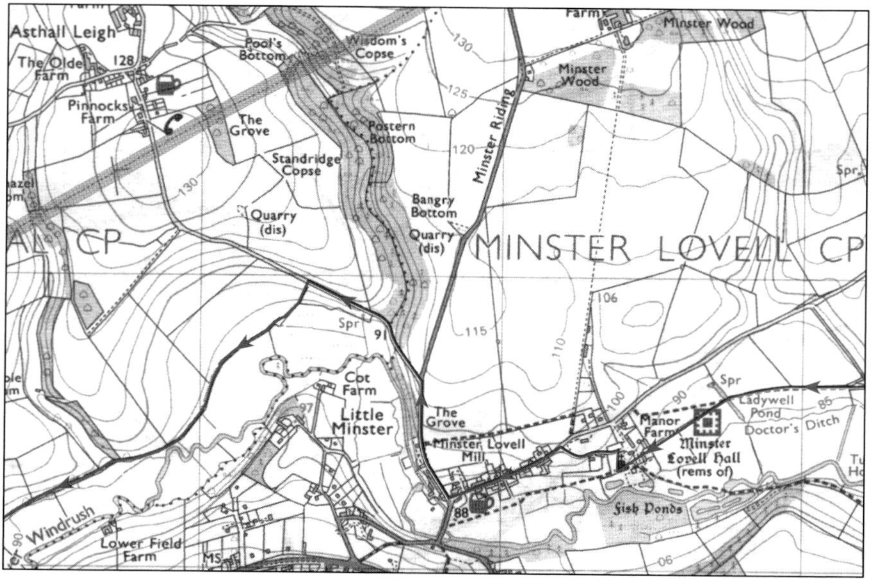

Access Point: Minster Lovell (car park west of the church), 4.25 miles. Pub, B&B, telephone. GR 323114.

Leave the footpath by turning right through the churchyard to turn left at the village road above.

St. Kenelm's church has a fine alabaster tomb of the 7th Baron Lovell with his head resting on his tourney helm (a helmet used in tournaments) and his feet on a lion, a symbol of courage.

On joining another road, turn left (W) to walk into the village past the Old Post House and past the green called Wash Meadow, a reference to the practice of sheep washing.

There are many ancient buildings with roofs of Stonesfield slates, including the The Mill and Old Swan Inn.

Turn right (NW) before reaching the River Windrush and pass the buildings of the former fulling and corn mills on the left. Beware of the fast traffic on this narrow road. Ascend the hill and bear left onto the road towards Asthall Leigh. After 600 yards, turn left (SW) along the bridleway descending to the river valley along the right side of the hedge.

This is a quiet, undisturbed area and we saw four herons here. Continue along the valley, then along a green lane, following the uphill (N) side of scrubland. On passing an elder copse to the right, there are numerous scattered mossy stones. This is the site of the remains of the Worsham Roman bath house, GR 307111.

Worsham Roman bath house

This was originally a bath house sited on the bank of the River Windrush when it flowed much further north than its present course. On excavation, the walls were found to be unusually thick, presumably to provide better foundations near the water. Hypocausts, a hot-room and a sunken bath with stoke holes for a furnace, have been found. (The Romans were ahead of us with their 'hot tubs'!) Later, the bath house became a villa with tiled floors and coloured plaster on the walls. Third and fourth century pottery and just five coins have been excavated, but no other metal objects found, (Victoria County History, 1939). The trackway beside the hedgerow just beyond the Roman villa linked it to Akeman Street, further uphill. In more recent times, this valley of Worsham Bottom was the hideout of the highwaymen, 'The Black Stockings', who held up the coaches from Witney on windy nights (Alun T. Jones).

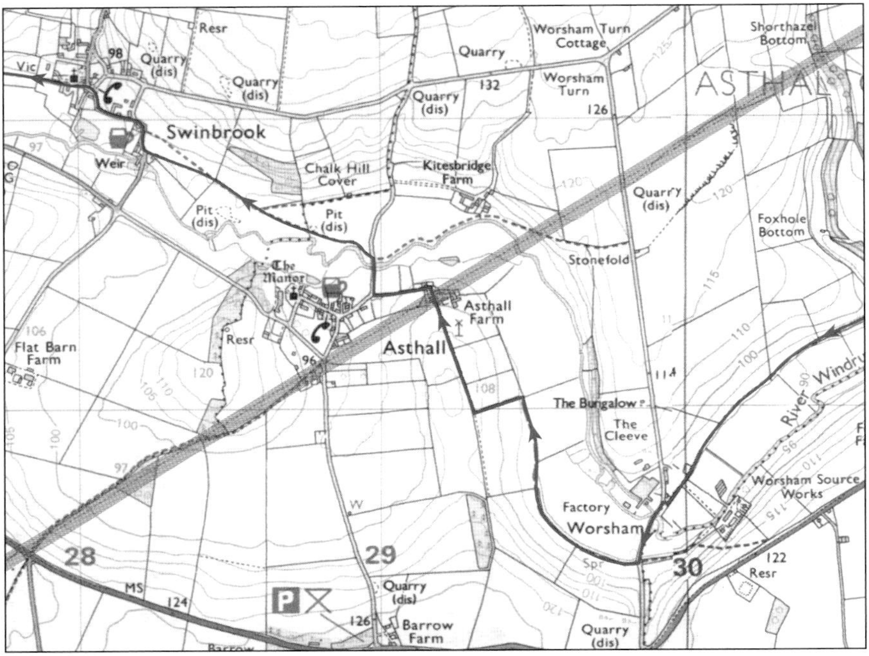

On reaching the road, turn left. On the right is the former Worsham Mill.

This was one of the network of Witney woollen mills making the renowned 'Witney blankets'.

Cross the River Windrush, then after 150 yards, turn right onto the footpath signed 'Asthall 1¼ miles'. Continue along the bridleway (NW) on the left side of a hedge with remarkably big, old, field maple and hawthorn trees in it.

Beyond the hedgerow to the right it is sometimes possible to see the former 19th century channels created to flood the water meadow, in order to improve the grazing (see also Day 6). There are beautiful views of the valley to the right. Further on, by looking ahead, the course of Akeman Street can be seen following the line of the hedgerow on the far, top side of the river valley as it descends from the north east to meet the river (see map). There was a Roman ford at GR 294115, (SE) of Kitesbridge Farm, but it is not on a public right of way.

Turn left, then right, beside the hedgerow to reach the farm buildings of Asthall Farm. The line of the Roman road (NE–SW) goes between the farmhouse and the barn, and under the wooden garden shed on the left, towards the village. Turn left (W) to join the road leading into the village of **Asthall**.

Access Point: Asthall, 7.5 miles (parking on verges of road south of village under an avenue of beech trees, 350 yards from route). Pub, telephone. GR 287112.

Asthall and the Mitford Sisters

Asthall (OE East Hall) village is worth exploring, so turn left to pass the Maytime Inn on the right and the ancient houses in the village. Excavations near the village have shown a Roman settlement with the remains of a marching camp, and Akeman Street passes just south of the village. We talked to a farmer, who told us that during dry weather it is possible to see the parch marks of the grid pattern of the former military camp in the field south of the village, and to see the route of the Roman road in the crop as it ascends (SW) to the A40 road. Asthall was the home of Lord and Lady Redesdale who lived in the Elizabethan manor house just beyond the church of St. Nicholas. The Redesdales took over most of the Fettiplace lands. Their daughters Unity, Nancy (authoress), Diana and Pamela Mitford are all buried in the nearby village of Swinbrook. Diana was first the mistress, then wife of Sir Oswald Mosley. Both she and Unity were friends and admirers of Hitler. The last survivor of the six sisters, Deborah, Dowager Duchess of Devonshire, owns The Swan in Swinbrook. Asthall church is of interest, with a Norman font, a rare double sedilia and several Norman and Early English architectural features.

Retrace your steps to the exit of the farm track from Asthall Farm to turn right (N) towards a small stone bridge over the River Windrush.

In both the upstream and downstream fields beside the road are the raised banks of the former mill leat. In the wall on the left before the bridge, there is a stone stile going down to a sluice gate. The wall is decorated with a carving of a rifle made by one of the Polish WWII prisoners of war who were billeted here.

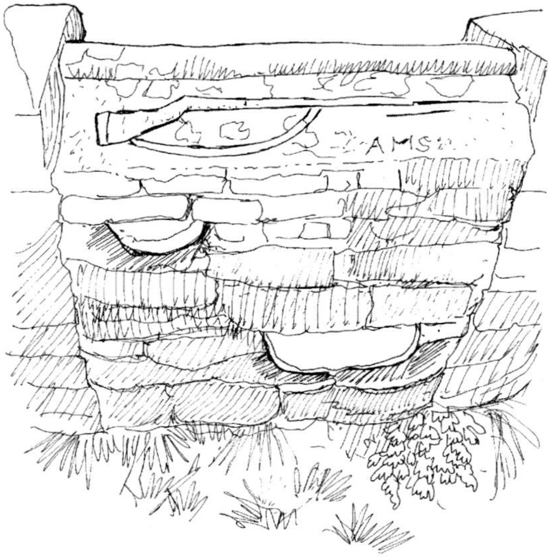

Rifle carving, Asthall

After the bridge climb over another stile to the left and bear across the field (W, 290°) following the north side of the stream to a gap in the hedge. Go right (NW) to meet a wall on the right, and continue in the same direction of the wall towards the village of **Swinbrook** (in Old English (OE) Pig brook). Where the path divides, take the left fork behind a house, over a stile into the road opposite The Swan inn. Turn right, then straight ahead at the T-junction, bear left at the village green and start climbing the slope past Hillside Cottage. Turn immediately left up the stone steps into the churchyard of St. Mary's Church.

Here there are bale tombs, so called because the curved tops are in the shape of wool bales. Inside the church are some remarkable 17th century monuments of the Fettiplace family. This is a rare example of two sets of triple monuments, the more rigid style being the earlier ones (1613), and the more realistic being the later style (1686).

The graves of Diana, Nancy and Unity Mitford are on the west side of the porch, Pamela's is near the NW corner of the church.

Walk out of the churchyard along the walled footpath (W) along a narrow footpath towards the church at **Widford**. Just before the wooden gate, the grassy terraces on the right side of the valley sides are the remains of the former Swinbrook Manor gardens.

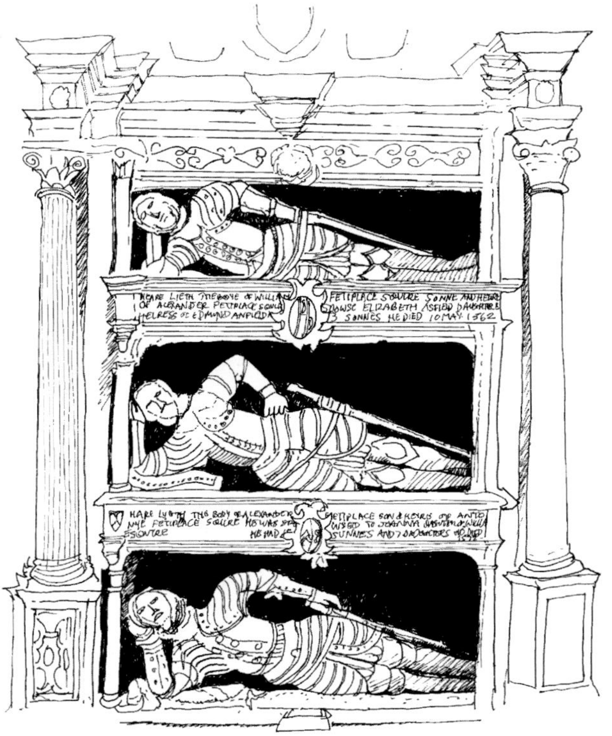

Fettiplace monument, Swinbrook

Widford

Widford (OE 'withig' meaning the ford by the willows). This was formerly part of Wychwood Forest, which was cleared in about 1862. The reason for siting the church here was possibly because the body of St. Oswald, who was King of Northumbria, rested here on its way from Lindisfarne to St. Oswald's Priory, Gloucester. He had been killed in battle in 642. The church is of Saxon origin and was rebuilt in about 1100 on the tessellated pavement of a Roman villa. There are 14th century wall paintings depicting a medieval cautionary tale of 'The Three Living and the Three Dead'. This was a story of three young princes, in the prime of life, who were walking through a forest and met three skeletons reminding them of the imminence of their mortality. This would have been particularly relevant after the devastating effect of the Black Death in 1348. The box pews are 18th century Georgian.

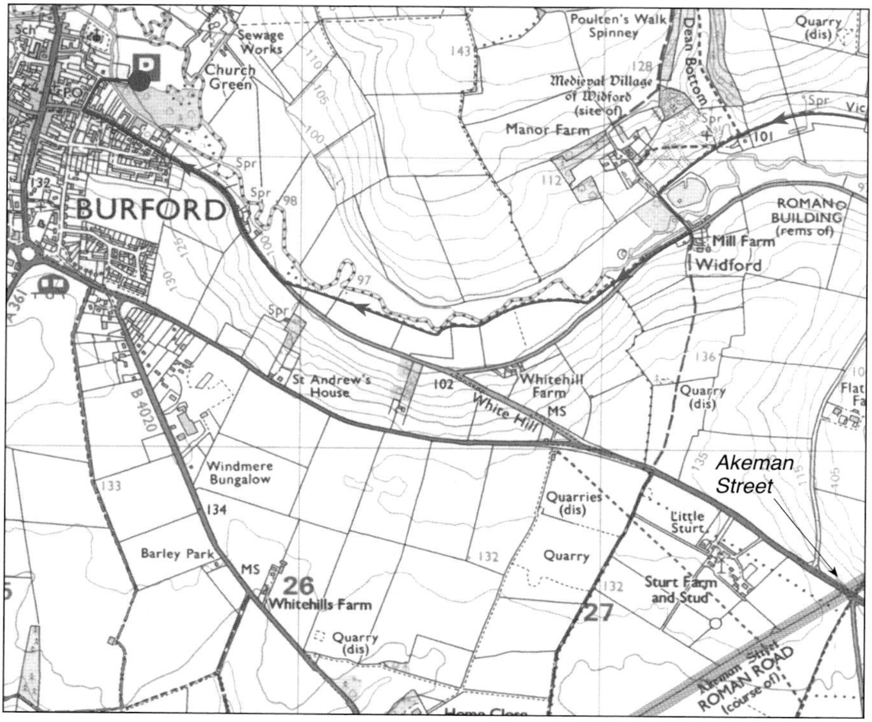

Leave the churchyard to walk across the fields.

The various humps and bumps are indications that Widford is a deserted medieval village; Domesday Book of 1086 shows that there were eleven households in this area.

Follow the river valley to turn left at the minor road over the River Windrush, past the Mill Race House with its Victorian letterbox, still in use, and turn right (SW) along the narrow lane. After 200 yards, fork right through a gate and into water meadows, to follow the footpath on the south side of the river.

This is a continuation of the Environmentally Sensitive Area where dogs need to be on a close lead to avoid disturbing the rich bird life here. We saw a pair of redshank and heard their call one snowy afternoon. Where the path meets the road, turn right to walk (W) towards **Burford**. In the town, turn right by the Royal Oak pub along Guildenford, and turn right at the T-junction to cross the former mill leat to the public car park.

Burford

Burford is a Cotswold town whose early prosperity was based on wool and building stone. Sheep grazed the surrounding slopes and in the churchyard there are more bale tombs. The ends of the tombs often have carvings of skulls to remind us of our own mortality. Quarries that exploited some of the finest Jurassic limestone are all around and this stone was used in the Oxford colleges and St. Paul's Cathedral. The church dates from 1175, though in 1649 it was used as a temporary prison for 340 rebel Cromwellian soldiers, called the Levellers, three of whom Cromwell had executed in the churchyard. The stone-built town runs upslope from the church with many medieval buildings lining the High Street. There are guided tours from the Visitor Information Centre and plenty of shops and tearooms.

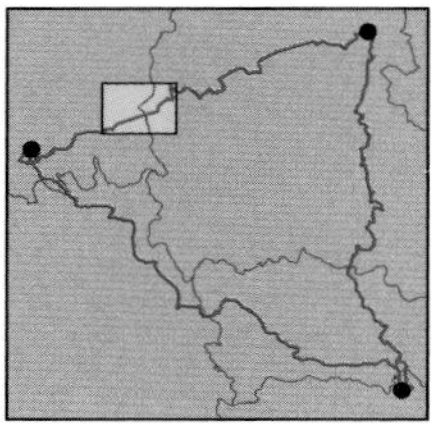

Day 4

Burford to Coln St. Aldwyns

Burford GR SP 254123 to Coln St. Aldwyns GR SP 145052

After leaving Burford, we pass through remote hamlets that have grown up around springs in the limestone uplands. These villages are part of three large estates through which we walk: Bradwell Grove, Hatherop and Williamstrip. We learn about a curious history of umbrella-making at Holwell, then join Akeman Street to descend into the valley of the River Coln.

Distance: 10.1 miles (16.2 km).

Maps: Outdoor Leisure 45 – The Cotswolds.
Landranger 163 – Cheltenham & Cirencester area.

Transport: Buses
- Oxford/Witney/Burford, 853.
- Witney/Burford, 233.
- Coln St. Aldwyns/Cirencester, 861/865/866.
  Traveline – Tel: 0871 200 2233. www.traveline.org.uk

Taxis:

Burford
- Fairways. Tel: 01993 823152 or 07751 472125.
- Charlies. Tel: 01993 845253 or 07719 010400.

Bibury
- Coln Valley Cabs/Rainbow Cabs. Tel: 01285 740070.

Cirencester
- Radio Cars. Tel: 01285 651117/650850.
- Cirencester Taxis. Tel: 01285 800006.

Car Parking: Burford – Car park near the River Windrush, east of the High Street and church.
Coln St. Aldwyns – Restricted parking beside the high stone wall in Church Lane, west of Coln Stores.

Accommodation/Public Houses/Refreshments:

Shilton
- Manor Lodge, B&B. Tel. 01993 841444.
  e-mail: enquiries@manorlodgeb&b.co.uk
  (2.4 miles from route – GR 267086)
- Rose & Crown PH. Tel: 01993 842280.

Eastleach Turville
- The Victoria PH. Tel: 01367 850277. (1.3 miles off route)

Coln St. Aldwyns
- New Inn PH. Tel: 01285 750651. www.new-inn.co.uk
- Deer Park Cottage, Hatherop Road. Tel: 01285 750692.

Bibury
- Cotteswold House B&B. Tel. 01285 740609.
- Bibury Trout Farm, café. Tel. 01285 740215. (both 2 miles off route)

Aldsworth
- Sherbourne Arms. Tel. 01451 844346. (3.25 miles off route)

For full accommodation list, contact Cirencester Visitor Information Centre.
Tel: 01285 654180. www.cotswolds.com

Wesleyan Chapel, Burford High Street

The outward appearance of this building, dated about 1715, is remarkable. It is an example of how local builders took the styles of great houses and applied them to a basic double-fronted house. "The baroque design with its giant fluted pilasters, its parapets and rustication gives it a monumental, and rather incongruous presence despite its small size." (J. Pilling, *Oxfordshire Houses*; 1993.)

Leave the car park by going over the former mill leat, turn right into Church Lane, past the church and the former Burford Grammar School (BGS) on the right, then turn left (S) onto Burford High Street. Climb the hill, after 150 yards passing the Wesleyan chapel on the left. It is worth crossing to the opposite side of the road to get a better view of the building.

Cross back to climb the left (E) side of the hill. In the sunshine the Cotswold stone buildings can turn to a pale golden colour.

'The Tolsey', the square timber-framed market hall at the end of Sheep Street on the right, dates from the 1500s. Wool merchants came to trade here from as far away as Flanders, Venice and Florence.

At the top of the hill, turn left at the A40 roundabout to walk (SE) along the pavement of Barns Lane for 200 yards. At the traffic island 100 yards before the Burford Lodge Hotel, turn right (S) to cross the A40 and take the footpath to **Signet**. Follow the path along the side of the golf course, then through two further fields.

This is high, open country and, when we walked in January, there were about fifty rooks, about the same number of wood pigeons feeding on the stubble, and yellowhammers in the hawthorn bushes.

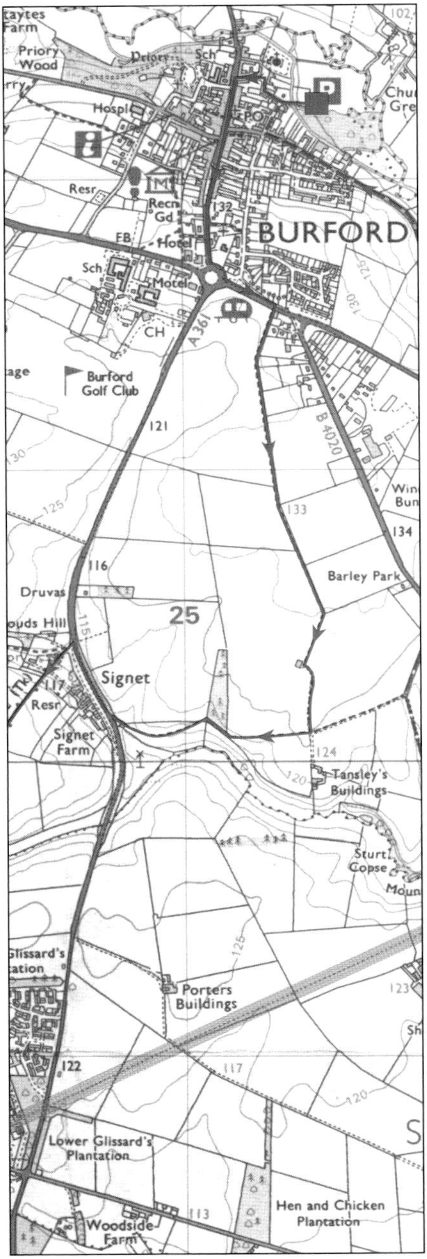

In the second field, the path crosses right to some farm buildings. Go between these, and continue on the stony track (S). Immediately before the track joins a tarmac drive, turn sharp right onto another footpath at GR 254101 (W, 268°) and keep right of a telegraph pole in the field. At the end of this field, bear further right to walk beside a wood, then along the edge of the field with the fence to the left towards a black barn.

Cross the road at this barn, taking care of the fast traffic, and descend a steep slope by a water hydrant with care into the hamlet of Signet. Cross the Shill Brook over an ancient clapper (ie stone-flagged) bridge.

'Clapper' is the dialect for 'a rough or natural bridge across a stream; stepping stones'.

Turn right (N) to walk beside the hamlet to reach a gravel track marked '**Holwell** 1'. Turn left (SW, 215°) past the duck pond and continue up the stony lane, known as Job's Lane.

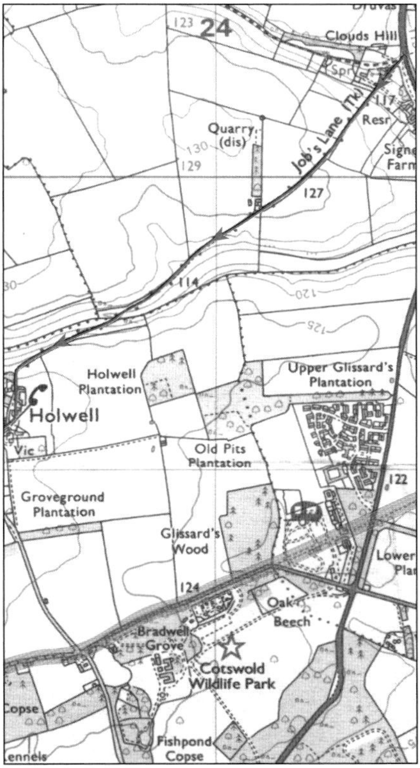

Job's Lane

Job's Lane (origin of name not known but could have related to someone who had the pestilence) was a well-used route from Burford to Holwell. A resident of Signet told us that the bread van used it until the 1950s. Job's Lane is bordered by limestone walls and multi-specied hedges. As we left Signet, we saw a stoat ferrying its young across the track. The stoat waited until its babies had all crossed. Stoats like to live in the dry spaces of stone walls. In September, there were dozens of red admiral butterflies and hoverflies feeding on the late-flowering ivy, starlings feeding on the elderberries and large parties of long-tailed tits feeding on the insects and larvae. Crab apples shone in the sunshine and we spotted a small copper butterfly feeding in the grassy meadow nearby.

Go through a metal field gate to continue along the grassy bridleway (SW, 240°) with the infant Shill Brook meandering on the left. There are thin, flaggy limestone walls (these stones would either have been gathered from the field surface or from shallow quarry 'delves' nearby). Cross the remains of a former bridge to climb towards Holwell.

An elderly resident said that he could remember smoking his first cigarette under this bridge, so it must have been more prominent then!

Go through two metal gates and up into the village. There is a barn on the left with a hand-carved oak window in the former wagon porch. Turn right to pass Lob's Cottage, passing the Old Brew House, Jompion Cottage, the village pump and a stone barn to reach the church.

These houses, though now privately owned, are still painted in the traditional khaki colour of the estate.

Access Point: Holwell Church, 3.75 miles. GR 232091.

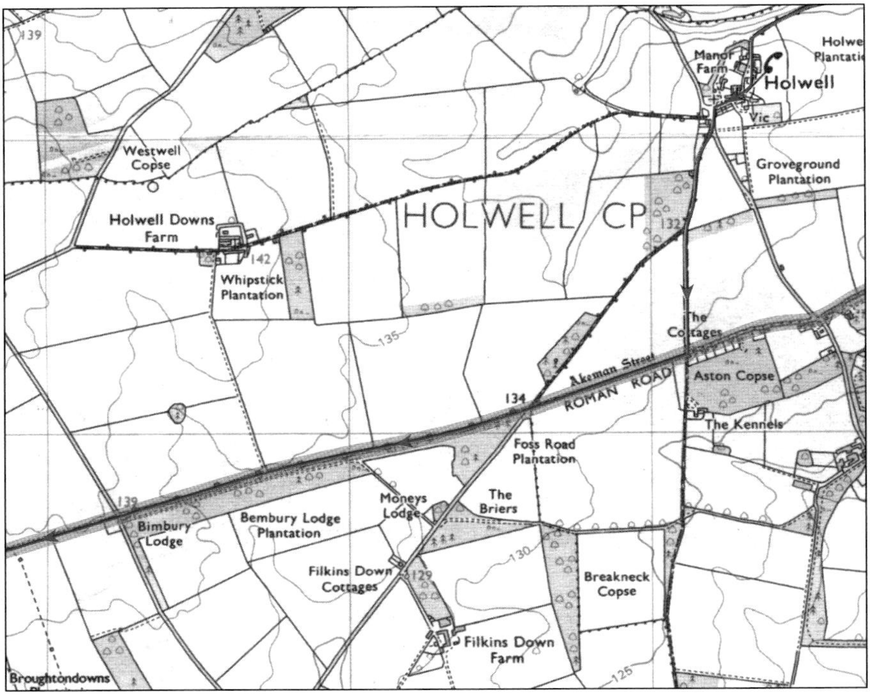

St. Mary's Church

Holwell's (OE holy spring or stream) church has an unusual history since it was rebuilt in 1895 by Squire W.H. Fox (1843–1920), whose family had a Yorkshire firm that made crinoline frames. When these went out of fashion, the family company ingeniously adapted the frames to umbrellas and made a fortune! Umbrellas with 'Fox Frames' were sold worldwide. Henry Fox and his wife Maria's pink marble gravestone is in the churchyard.
Though the present population consists of only seventeen households, the map inside the church which details the location of graves indicates that it was once much bigger with everyone occupied in estate work. The sizeable team included the carter, coachman, stud-groom, head gardener, game keeper, farm workers, vicar, sexton, chauffeur and, of course, the squire and his wife. One epitaph is accompanied by the sad story of a seventeen year old lad who fell off a wagon in the rickyard.

Access to the church: Apply to the Reverend H. MacIness (01993 845954) or M. Galione at Lob's Cottage (01993 822364).

Akeman Street, Holwell

Turn left (S) by the war memorial to pass the village pond on the right (W). There was no piped water to the village until the 1950s, so the spring with its ivy-covered pump house on the far side of the pond, now just discernible, provided water for the inhabitants. *Do not* take the first footpath to the right, but walk past the Old School Lodge and through a metal gate to join a path that goes south (196°).

The irregular surface of the field to the left has been created by surface quarrying of limestone for building. This is also part of the route of the d'Arcy Dalton Way. At the division of the paths, bear left to continue on Dead Man's Walk to reach the road.

The name Dead Man's Walk indicates that the path is a former coffin way linking villages that had no burial grounds. In this case, the coffins were carried four miles to Broadwell church north of the River Thames, until Holwell church was built in 1825.

Turn right (SW) at the road to follow the straight Akeman Street under an avenue of lime trees. At the point where the road bends to the left, continue straight on down a 'Failed Road' (Akeman Street), passing a wood on the left.

The left- and right-handed bryonys

As we walked beside the hedges, we had fun identifying black bryony and white bryony, both climbers. The black bryony belongs to the yam family and twines clockwise and has heart-shaped leaves, no tendrils, yellowy-green flowers and bright red glossy berries. The white bryony is part of the gourd family, twines anti-clockwise, has ivy shaped leaves, tendrils, greenish-white flowers and also red berries.

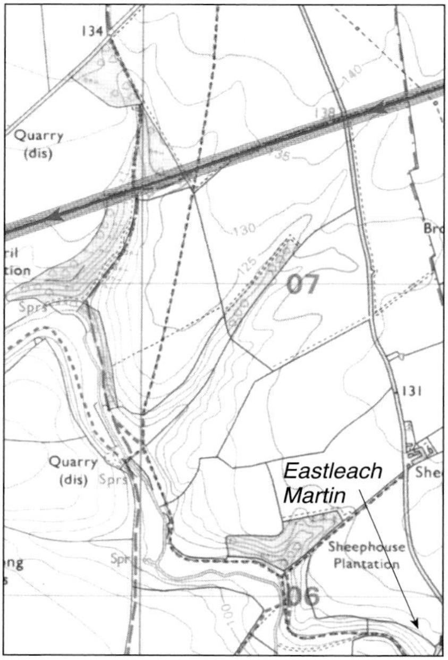

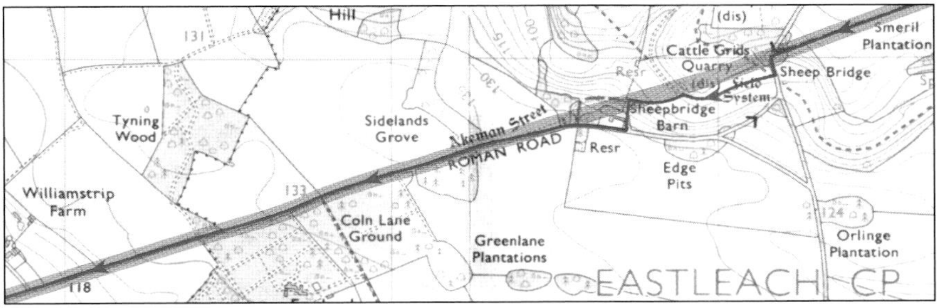

At Bimbury Lodge, cross the minor road to follow the bridleway in the same direction (SW). Just after the pylons, go through a gap in a wall. This is the Oxfordshire/Gloucestershire boundary. The route then crosses a minor road into a large field. Follow the field boundary for 200 yards to turn right before a metal gate into the bottom of a valley. Turn left into the corner of Smeril Plantation (N.B. the wood has been extended since the map was printed).

The line of Akeman Street (the bridleway) is straight across the field entering the wood 50 yards north-west of the corner of the wood down a slope. The gap in the wood can be difficult to find. Ignore the well-defined

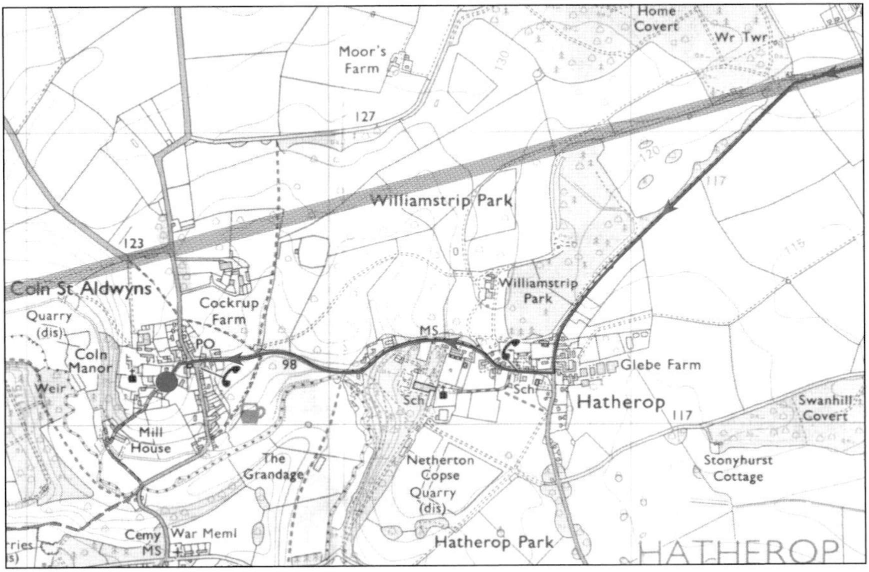

north/south bridleway, part of the *Seven Shires Way*, a 234 mile walk around the Oxfordshire county boundary that crosses Akeman Street in the wood.

On leaving the wood continue along the line of Akeman Street with the stone wall to the left and descend a steep, wooded slope to the road. Akeman Street continues through the wood on the other side, but we turn left down the steep hill and then turn right over the cattle-grid just before Sheep Bridge.

This is the valley of the River Leach, with examples of well preserved medieval lynchets along the contours of the slopes (for explanation of lynchets see Day 8).

Access Points: Sheep Bridge, 6.6 miles. GR 191069. (N.B. no car parking space available). Eastleach Turville, 1.3 miles from route. Pub, telephone. GR 198052.

Follow the valley bottom, then where the track bends right, bear left across a ford to follow the route of Akeman Street as it climbs as a sunken green way up the slope to Sheepbridge Barn. Aim for a small wooden gate in the wall on the upward slope. Go through this gate which leads into the Hatherop estate (note the sage green coloured paint of the estate colours), and continue along the sunken way to a projecting wall corner at the end of a small coppice. Turn left, going behind Sheepbridge Barn, up the slope to the gate onto the road above.

Sheep Bridge Valley

N.B. If the ford is flooded, you will need to retrace your steps back to Sheep Bridge. Turn right (S), then right (SW) up the steep hill signed 'Hatherop 2½ miles', and rejoin the route at Sheepbridge Barn.

Turn right (W) to walk along the road. Fifty yards beyond the cottages we rejoin Akeman Street from where we start a 2.2 mile section of road walking as we follow the Roman road. This is a high, quiet road bordered by ancient stone walls covered with thick moss.

There was 'Old Man's Beard' (wild clematis), coppiced hazel, dogwood, elm trees and ancient laid sycamore trunks in the hedges. In July, we saw some amazingly large specimens of woolly thistle on the verges here, with flower-heads up to 7cm in diameter.

Woolly thistle

Hatherop Church carving

Go past Eastleach Folly at 333 Akeman Street and then Williamstrip Farm to reach the gates of Williamstrip Lodge (painted in the cream Williamstrip estate colour) where Akeman Street continues its straight course. Follow this long road that veers left (SW) and into the village of **Hatherop**. Turn right towards **Coln St. Aldwyns**. On the left is the primary school, the former drinking fountain and the footpath that leads to Hatherop church.

It is worth a short diversion (300 yards) to see this unusual church which was built in 1854 by Henry Clutton in a perpendicular-cum-French Gothic style. The quality of the carvings both inside and outside is beautiful.

On returning to the village street from the church, turn left (W) past the remains of the old preaching cross on the right side of the road, the 'flower-pot man' on the left, and Hatherop Castle School. Nancy Mitford, (see Day 3) attended this school for a short time. Descend the hill past a former mill on the left towards Coln St. Aldwyns.

At Park Lodge, near the bottom of the hill, it is worth making a 200 yard diversion to see a beautiful view of Williamstrip Park House and a traditional English parkland. Go through the wide wooden gate in front of the Lodge (also painted cream) to take the footpath (N) climbing to the top of the slope. The house, with its elegant external staircase, copper roof, pediments and Georgian windows can be seen to the north.

Flowerpot man

Continue (W) into the village. On reaching the chestnut tree at the small triangular green and the Coln Village Stores, continue in the same direction to arrive at Church Lane.

This village has been here since Norman times. The New Inn is down the street to the left of the triangular green and dates from the reign of Queen Elizabeth I, when she decreed that there should be an inn within a day's travel of every centre of population for the comfort and security of her subjects.

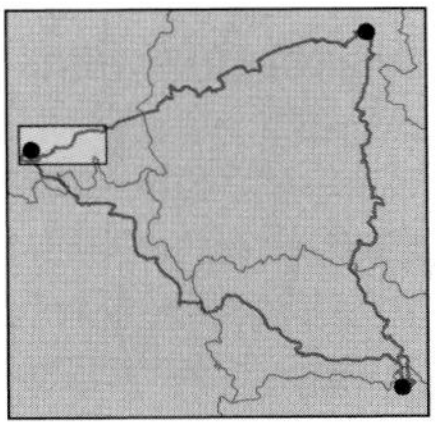

Day 5

Coln St. Aldwyns to Cirencester

Coln St. Aldwyns GR SP 145052 to Cirencester GR SP 020012

We first follow close to the route of Akeman Street as it heads south-west across the open Cotswold Hills towards Cirencester (the Roman town of Corinium). We then leave its straight course and approach the town via ancient villages built close to the Ampney Brook and the River Churn, arriving at the huge Roman amphitheatre on the south side of the town. There is an opportunity to visit the town's museum. This section could be divided into two halves by parking at the access point in Ampney Crucis which would leave more time for the museum.

Distance: 11.5 miles (18.4 km)

Maps: Outdoor Leisure 45 – The Cotswolds.
Explorer 169 – Cirencester & Swindon.
Landranger 163 – Cheltenham & Cirencester area.

Transport: Buses
- Cirencester/Coln St. Aldwyns/Hatherop, 865/866.
- Ampney Crucis/Cirencester, 861.
  Traveline – Tel: 0871 200 2233. www.traveline.org.uk

Taxis:
Bibury
- Coln Valley Cabs/Rainbow Cabs. Tel: 01285 740070.

Cirencester
- Radio Cars. Tel: 01285 651117/650850.
- Cirencester Taxis. Tel: 01285 800006.
- Brian's. Tel: 01285 655299.

Car Parking: Coln St. Aldwyns – Restricted parking beside the high stone wall in Church Lane, west of Coln Village Stores.
Cirencester – Junction of Cotswold Close with Cotswold Avenue on south side of amphitheatre. N.B. there is no notice about the amphitheatre, just a small wooden gate and fence near the entrance.
Cirencester – For the museum and town. Car parks at the Leisure Centre (GR 017016) or Old Station (GR 018017). Charge £5 per day, free on Sundays.

Accommodation/Public Houses/Refreshments:

Ampney Crucis • The Crown of Crucis Hotel. Tel: 01285 851806.
Siddington • The Greyhound Inn PH. Tel: 01285 653573. (600 yards from route)
• Dobbies Garden World, café and restaurant. Tel: 01285 884300.

For full accommodation list, contact Cirencester Visitor Information Centre. Tel: 01285 654180. www.cotswolds.com

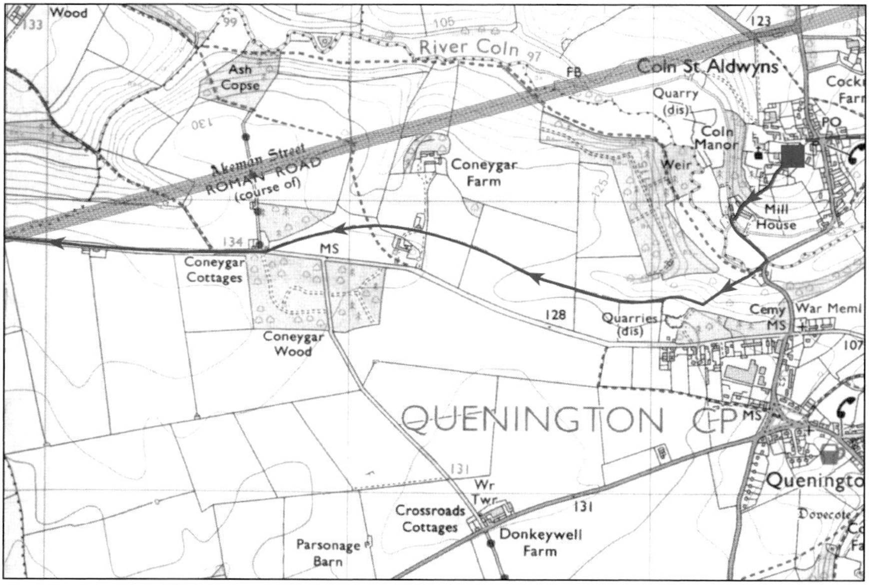

Go along Church Lane (SW) towards the church and past the almshouses built of stone and timber from Williamstrip House (see Day 4) as a memorial to Lucy Catherine, Countess St. Aldwyn 1851–1940. Pass the lane to the church and continue in the same direction (SW) to cross the bridge over the mill leat from the River Coln and turn left (SE) to the road.

The continuation of the mill leat can be seen winding through the valley in its raised channel (NE). Turn right at the road to cross the main channel of the River Coln and right again through the wooden gate by a lodge. Bear left up the bridleway (240°) among parkland trees.

We heard the mew of buzzards in the tall beech trees on the sides of the valley.

Follow the track to go under the trees to a corner of a stone wall. Go alongside this wall to pass through another metal gate and across the middle of the next field (NW, 290°). Cross another field in the same direction to pass left of the small stone cottages with a fine medieval barn, south of Coneygar Farm.

In Middle English, Coneygar means rabbit warren. Rabbits were introduced by the Normans.

Go through the metal gate by these cottages to walk across the field beyond, bearing slightly left towards the road (248°) to meet it just before Coneygar Cottages.

The latch of the small wooden gate onto the road was crafted specially to make it easy to press open when on horseback. We admired the blacksmith's work from a different age, in making a metal cup with a small drain in it so that the hunting crop did not get wet!

Gate latch, Coln St. Alwyns

Turn right along the road and walk to the first bend. Akeman Street meets the road at this point. At GR 118048, where there is a small section of wall in the hedge on the right, until recently the pronounced linear mound of the agger could be seen in the field. Beware of the fast traffic.

A wildflower verge
This bend also marks the start of the Experimental Verge, an initiative to encourage biodiversity of wild flowers being conducted by Gloucestershire County Council. When we passed it in September, flowers included agrimony, autumn hawkbit, deadnettle, knapweed, rosebay willowherb, St. John's wort, scabious, thistle, toadflax and yarrow. The hedge species included elder, field maple, ash, hazel, oak, bramble, hawthorn, whitebeam, crab apple and bryony. We saw a brimstone butterfly (so called because of its sulphur yellow colour) feeding on the knapweed, and bumble bees on the thistles.

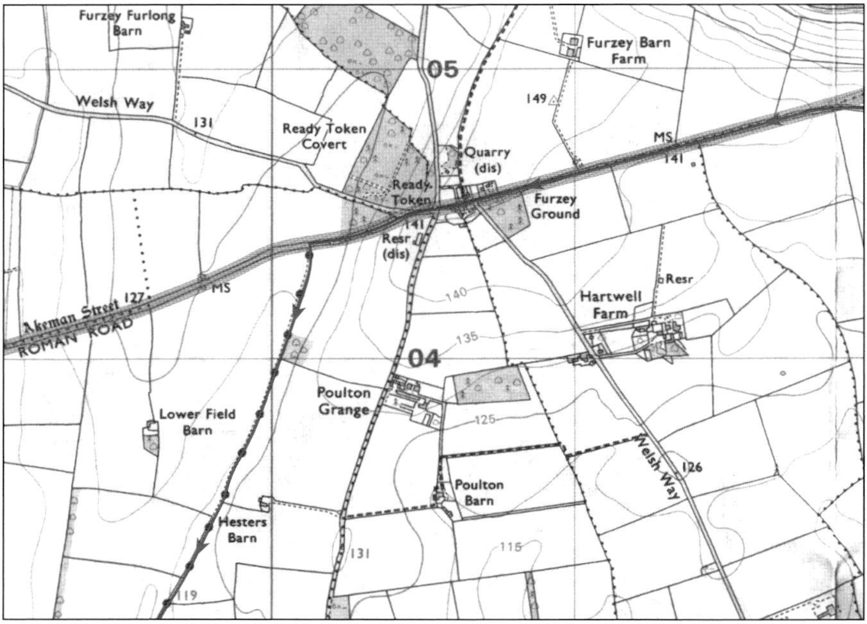

Further on, the milestone on the right has a bench mark. Here, as the map shows, we are 141 metres above sea level. Continue along Akeman Street to reach the group of buildings at **Ready Token**.

The name Ready Token meant a pub requiring real money. This settlement had a spooky reputation for highwaymen: there is a story of a skeleton being found bricked up in the wall of one of the houses.

At the junction, continue (SW) in the direction of Barnsley. Go over the crossroads, then at the next road junction bear slightly left (250°) to go down the hill, still on Akeman Street. Where the slope flattens and 350 yards after the fork, turn left onto the first track on the left, through field gates to join a byway for 1.6 miles (SW). Keep on the main track (SW) until the outskirts of **Ampney St. Mary** are reached.

This grassy way is bordered by a hedge and verge rich in species. In August, there was burdock and high stands of blue-hued teasel flowers, the nectar of which feeds the bees, and in winter the seeds are a valuable larder for goldfinches and other seed-eaters. It is thought that goldfinches carry a 'map' in their brains of where these rich food sources are, and remember them year after year. We saw peacock and painted lady butterflies here.

At the edge of the village, where the track makes a T-junction with a minor road, cross the road and over a ladder stile, straight across the field in the same direction to a kissing gate opposite and through a gate out onto the village street. Turn left, then right down a narrow path marked with a staddle stone.

At the triangular green with its Queen's Jubilee sugar maple tree, keep straight ahead (S) towards a large tithe barn. Turn right (NW) at Elm Tree Cottage and follow the village street. Pass the telephone box and Manor Farmyard.

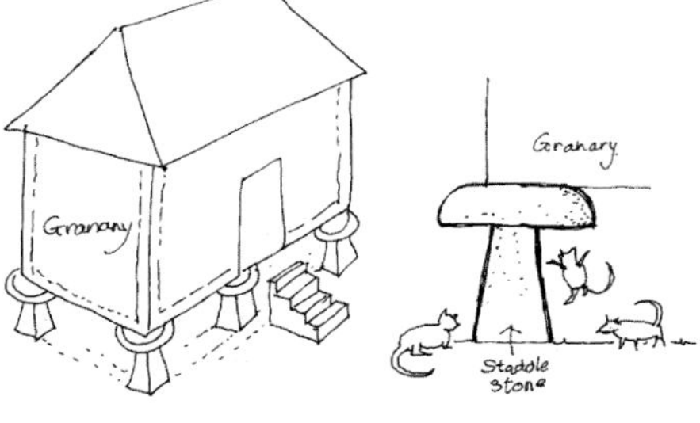

Staddle stone, Ampney St. Mary
These were placed to raise granaries above vermin

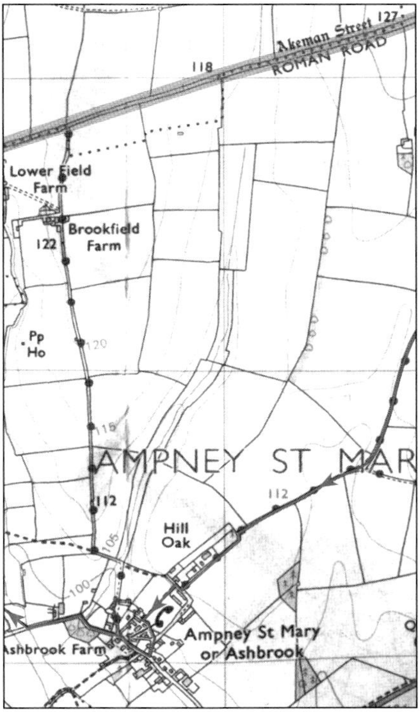

Is the village called Ampney St. Mary or Ashbrook?
On the OS map both names are listed. This is because during the time of the Black Death, the residents of the former site of Ampney St. Mary village, south of Ampney Crucis (where now only a tiny 13th century church with its medieval wall paintings remains, at GR 075015, south of the A417), were first to catch the plague. This community moved away from the damp surroundings of the valley of the Ampney Brook up to Ashbrook, bringing the name of their village with them. Even today some of the residents whom we met still refer to it as Ampney St. Mary and others as Ashbrook. Thus the Ordnance Survey map records the continuing confusion!

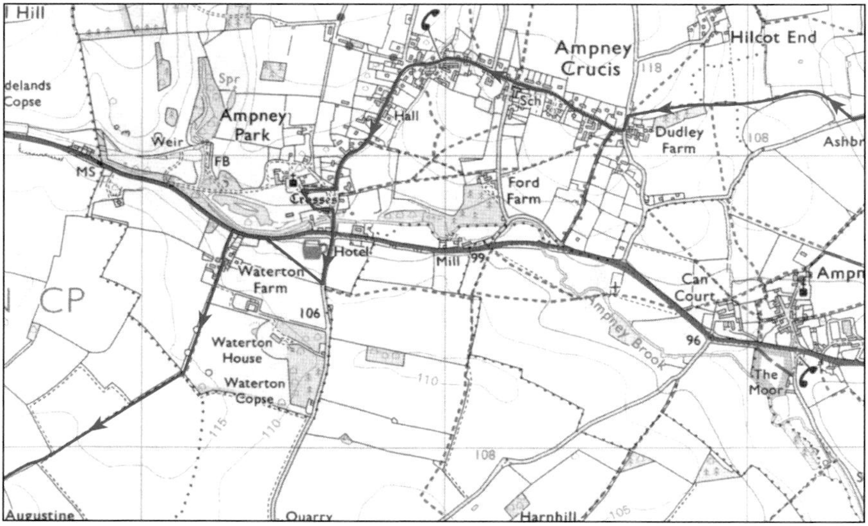

Continue through the village past the pond on the left, and Forty Farm with its milk-churn stand outside. The curious name, 'forty', originates from fort or forp and ey (OE) meaning 'a spur of land projecting into the marsh'. Walk 50 yards past the entrance of Ampney St. Mary Manor on the left. Here, turn right through the hedge and go diagonally left through a field full of thistles.

When we walked in September there was a charm of goldfinches feeding on the thistle seeds, and several species of butterflies also enjoying the flower heads.

Go through a small wooden gate, then keep left along the hedgerow following it over the footbridge in the next hedge, then walk (260°) across the next large field. N.B. this is not the same as on the OS map since a wood and hedge east of Dudley Farm have been removed since surveying took place. Aim right of a group of buildings and into **Ampney Crucis**. Turn left on the road and almost immediately right, to walk along the village street. Pass the cemetery where we admired the black and white timber work of the chapel.

Access point: Ampney Crucis, 5.7 miles, near cemetery chapel. Bus 861 to Cirencester, telephone. GR 074022.

Continue (NW) along the long (nearly 0.75 miles) village street of Cotswold stone-built houses past a triangular green and keep on the main village street passing Ampney House on the left with its twin haylofts. Pass cottages called The Old Bakery, Bakery Cottage and Cobbler's Cottage. Go past a triangular green with a wooden bench on it, and along to a house on the right called 'Five Bottles'. This recalls the fact that the five bottle ends built into the top of the gable end were the last to be produced in the former brewery. The Malt House next door was originally the mead house and the house opposite, the Hops house, thus indicating the stages of brewing beer.

Go round the next corner keeping to the pavement and continuing down the hill to pass Gardener's Cottage and Nurse's Cottage. Soon after Nurse's Cottage, turn right under an iron lych gate at the site of the remains of an ancient preaching cross, to follow the footpath (W) beneath the yew trees to the church.

From the footpath opposite the church, turn left downhill (SE) along the back lane past the Old Rectory on the left. There is a red King Edward VII letterbox in the wall, an unusual sight as he reigned for only nine years, from 1901 to 1910. At the war memorial, cross the stone bridge over the Ampney Brook with its crystal-clear waters. The hotel, The Crown of Crucis, and the bus stop for Cirencester are nearby.

Access Point: Ampney Crucis, The Crown of Crucis Hotel, 6.75 miles. Pub, bus, telephone. GR 066017.

Cross the A417 with great care, to continue (S) along a small lane towards Driffield. After 200 yards, turn right up some wooden steps in the bank and cross the small fields bearing slightly right (NW) downhill to meet the road at double wooden gates. Turn left over a traditional

Ampney Crucis Church
The dedication of this church to the Holy Rood (Holy Cross) is rare and ancient. At the time of Domesday Book in 1086, the village was already known as Ampney Rood. The preaching cross outside dates from 1415 and has four carved sides. Inside the church is a Saxon doorway, with its typically tall, narrow shape. There are Norman features and a fine tomb and remnants of interesting medieval wall paintings.

Preaching Cross, Ampney St. Crucis

stone slab stile, cross the road very carefully and go west (left), then cross again to take the track (S) up to Waterton Farm. Go through the farmyard and metal gates, to walk along the right side of a field.

We saw two buzzards here, distinguishable by their characteristic rounded tail and their flap-flap-flap-glide flight.

Continue to the end of the second field. At the gap in the stone wall, go into the next field. Continue following the hedge until reaching the part where the field opens out. Go straight across here (SW, 240°) to a projecting hedge corner opposite, to follow the hedge (SW) to the very corner of the field.

At this point, turn right to go through a small gap over a footbridge, and turn left alongside the hedge (SW). Continue alongside two fields on the south-west side, then through a wooden gate into a third field, to bear half right across the field (NW, 310°). Go towards the road, A417(T), and a green road sign.

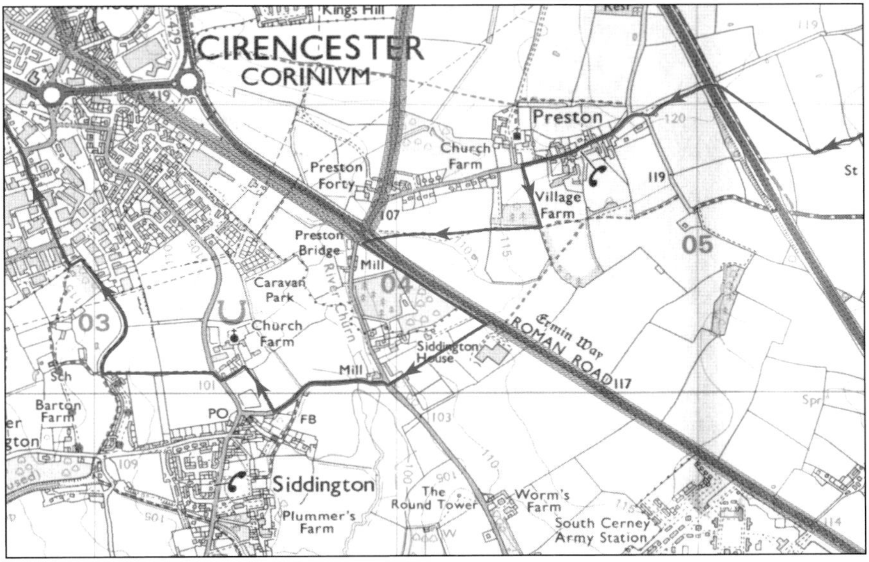

Should the crop be impassable, it is possible to continue along the left side of the field, then right along the fenced bridleway beside the road. Cross the road with care. Turn left at a substation on the other side, then right to walk away from the road with a hedge on the right. On reaching a minor road, bear right, then left (SW) towards **Preston**.

This village has several old stone houses with characteristic features, for example the weather vane of Bo Peep and her sheep at the Old Farmhouse on the right.

Access Point: Preston village street, 8.5 miles. Telephone. GR 046008.

It is possible to make a 100 yard diversion to the church via a narrow path and beside it is a millennium stone that details how, in the year AD 1000, the village population was 100; in the year 2000, it was 250.

Keys can be obtained from the Old Rectory, Mr Alaister Painter (01285 650624).

Continue along the street (SW) to the wide entrance of Village Farm on the left, with a waymark on the far side. Just beyond here is the entrance to the church on the right.

Back at the waymark sign turn south to walk alongside the wall, then having passed a wood on the right, and just before a small wood on the left, look for an old Cotswold stone stile. Turn right here to join an east/west footpath. Go beside a pine wood, bear slightly more left across a field (W, 260°) to turn right to follow a ditch to the stile by a road junction.

There is a crossing place over the Roman road, the Ermin Way, now the busy A419(T). We make a 600 yards diversion (SE) in order to avoid the narrow, dark and dangerous lane to Siddington. This route has the advantage of spotting the only 'ha-ha' on the Roman Way! Turn left (SE) alongside the road and walk on the pavement beside the parkland of Siddington House.

Turn right (SW) on the footpath just before Dobbies Garden World to arrive at the boundary of Siddington House. Go through a wooden gate and walk along the base of the 'ha-ha' of Siddington House.

Ha-ha, Siddington House

Around the turn of the 17th into the 18th century the desire to have an uninterrupted view across the landscape, combined with the need to stop grazing animals straying into the gardens, prompted the invention of the ha-ha. These are sunken ditches with a wall on one side that does not rise above ground level. The origin of the name comes from the surprised "ah ha" on spotting one!

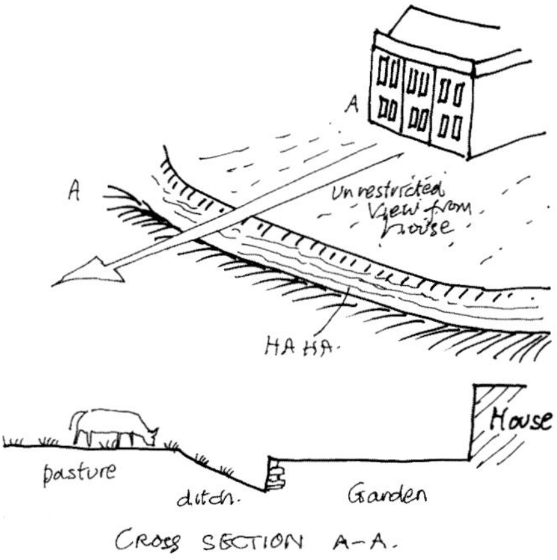

Cross the lawn, past the helipad and continue in the same direction over a drive between two conifers into another narrow, sunken path to arrive at the road. Beware of the fast-moving traffic, and cross towards the village of **Siddington**, passing the mill on the right.

Cross the bridge over the River Churn. This is a dangerous, narrow, winding road. We crossed and re-crossed to the outside of each bend to give oncoming traffic maximum warning of our presence. Further on, the manor house can be seen across the meadows to the right. Just where the road bends right at Prospect Cottage, turn right (NW) over a stile to walk towards the manor house. At the end of the field, the route goes immediately left along Church Avenue.

Here is an opportunity to make a 100 yard diversion to visit the church and its medieval barn.

Access Point: Siddington, Church Avenue, 10.0 miles. Telephone, pub, PO, shop, B&B. GR 034001.

Siddington Church
Siddington church has a remarkable carved south doorway. Above the apex of the hood-mould is a demon's head with horns, and there are fifteen Scandinavian-influenced beakheads. The Norsemen who carved this would have been importing their traditions from their native lands. The tympanum (the semi-circular space between a door lintel and the arch above it) represents God seated on a throne presenting a large key to St. Peter with his right hand and with his left, a book to St. Paul.

Keys with Michael Painter (01285 650624) or Alan Howe (01285 657933).

Retrace your steps to go along Church Avenue, turn right (NW) at the road, then almost immediately left across the road, to walk west (290°) on the footpath with the hedgerow on the left. Walk through a partly dismantled railway bridge and along the edge of a field in the same direction, to arrive at a crossroads of paths. *Do not* cross the canal bridge but turn right (N) to follow the route of the disused Thames and Severn Canal (see Day 6).

The age of the trees in the canal bed gives an indication that this canal has been abandoned since at least the 1930s.

Access Point: Cirencester (south), Corinium Centre, Love Lane on the industrial estate, 50 yards left (W) of path exit, 10.6 miles. Bus stop (51) Love Lane. GR 028005.

Tithe barn, Siddington

One of the oldest barns in England

Beside the church to the left, the triangular end of a low stone barn can be seen. The property is owned and managed by the Bathurst estate.

Permission to visit needs to be obtained (01285 653135).

Go through the small wooden gate and walk beside the barn to its huge wagon porch entrance. Inside, the roof timbers and the wooden joints have been dated to the early 13th century. It is a fine, five-bay, aisled barn with a massive roof of Cotswold stone slate. It was given to the Knights Hospitallers, part of the Knights Templars estate.

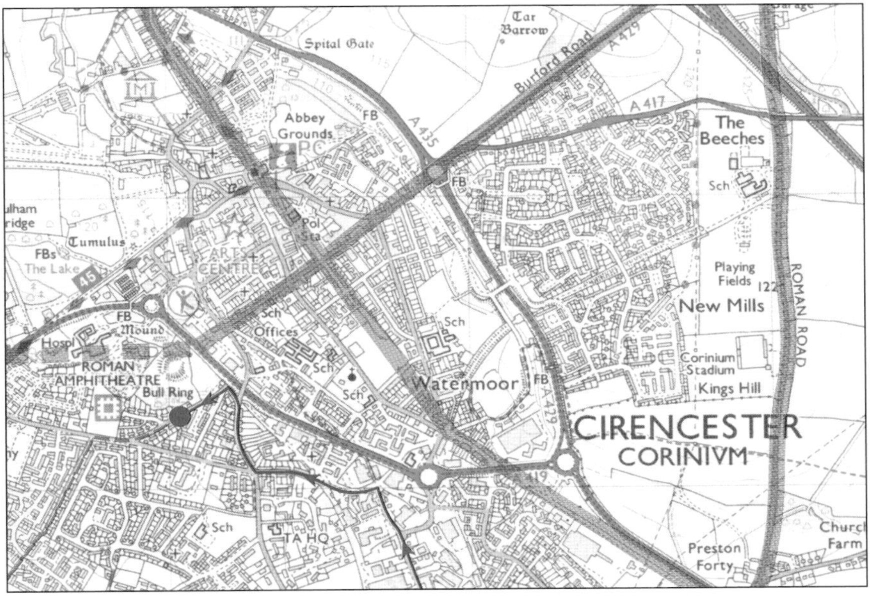

To continue the route to the amphitheatre and the town centre, turn right (N) along Love Lane crossing Elliot Road, Midland Road and up to the garage with its shop. This was formerly the route of the industrial canal.

Bear left (NW) uphill after the garage to pass Meadow Road on the right. Take the first right along Somerford Road, then left along Cotswold Avenue to where there is a gap in the stone wall, which is the entrance to the site of the Roman amphitheatre.

Access Point: Cirencester amphitheatre, 11.5 miles.

To visit the centre of the town and the museum, return along Cotswold Avenue (NE) to rejoin Somerford Road. Turn left (N) across the bypass bridge, up Querns Hill and enter Sheep Street. There are some fine stone houses on the right such as the Old Rectory, and on the left is the Memorial Centre with its roll of honour for those who died in World War I. The Old Station car park is to the left and the Cirencester Museum is further north beyond Sheep Street along Park Lane.

Corinium Museum, Park Street, GL7 2BX. Tel: 01285 655611. Mon–Sat, 10am–5pm, Sun, 2–5pm, shop and café. GR 021020.
www.cotswold.gov.uk

Cirencester Roman Amphitheatre

The amphitheatre was one of the largest in Roman Britain. It is an oval enclosure with seating made of stone and wood which would originally have risen 10 metres high. It might have accommodated up to 8,000 spectators from the town and surrounding countryside. The arena was used for games, including gladiatorial combats, bear baiting, animal hunts, boxing and wrestling, as well as for religious and other processions. Outside the arena, a macellum or market would have thrived with a variety of tented stalls selling merchandise and refreshments.

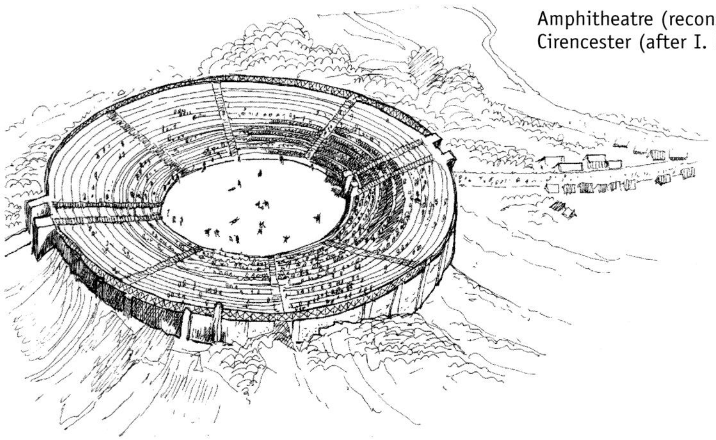

Amphitheatre (reconstruction), Cirencester (after I. Lapper)

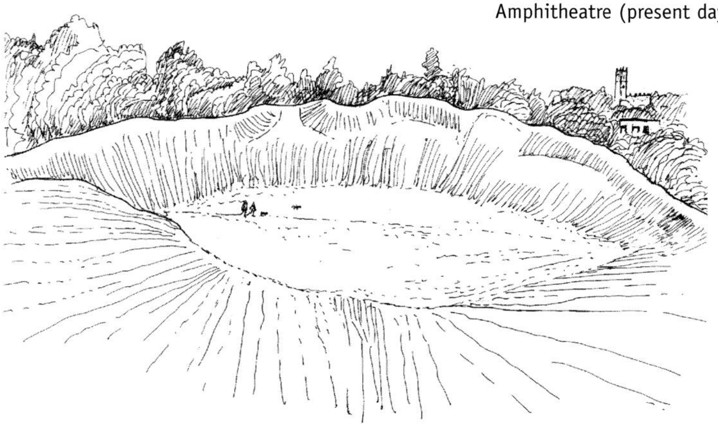

Amphitheatre (present day)

Corinium Dobunnorum (Cirencester)
Corinium Dobunnorum was first established as a Roman fort at the crossing of the River Churn. It became an administrative centre from around AD 75 and was subsequently enclosed by defences, including the last visible but impressive, remains beside the road in 'Corinium Gate', GR 028022 where Akeman Street (now the Burford Road) enters the town.
When Britain was divided into four provinces, Corinium became the capital of one of them and was the second largest town in Britain.

Roman soldier's tombstone, Corinium Museum
The stone commemorates a member of the cavalry unit stationed in the fort. The Latin inscription reads: "Sextus Valerius Genialis, trooper of the Cavalry Regiment of Thracians, a Frisian tribesman, from the troop of Genialis, aged 40, of 20 years service, lies buried here. His heir had this set up."

A change of direction
Corinium was the meeting place of three major Roman roads: Akeman Street from Verulamium in the east, the Fosse Way from Lincoln to Exeter and the Ermin Way from Gloucester to Silchester. From Day 6, we turn south-east to follow the route of the Ermin Way which has been so-called since the 19th century antiquarians developed the name from that of Ermine Street (OE: the road of Earn(a)'s people), which runs from London to York.
Before we set off, there is a chance to enjoy a re-creation of a Roman garden in an outside space at the museum. The Romans introduced many plant species to Britain, including daffodils, plums and walnuts. Plants grown in Roman gardens were often chosen for their healing powers. The dog rose was one, so called because the Romans thought that the root of this plant cured rabies.

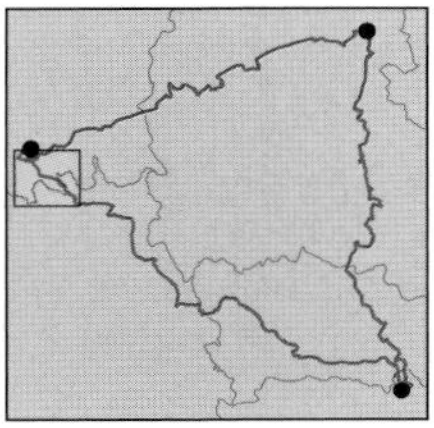

Day 6

Cirencester to Cricklade

Cirencester GR SP 019012 to Cricklade GR SU 100934

The Roman road, the Ermin Way, runs south-east along the north side of the day's walking, crossing the flat alluvial plain created by the River Churn. When the water level is high, it might be worth checking in advance that the paths are passable. Surprisingly, many of the buildings in the villages through which we pass are made of stone that was brought here from the Cotswold Hills. We follow the path beside canals and the Rivers Churn and Thames to arrive in the 9th century Saxon burh town of Cricklade.

Distance: 9.7 miles (15.5 km).

Maps: Explorer 169 – Cirencester & Swindon.
Landranger 173 – Swindon & Devizes.

Transport: Buses
- Cirencester/Cricklade, 50/51.
  Traveline – Tel: 0871 200 2233. www.traveline.org.uk

Taxis:

Cirencester
- Radio Cars. Tel: 01285 651117/650850.
- Cirencester Taxis. Tel: 01285 800006.
- AAR Services. Tel: 01285 658189.

Swindon
- V Cars. Tel: 01793 701701.
- United Radio Cars. Tel: 01793 611111.

Car Parking: Cirencester – Junction of Cotswold Close with Cotswold Avenue on south side of amphitheatre. N.B. there is no notice about the amphitheatre, just a small wooden gate and fence near the entrance.
Cricklade – Town Hall free car park in the High Street, (on approaching the town from the A419, turn left at the T-junction, the Town Hall is 100 yards west). Alternative parking is either in 'Waylands', the road south of the Town Hall, or in the car park in Stockham Close (GR 107935) near the roundabout on outskirts of the east side of the town near the A419.

Accommodation/Public Houses/Refreshments

Chesterton
- Chesterton Farm Shop – Refreshments.
  Tel: 01285 653003.

Siddington	• Greyhound Inn. Tel: 01285 653573. (0.5 miles from route)
South Cerney	• Eliot Arms Hotel. Tel: 01285 860215.
	• The Old George Inn. Tel: 01285 869989.
	• Pippins B&B. Tel: 01285 860902. www.southcerney.org.uk
Cerney Wick	• Crown Inn (B&B). Tel: 01793 750369.
Cricklade	• Tourist information. Tel: 01793 751394. www.cricklade-tc.gov.uk
	• The Old Bear Inn. Tel: 01793 750005.

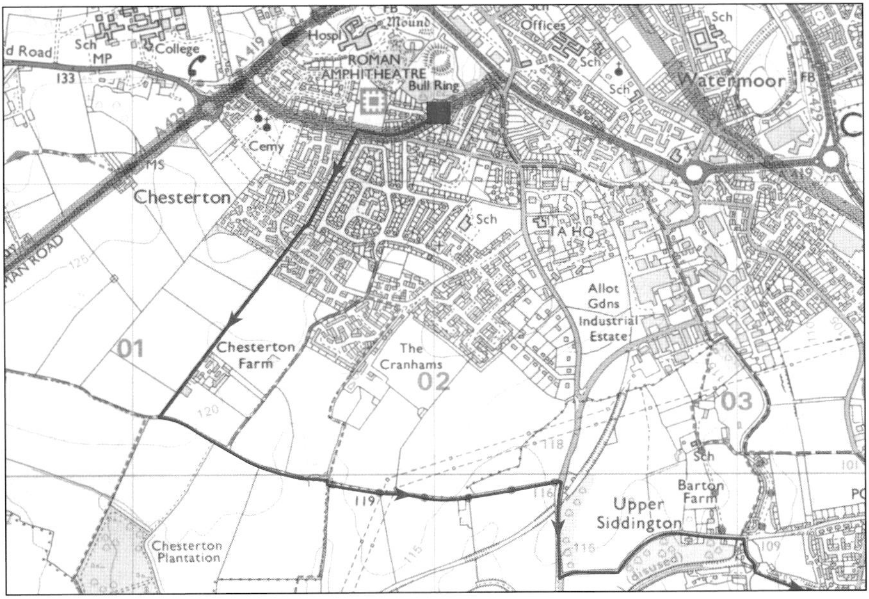

Walk (SW) on the road, slightly uphill from the amphitheatre to turn right into Chesterton Lane. The name Chesterton refers to a Roman station within the ancient city boundary of Cirencester. (See Day 1, Chesterton.) After 100 yards, at the dead end sign and just before Four Acres View begins, turn left (SW) down a track at the back of houses.

Continue down this track crossing over an estate road and on to pass Chesterton Farm with its large stone built barns, external staircase and farm shop. The tall chimney was built for the former steam engine that powered the corn mill. 250 yards beyond the farm, at a track junction, turn left (SE) to follow the bridleway.

Beside the track is a field margin that has been planted with native tree species; we saw field maple, elder, hawthorn, oak, privet, whitebeam, dogwood, cherry, hazel, beech, ash and guelder rose. There were sloes in the more ancient hedge on the left, and flowering ivy on the stone wall to the right. Here we saw three buzzards wheeling overhead.

Continue (E) under the electricity transmission lines and along the permitted path. At the minor road, turn right (S) for 300 yards along the busy, narrow road. Take great care as the traffic is fast: we recommend walking on the verges. Turn left to take the road to **Upper Siddington** passing the old ash trees that border it. On nearing the village the stone-gabled building of Barton Farm on the left with its fine stone-tiled shelter shed and external staircase is passed.

Before the village green, turn right going beside the children's playground to approach the canal. Turn left and descend the steps on its far (S) bank to walk east.

Orpheus Mosaic

Barton Farm is the site of a former Roman villa which possessed the remarkable Orpheus mosaic that is now exhibited in the Corinium Museum in Cirencester. Orpheus charmed animals, including this tiger, with his music.

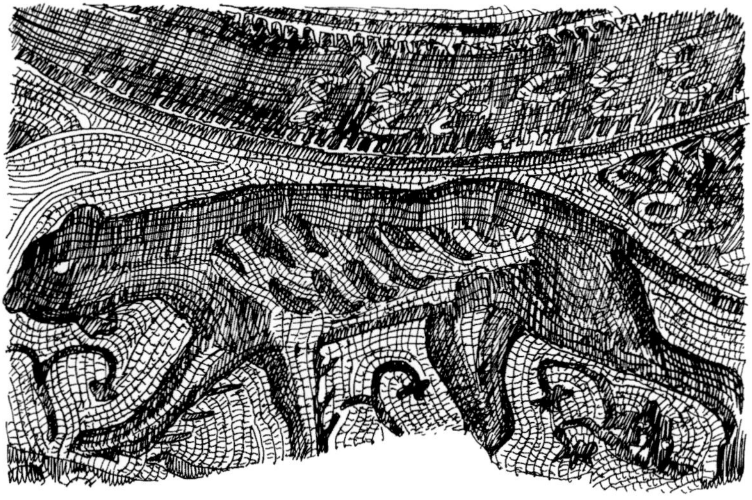

Tiger, Orpheus mosaic, found at Barton Farm, Upper Siddington

Some history of the Thames and Severn Canal is evident here. Before the canal, is the Canal House with its distinctive small windows, built to minimise the impact of window tax (from where the expression 'daylight robbery' originates). There are the remains of a winding hole. These were designed to overcome the problem of turning long narrow boats and barges. There was plenty of room at the larger canal basins, but in the outlying regions the canal was widened by building a short arm to allow the bow to be placed in the arm and the stern punted or towed round.

Winding hole, Upper Siddington

Continue along the towpath to the village street. The house 'Greenways' is on the left, on the site of Siddington Bottom lock. The house is built on girders across the canal lock! The Greyhound Inn is 100 yards along the road to the right.

Access Point: Siddington, 2.7 miles. Shop, post office, pub, telephone. GR 033994

Cross the road and over metal poles on the other side to continue following the canal towpath signposted to **South Cerney**.

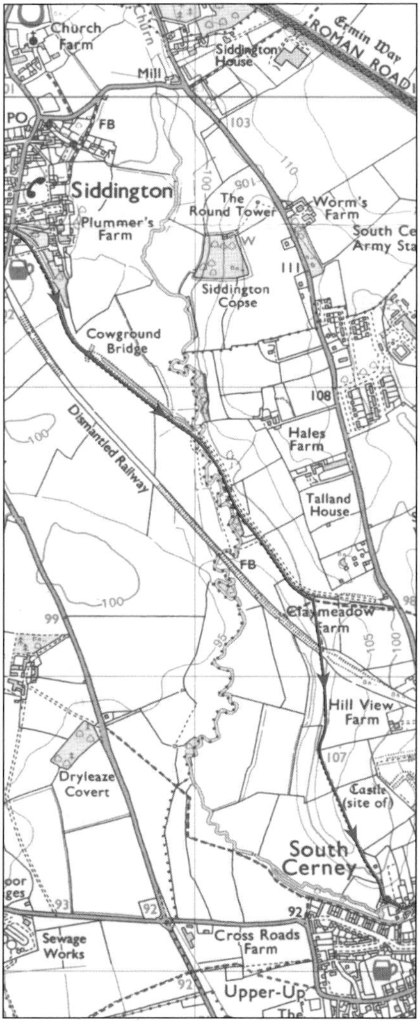

This is a delightful wildlife corridor with watercress, comfrey and umbelliferae. 350 yards beyond the road, turn left (NE) beyond the farm gates between two Leyland Cypress trees, there is a view of a building that looks like a castle. It is The Round Tower (GR 042996), an 'eye catcher' or folly for the Siddington House estate.

Continue along the towpath under the brick canal bridge and on for a further 200 yards to where the canal would have crossed the River Churn via an aqueduct. Sadly, a bomb landed in the middle of it in World War II and destroyed the aqueduct. There is a commemorative plaque on the far side of the bridge.

'An early bite'

In the flood meadows to the right are signs of medieval water management. The channels, still visible, would have been used to flood these meadows in the winter to avoid ground frost delaying the growth of the early spring grass and to provide a rapidly moving sheet of water to oxygenate the grass and so stimulate its early growth. The layer of water would also have protected the young shoots. Once the grass was long enough, the meadows would have been drained so that cattle would have had a nutritious 'early bite'.

Continue on the towpath, then just before reaching a seat commemorating David Fox's life, turn right over a wooden stile to bear left (170°) through a metal gate to walk diagonally across a field (S) following the line of the path on the map.

Go over a stile by a wooden gate and across a dismantled railway, then through a metal field gate. Follow the track for only 50 yards, then leave it to bear left uphill (180°) climbing gently to a protruding hedge corner. Walk another 50 yards to go through a metal gate and bear left (160°), keeping beside the hedge on the left. Go over a stile to walk along the top of the promontory.

Keep along the hedge going over a stile to arrive at a concrete drive, turn right, and turn left into School Lane to the village of South Cerney with the River Churn to the right. There is a characteristic Cotswold stone 'plank' fence at the cottage near the village hall.

Access Point: South Cerney, 4.6 miles. (Station Road, at junction with main village street, Clarks Hay.) Shop, post office, pubs, buses, telephone. GR 049970.

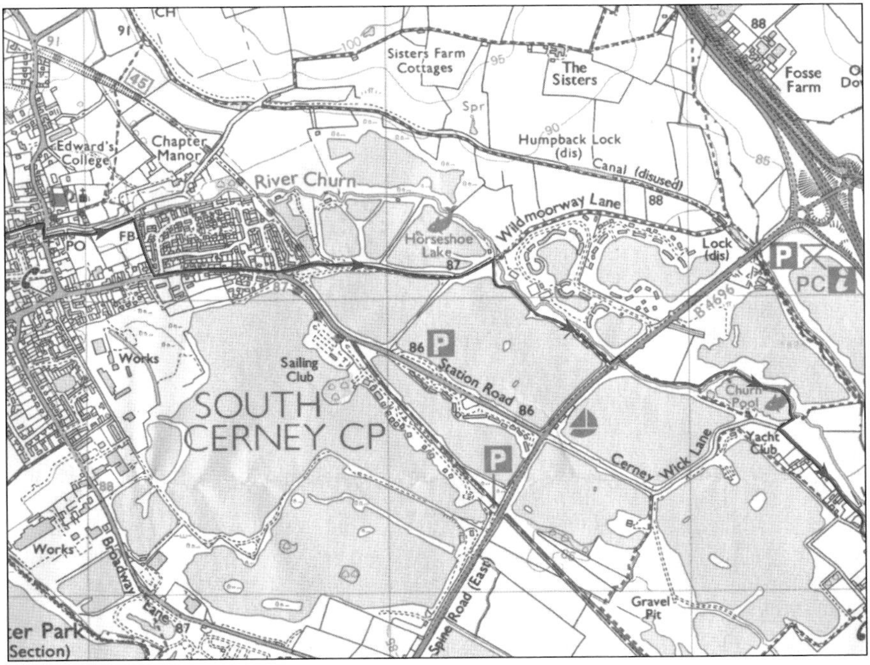

A rare crucifix in All Hallows church

To see this treasure, turn left, then right alongside Atkyns Manor with its fine topiary yew hedges. The church is Norman with a tympanum, chevron-mouldings and beakheads in the doorway. One of the most remarkable features is a resin copy of the head and feet of the celebrated South Cerney crucifix now preserved in the British Museum. This is believed to be one of the earliest pieces of wood-carving of this type found in Britain. Nearly all the bigger churches would have had such a crucifix on the rood (choir) screen in the 12th century. This one is dated about AD 1130. As you return to the village street, the stone louvres can be seen on both the church and manor roofs.

On reaching the main village street, Silver Street, turn right, then left (E) along a road called 'Bow Wow', (this is a local name for a boundary) following the River Churn on the left. The stream on the right is the mill leat and is slightly higher than the river. After 300 yards, turn right over a footbridge in front of the mill to follow a path (S) at the back of a housing estate.

At Station Road turn left (E) for 400 yards to the edge of the village to bear left along the track 'Wildmoorway'. After 600 yards, just before a wooden bridge and opposite the second gate of the Watermark Fisheries, turn right along the waymarked footpath. This path follows the edge of the lakes then swings south-east alongside a lake to the Cotswold Water Park West where a track from the left joins the path. Keep right to stay by the large lakeside.

Access point: Cotswold Water Park Visitor Centre, 6.4 miles. Café, information centre, tours of the area. Tel: 01793 752413. www.waterpark.org
600 yards (NW) from route along B4696. GR 072971.

Cotswold Water Park

This area consists of 73 lakes formed by gravel extraction in the alluvial river basin. The lakes are used for water sports of all kinds but also provide a sanctuary for water fowl. We saw great crested grebe, little grebe, mallard, pochard, shoveller and smew. Reed mace (bulrushes), thistles, valerian and Himalayan balsam grow on the banks providing, in turn, a food source for butterflies.

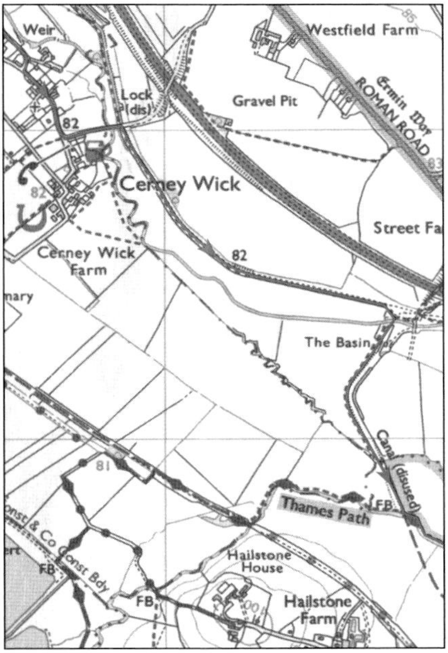

Turn left (NE) onto the B4696, cross it, and almost immediately turn right down some wooden steps to follow the left bank of the River Churn. After 300 yards cross to its right bank and follow the path around the north side of the Churn Pool. There are views back to the Cotswold Water Park Visitor Centre with its numerous solar panels on the roof.

At the far side of the pool, follow the river for 20 yards to turn sharp right, not over a stile into a field. Instead take a narrow path which doubles back (SW) to meet the road. Turn left and walk into the village of **Cerney Wick**. The Anglo-Saxon origin of this name is 'a dairy farm'. There are several stone buildings, for example, Baker's Farmhouse with its semi-circular bread oven protruding from the external wall. At the Crown Hotel, turn left along the street to reach the canal.

Turn right (SE) to follow the towpath for one mile. The former Latton Canal Basin is reached. This provided a link and space for change of cargoes from the Wilts and Berks Canal to the Thames and Severn Canal. Turn right through the gate. N.B. The footpath has been diverted to east of the lock-keeper's house, not west as on the map. Follow the footpath signs (SW) along the path of the former Thames Link Canal. A bridge over a stream is reached. Continue 200 yards to the bridge over the River Thames. Turn left before the bridge to walk along the left (N) bank of the river.

Thames and Severn Canal

This canal was opened in 1789, but with the competition of the railways carrying freight the canal trade reduced so much that the canal company put forward a bill to turn itself into a railway. Its fortunes continued to decline: in 1864 the last dividend was paid by the company and in 1900 the canal was closed to commercial traffic.

Lengthman's Houses

The circular stone building to the left of the canal bridge at Cerney Wick is one of five lengthman's houses built along the course of the canal in 1790. They were called lengthman's houses because the occupant was responsible for looking after a particular length of the canal. The traditional circular shape was due to a suspicion that the devil, or evil, could find no corner in which to hide! Besides this one, there are circular lengthman's houses at Sapperton Lock, Chalford, Marston Macey and Inglesham. There are plans by the Cotswold Canal Trust to restore and re-open the canal.

For further information visit:
www.cotswoldcanals.com

Lengthman's House, Cerney Wick

North Meadow

The meadow to the left is North Meadow, one of the finest uncultivated ancient flood meadows in Britain. It is ancient 'Lammas' land which means that certain townspeople had the right to graze their animals from Lammas Day (August 1st) until February 2nd, the land reverting to meadow in the summer so maintaining the traditional hay cutting and grazing management. It is now a national nature reserve, owned by English Nature, and is famous for its snake's head fritillaries which flower in April.

Follow the Thames Path into **Cricklade** heading towards 'Bottom School' a former schoolhouse at the bottom of the town! Enter the town along the course of the north wall. Turn right at the site of the former northern gate and passing the Catholic church to the right, walk south along the High Street.

There are several pubs and cafés here and St. Sampson's Church with its fine tall tower to the right. It is justly known as 'the glory of North Wiltshire'.

Pass the Jubilee Clock, built with public subscription in 1898 to commemorate Queen Victoria's Diamond Jubilee in 1897, and onto the town hall 150 yards past the clock and road junction in the same (SW) direction. There is an interesting town trail (leaflets from the Town Hall).

Jubilee clock, Cricklade

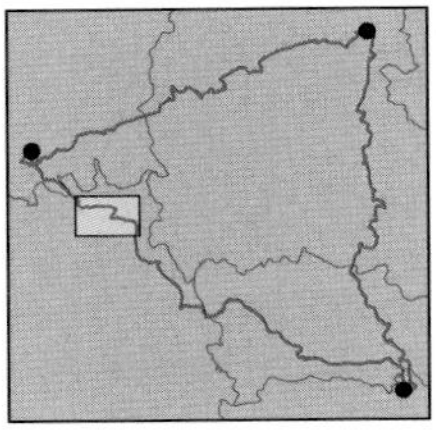

Day 7

Cricklade to South Marston

Cricklade GR SU 100934 to South Marston GR SU 194879

The route continues in the low-lying river meadows of the Rivers Key and Ray which are tributaries of the River Thames to the north. It is part of the Upper Thames Environmentally Sensitive Area and is a remote, quiet place. Since the land can be water-logged when the water table is high, it may be advisable to walk in Wellington boots or to put them or a dry pair of socks in the rucksack! The route climbs to the high point of Castle Hill from where there are fine views of the whole area.

Distance: 10.5 miles (16.4 km).

Maps: Explorer 169 – Cirencester & Swindon.
Landranger 173 – Swindon & Devizes.

Transport: Buses
- Swindon/South Marston, 65.
  Traveline – Tel: 0871 200 2233. www.traveline.org.uk

Taxis:
Circencester
- Radio Cars. Tel: 01285 651117/650850.
- Cirencester Taxis. Tel: 01285 800006.

Swindon
- V Cars. Tel: 01793 701701.
- United Radio Cars. Tel: 01793 611111.

Car Parking: Cricklade – Town Hall free car park in the High Street (on approaching the town from the A419, turn left at the T-junction, the Town Hall is 100 yards west). Alternative parking is either in 'Waylands', the road south of the Town Hall, or in the car park in Stockham Close (GR 107935) near the roundabout on the outskirts of the east side of the town near the A419. South Marston – Village car park, by the footpath sign, south of the village school on the west side of Old Vicarage Lane and north of the playing field.

Accommodation/Public Houses/Refreshments:
Broad Blunsdon (300 yards from route)
- The Heart in Hand PH. Tel: 01793 721314.

- Portquin B&B. Tel: 01793 721261.
- Blunsdon House Hotel. Tel: 01793 721701.

Stanton Fitzwarren
- Stanton House Hotel. Tel: 0870 084 1388.

South Marston
- The Old Post Office B&B. Tel: 01793 823114.
- Carpenters Arms Motel. Tel: 01793 822997.
- The South Marston Hotel. Tel: 01793 833700.

Cricklade
- Cricklade Museum. Tel: 01793 750686. www.cricklademuseum.org

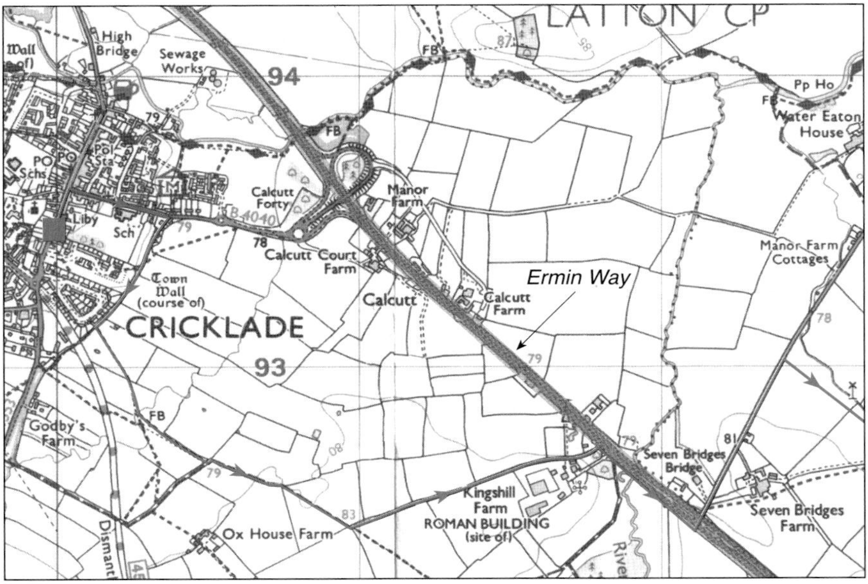

Turn right (NE) along the High Street. The first building that you pass just on the edge of the village hall forecourt is a small stone building, a former weigh house. There are some fine buildings in Cricklade; number 23 High Street, on the opposite side of the road, has a baroque doorway with a characteristic 'broken arch' and fine urn in it. Turn right (SE) at the Jubilee clock along Calcutt Street for 0.25 miles passing the Cricklade Museum on the left, then, at the row of cottages turn right (SW) along Spital Lane parallel to the course of the former Saxon town earthwork fortifications which provided the base for walls built on top of them.

Spital is derived from the Latin for hospital and in medieval times travellers, the elderly and the ill would have been accommodated so that a hospital in those days would have been a mixture of a hotel, a workhouse and a hospital, significantly located on the edge of the town.

Cricklade Museum: Open Wednesdays 2–4pm (summer only) and Saturdays 10–12 noon. Contains Roman artefacts including huge roof tiles from a luxury villa near what is now Kingshill Farm (on the route, GR 117925).

Go through a metal gate (SW) along a path behind the houses. Continue walking behind the houses, through two more gates, to turn left over a wooden stile just after the second gate at GR 101931, before reaching the brick bridge of a dismantled railway line. Ignore the well-trodden path going parallel along the left side of the field but bear diagonally left (SE, 156°) to a stile in the hedge three quarters of the way down the right side of the field. The field is longer than shown on the OS map as the original field boundary no longer exists.

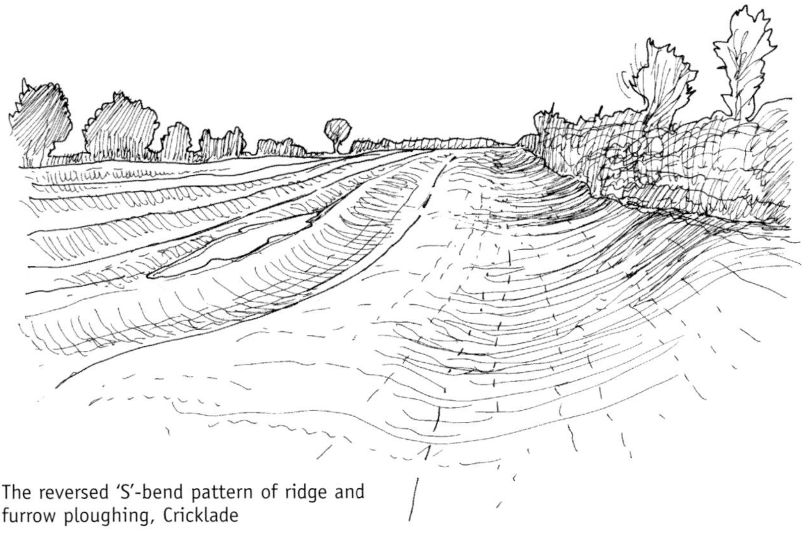

The reversed 'S'-bend pattern of ridge and furrow ploughing, Cricklade

The river meadows to the left still have the remains of the ridges and furrows created by medieval ploughing close to the town walls. In some fields, reverse S-bends can be seen showing where the farmers began to turn the plough team.

Saxon town walls, Cricklade
After 100 yards, at the first field boundary (GR 102933), where a path joins from the right, it is worth walking back a few paces to look over a small wooden gate across a school playing field on the right (W). Here are the remains of the Saxon earthworks (9th century) with poplars now growing on top of them. Cricklade is a rare surviving example of a burh or fortified town built to protect Wessex from the Danes in the 880s. It is one of the most intact examples of a late Saxon town in Britain.

Continue in nearly the same direction diagonally left (SE, 168°) across the next field to the footbridge over the River Key in the far corner. From the footbridge take the left-hand path to bear slightly more left (SE, 123°) to the corner of a hedge just right (S) of a metal field gate 50 yards away.

This flood plain shows all the characteristics of an enclosure landscape with its mainly straight hedges.

Do not go through the metal gate at the hedge corner, but follow along the right side of the hedge (SE, 120°) crossing two stiles. On reaching a bridleway, turn sharp left and after a few paces, go through a metal field gate to turn right (SE) along the left side of a hedge. Half way (300 yards) along this field, turn right to go through a metal gate in the hedge beside a tall tree in the hedgerow.

On the other side, turn left and immediately through a metal gate to bear diagonally left across the field (SE, 120°) aiming left of a large oak tree in the far hedgerow. After the gate (GR 109924), turn left (NE, 74°) along a bridleway. Go through double metal field gates between two old hedgerows and continue through a metal gate to the buildings of Kingshill Farm. Pass between these to the A419(T). There was a fine Roman villa to the east of Kingshill Farm (see Cricklade Museum, page 74).

The busy road follows the line of the Roman Ermin Way that ran between Cirencester and Silchester. Cross it with great care and turn right to walk along the verge for 0.25 miles crossing the Seven Bridges Bridge over the River Ray that flows north to the River Thames and then to the Castle Eaton road.

The name Seven Bridges probably originates from a wide seven-arched bridge before the days of river management.

Turn left to follow the narrow (Castle Eaton) road for nearly half a mile (NE). Pass Seven Bridges Farm with its fine lime tree avenue and the cottages beyond, to turn right through a bridleway gate.

Walk (SE, 122°) with the stream to the left (N) across two fields to go through a third bridleway gate.

Turn left with the hedge to the left then, at the end of the next field, turn left through a metal gate, over a ditch and along the farm track. Before the next metal gate, turn right over a wooden stile to walk on the right side of the hedge (SE).

A stile leads into a copse, which was water-logged on the day that we walked it. The path beyond here forms the county boundary between Wiltshire to the west and Swindon Unitary Authority to the east.

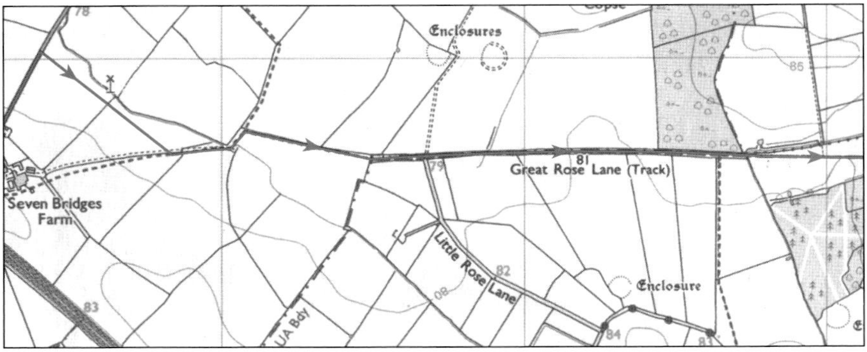

Ermin Street, Blunsdon Hill 2006

This part of the flood plain is a quiet, remote landscape of water meadows all below the 80 metre contour. We saw roe deer, hares and buzzards. Some of the hedges have many species including field maple, hazel, sloe, rosehip and guelder rose.

Continue east along Great Rose Lane, which is reputedly a Roman road for transporting heavy goods as an alternative to the steep gradient of Blunsdon Hill on Ermin Way (GR 138909).

Go along the track (E) on the south side of Water Eaton Copse, through a wooden gate (E) and into an open field. Here the bridleway branches half right (92°) away from the hedge boundary. Cross the field towards a gap in the hedge at the far opposite corner, north of the

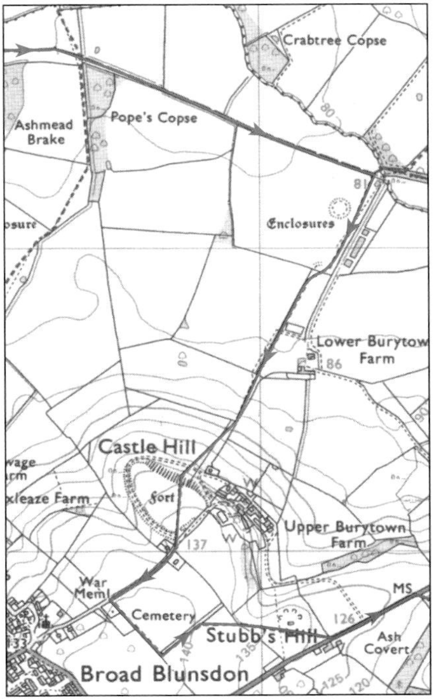

east end of Ashmead Brake and along (SE) to reach the north side of Pope's Copse. Watch out for an owl box high in a large oak tree beside the track.

Follow a gravel track for more than half a mile. Just past the nesting box 221 and 50 yards further on (GR 164922), turn right over a footbridge in a gap in the hedge. If you reach a crossing bridleway with a pond at the junction, you have gone too far. Follow the left side of the field (SW) past what were once ancient enclosures but which have been ploughed out.

Bird Life

A local farmer told us that 110 species of birds have been identified by RSPB volunteers on 3,500 acres of farm and woodland. This is about a third of all UK species. The small nesting boxes are for about 400 tree sparrows, the largest colony in England, and the larger boxes have had little owls, barn owls, tawny owls and other raptors nesting in them. Long-eared owls winter here.

Dog-leg right and left around the rubbish dump just before the next hedge, through a metal gate and along the right side of the field towards Castle Hill ahead. Lower Burytown Farm derives its name from 'bury' meaning castle or enclosure. Leave the field via a metal gate in the corner and climb up the slope and over a stile with the hedge on the left, through another metal gate and uphill to the waymark post.

Bear left (S, 190°) to the far left field corner, crossing the ramparts to a waymark and gate leading into a lane. Turn right (S) past some cottages, and continue for 400 yards, then left (SE) before the stone wall of a cemetery.

Access Point: Broad Blunsdon church, 6 miles (300 yards from the cemetery). Telephone, B&B, pub, hotel. GR 155908.

Follow the path beside the cemetery for 200 yards then turn left again (NE) to follow the left side of a field. At the waymark 200 yards further on, bear right (E, 96°) to cross the corner of the field to a kissing gate. Continue in the same direction (E) towards the gun emplacements on the top of Stubbs Hill.

These are part of the World War II anti-aircraft gun batteries that were built to defend Swindon and the approaches to London (see Day 12, the Blue Line).

Beyond them, continue in the same direction to cross a stile and onto the busy B4019. Cross this road, turn left and, due to fast traffic, walk with

Bury Croft hill fort, Broad Blunsdon
On the summit of Castle Hill is an Iron Age hill fort with double ramparts and defensive ditches. The Thames Valley floodplain can be seen below to the north with the industrial buildings to the north of Lus Hill being those of Fairford Airport. Cricklade church tower can still be seen (NW).

great care on the right hand verge for 380 yards. Pass the entrance to Castle Hill Court, then just after a milestone on the left verge, turn right at a waymark.

The milestone indicates Cricklade 3, Highworth 3, London 79 miles, as this road was one of the main coaching routes to London. It is as busy now as it was then!

Go through a gate to descend the valley along the right side of a field to go through the next gate and then down another field with the hedge to the left. Cross a small stream via a footbridge to climb gently uphill along the left side of the field. At the far hedge, turn left to follow a footpath (E) with the hedge on the right.

Continue through several small gates keeping on the left side of the hedge. This is part of an old enclosed landscape where the original small narrow fields still remain. At the fingerpost, turn left to **Stanton Fitzwarren**. Mill Copse, the wood on the right, is an ancient hazel coppice with a clearly defined woodland bank originally built to keep deer out.

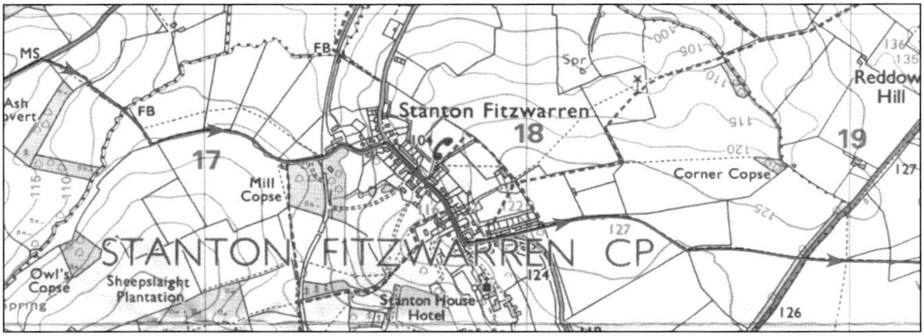

When we passed in April this wood was carpeted with white star-like wood anemones, primroses and celandines. The mill was once a flour mill and used the overflow water from a lake created in the 1860s when the earth was removed to build the railway.

Go down Mill Lane, over the course of the dismantled Highworth to Swindon railway (the house called 'The Old Station House' is on the left). Pass Mill Cottage on the right to arrive at the main street. Turn right (SE) along the main street past the bus stop and up the hill.

The Old Rectory on the right has tall brick chimneys, which were added to increase the draught in the fires when households switched from using wood to coal.

Follow the road round where it bends to the left (E), (there is a medieval stone barn at this corner) ignoring the road 'Trenchyard' ahead.

A diversion along Trenchyard, however, to the church and to the hotel for cream teas is recommended. The church, built in the 11th century is dedicated to St. Leonard and has a fine Norman decorated archway and a Norman font.

Access Point: Stanton Fitzwarren church (200 yards from route), 7.75 miles. Telephone, hotel. GR 179901.

Village pump, Stanton Fitzwarren
There are two former village pumps on the left side, one 50 yards beyond the telephone box and before the waymark signed 'Kingsdown 2'.
This pump is dated 1902 (King Edward VII's reign).

On the road out (E) of the village, bear left at The Avenue to join the footpath leading to Sevenhampton, ignoring a footpath after 100 yards off to the left (N). Instead, keep to the hedge boundary until, after 250 yards, there is a waymark pointing diagonally right (SE, 120°) across the field to a gap in the far hedge. Go through the gap, and turn left (E) past the waymark to the corner of the field. Bear slightly more right (E, 100°) across the open field to a metal gate at the busy A361 road.

Cross the road, and continue (E, 110°) across a field, over an asphalted track and on towards the farm buildings. At a gateway, go over a small stile to the right of the gate, into a paddock bearing right across it towards some mobile homes to the right of a corrugated iron barn. Go through the metal farm gate out of the paddock to turn right at the trunk of an old ash tree passing the farm buildings. This is Queenlaines Farm named after the track that has existed since the 12th century. Go (SE, 160°) along the main farm track (Queens Lane) to a minor road.

Continue along the track beyond, with the hedge to the right. There are fine views of the Berkshire Downs ahead with the Iron Age hill fort of Liddington Castle half right (S, 155°) and the Honda factory in Swindon to the right (SW, 220°).

Keep south, to where the track bends left by a ruined building. Continue ahead (S, 180°) under a wire fence and across a field, over an overgrown stile to cross the next field (S) over another stile. There is a track 50 yards away to the left, but it is not on the public right of way. At the open field (GR 196891), bear left (S, 180°) across the field, aiming for a gap in the far wooded hedgerow. There is a footbridge in the hedge just left of the gap.

Go down the hill in the middle of the field due south (180°) aiming left of **South Marston** church tower. The foot bridge over the brook is situated three-quarters left (E) along the hedge at the far end of the field. After crossing the footbridge, follow the fenced footpath to a lane, to turn sharp left and right over a footbridge to arrive at the church. The church has Norman north and south doorways and a 13th century chancel. Turn right into the lane, then left into Old Vicarage Lane, and right into the car park beyond the village school.

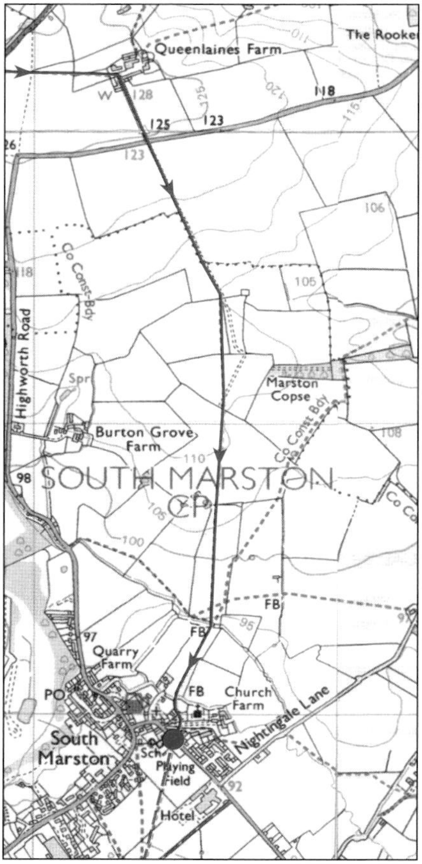

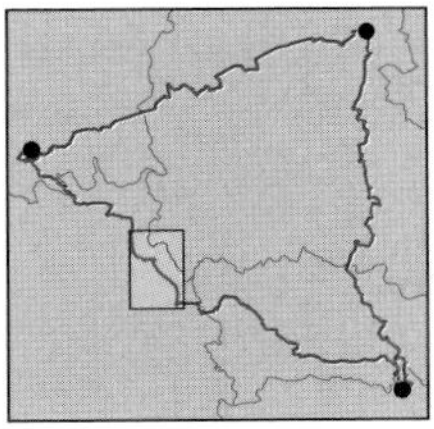

Day 8

South Marston to Aldbourne

South Marston GR SU 194879 to Aldbourne GR SU 264757

A day of crossing the valley of the River Cole passing the site of a Roman 'mansio' on the Ermin Way. There is a climb to the open Wiltshire Downs before following a chalk valley down to Aldbourne. The route from South Marston to the Ermin Way is a complex network of footpaths, so extra time may be needed for this section.

Distance: 11 miles (17.6 km).

Maps: Explorer 170 – Abingdon, Wantage & Vale of White Horse.
Explorer 157 – Marlborough & Savernake Forest.
Landranger 173 – Swindon & Devizes.
Landranger 174 – Newbury & Wantage.

Transport: Buses
- Wanborough/Hinton Parva, 47. www.thamesdown-travel.co.uk
- Aldbourne/Wanborough/Swindon, 48A. Traveline – Tel: 0871 200 2233. www.traveline.org.uk

Taxis: Swindon
- United Radio Cars. Tel: 01793 611111.
- V Cars. Tel: 01793 701701.

Car Parking: South Marston – Village car park, by the footpath sign, south of the village school on the west side of Old Vicarage Lane and north of the playing field.
Aldbourne – By the village pond or near the Old Forge in South Street, north of the pond.

Accommodation/Public Houses/Restaurants:

Lotmead Farm
- Tea Rooms (9.30am–7pm, summer only). Tel: 01793 790137

Lower Wanborough
- The Cross Keys PH. Tel: 01793 790302.
- Great Moorleaze Farm B&B. Tel: 01793 485838.

Wanborough	• The Brewers Arms. Tel: 01793 790707.
	• Harrow Inn (B&B). Tel: 01793 790622.
	• The Plough. Tel: 01793 790523.
Upper Wanborough	
	• The Black Horse. Tel: 01793 790305.
Aldbourne	• Blue Boar Inn. Tel: 01672 540237.
	• Crown Hotel. Tel: 01672 540214. www.crownataldbourne.co.uk

From the car park, go diagonally left (S, 190°) to cross the playing field, right of an oak tree, and over a footbridge. Keep in the same direction again going diagonally left to cut off the corner of the field, aiming for half way along the left hedgerow. Cross the footbridge to bear diagonally right across the next field (SW, 172°) with Manor Farm to the right (W). Cross the horse paddocks to the metal gate. Turn right onto the bridleway, then left (S) by a metal gate, along a narrow lane.

Before the next metal gate, bear right through a metal gate by an overgrown stile. Take the right-hand (S) path where the paths divide at the beginning of the field. Bear right across the field to go past the corrugated iron field shelter. Fifty yards before the end of the right-hand hedge (or three quarters of the way along the field hedge), go over a stile in the hedge. Bear right to cross the next field (S, 160°) aiming right (W) of South Marston Farm. Go over a stile beside the drive and through a wooden gate to continue in the same direction (S) across a small field along the right side of a garden, to a double stile in the hedge. Beware of the geese.

Cross the track into a horse paddock. From this track, go diagonally left across the field and another stile (S, 190°). After the stile and footbridge, turn sharp left (S, 156°) beside the hedgerow towards the London to Bristol railway line. Cross the railway tracks with great care, then go

The Great Western Community Forest

The River Cole Path, which we have now joined, is part of the Great Western Community Forest. This is one of twelve forests in England where local people, schools, businesses and community groups are working together to create a better environment. It covers 168 square miles in and around Swindon. A mosaic of woodland, green spaces and areas for wildlife has been created and we saw hares, roe deer and herons here. For more details contact: Swindon Borough Council. Tel: 01793 466321. www.forestweb.org.uk

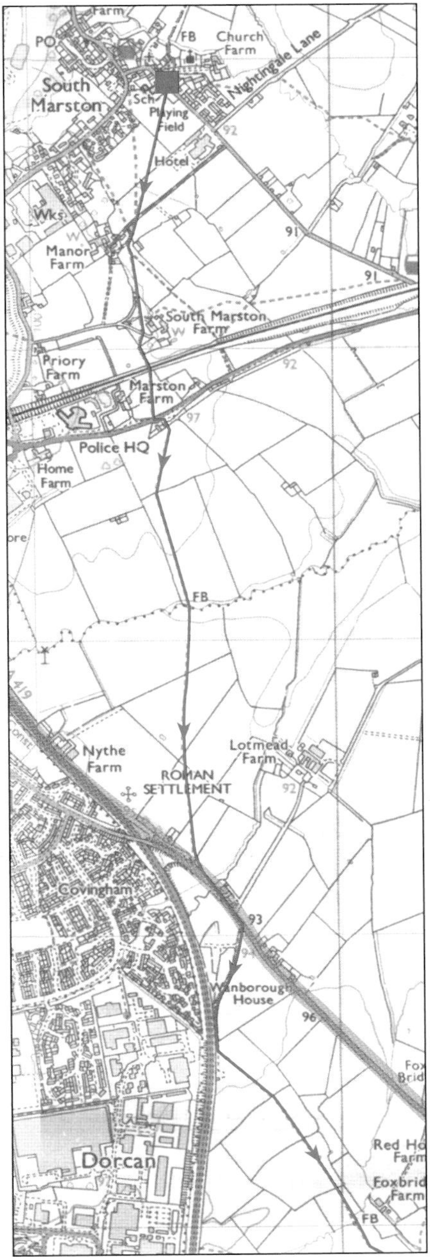

diagonally right aiming for the right side (W) of a white house ahead. Go over the stile in the hedgerow to cross the A420 road also with great care.

Go diagonally left on the footpath as it enters a farm track. The rear of the two houses is called Lock Keeper's Cottage, a reminder of the former canal to Swindon. Go over a metal gate. Looking right (W) from the gate, the raised embankment of the canal is visible and near the cottage garden are the big stones of the former lock.

From the field gate bear diagonally right (S, 192°) to the opposite far corner of the field, left of the two tall oak trees. Liddington Castle Hill, an Iron Age hill fort, can be seen ahead. Go over the stile right of the field gate, and then keep near the wire fence on the right side of the next field to continue walking south-east.

Sarsen Stones

In winter, on the other side of the wire fence, it is possible to see two big sarsen stones which have been dragged to the edge of the field by farm machinery. Sarsen stones are the boulder remnants of a hard siliceous (quartz) sandstone crust that once overlaid the chalk hills of the Wiltshire Downs. Because these stones were so hard and difficult to move, they made good markers or signs for ancient boundaries.

Cross the stile and footbridge over the tributary of the River Cole which flows north into the River Thames. There are more sarsen stones in the brook. From the footbridge, continue south (188°) by walking straight ahead across the field and over the remains of a traditional Cotswold stone slab stile in the hedgerow. In the next field, bear slightly diagonally right to a footbridge in the hedge. In the next field, although the footpath continues south near a marker pole within a fruit farm, it is easier to go left along the asphalt track to the Lotmead Farm Tea Rooms.

We enjoyed a welcome cup of tea here, appropriately, as this was the site of an ancient mansio where the Romans would also have stopped for rest and refreshments.

A Roman Mansio

As part of the Roman town, Durocornovium (see below), this Roman mansio or posting station (Latin = manere = to remain or to stay) GR 195854 was a large building incorporating stabling, lavish rooms and baths, that provided a change of horse and rest for the couriers and other government officials travelling from imperial Rome to Corinium and beyond. These stations were approximately 25 miles apart and were part of the 'cursus publicus', the Roman equivalent of the Royal Mail.

Go past (SW) the metal water tank (with EXIT painted on it) and along a track and over a metal barrier just east of a brick-built house. Turn left (SE) onto a minor road which joins the road to **Wanborough**. This is part of the Roman Ermin Way. Here was the Roman town of Durocornovium, GR 195855, which is marked on the OS map.

Durocornovium and Wanborough

Durocornovium was a Roman small town. It extended for about a mile on either side of Ermin Way south-east of Covingham on the outskirts of Swindon. It was occupied from AD 50–450. A mansio and timber-framed buildings were arranged within a grid of streets following Roman custom. Industries, such as iron working, bread-making and flour milling were established.

Excavations from nearby Wanborough have revealed that gods were worshipped: a stone carving of the god Mercury was found and pottery decorated with faces showing the ancient Celtic head cult. A curse to an enemy written on a sheet of lead shows that superstitions persisted.

These and other finds are housed in the Swindon Museum. Open Mon–Sat 10am–5pm. Tel: 01793 466556. www.swindon.gov.uk/art-museumandartgallery

Cross this Roman road onto the footway and walk for 350 yards, past the lane entering from the left to Lotmead Farm. Just past the 30mph repeater sign on the right is a waymark post with a kissing gate beside it (before reaching the childcare centre and nursery). Go through the gate to climb up the left bank and walk along the tarmac track (SW) near the ring road.

Go through a metal gate. 100 yards before reaching the pumping station, there is a waymark high above on the right bank. Here bear diagonally left across the field (134°), left of the telegraph pole, to the gap in the far hedge.

When we walked across this set-aside field in May, it was full of sow thistle and camomile which provide a good seed supply for birds.

This field is designated as a Flood Relief Area and in wet weather it could be flooded. If so, it may be necessary to retrace the path back to the Wanborough Road by turning right (SE) to walk along Ermin Way into Wanborough.

After the remains of a stone stile in the hedge, cross the next field slightly right (SE, 144°) to the footbridge ahead, to enter a woodland created by the Forestry Authority. Travel in the same direction (SE) ignoring the paths branching off to the left and right.

The tree species planted are ash, field maple, silver birch, oak, alder, guelder rose, hawthorn and whitebeam.

Leave the wood via a wooden stile. N.B. The area around this stile can be flooded, so it may be necessary to divert 80 yards to the right and exit the wood over a wire fence. Continue walking parallel to the hedgerow on the left with views of **Wanborough** church tower and spire ahead, and a fine line of tall poplars to the right.

Wanborough church is one of only three churches in England to have a separate spire and a tower, one being nearby at Purton, and the other at Ormskirk in Lancashire. There is an old wives' tale of two spinsters who both wanted to donate to the church and each wanted recognition for their gifts. They could not agree, so one had the spire built and the other a tower!

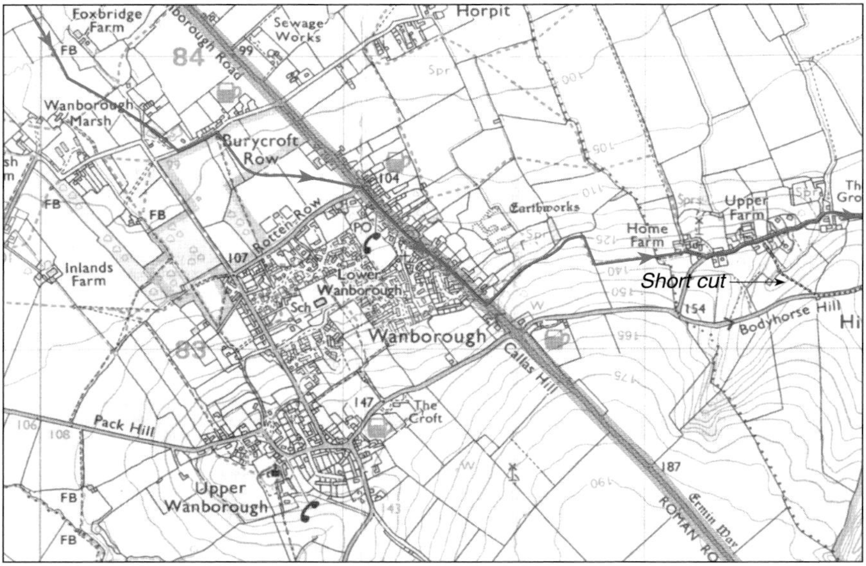

On examining the map and climbing the numerous stiles there is evidence that, apart from the noisy A419 road, this is an unchanged landscape of small fields with many drainage ditches. The place names Wanborough Marsh, Marsh Farm, Inlands Farm and Moor Leaze indicate that this has been a wet area due to the underlying clay soil.

Cross a gated footbridge and continue past the left-hand hedge corner (SE) past a fallen tree to continue (SE) crossing double stiles in the middle of the hedgerow. (N.B. Do not go on the footpath through a wide wooden gate on the left side of some wooden railings.) Cross the next field to go between ponds and some tall willow trees. Enter a horse paddock via a stile and walk along the right side of the fence in front of a brick-built house. Cross the stile and lane to walk on the right side of some pens. Turn left onto a road to pass a thatched cottage called 'Cattaways'.

This cottage shows an interesting mix of building materials since it is made of chalk clunch blocks, then below the roof is a mixture of sarsen rubble, with a brick-built extension to the left.

Almost immediately after 'Cattaways' and 50 yards before the Cross Keys pub, turn right through a kissing gate to bear left at the interpretation notice of Warneage Wood. Follow the footpath diagonally left (SE) through the woodland to its edge. Turn left (E) across a sports field along the right side of a pond to a kissing gate in the hedge.

In the field beyond, in the rough grass, there was a charm of 40–50 goldfinches feeding on the thistles in October.

Wanborough (OE wagen = wagon, beorg = hill or burial mound)
The architecture in this village is a combination of thatched cottages with walls made of a mixture of yellowish-orange sandstone and sarsen blocks in a hard mortar. Thatching was used because it was relatively light in weight. The Maltings and The Old Malthouse on the left of Ermin Way indicate a brewing past. The pubs called The Plough and The Harrow were coaching inns in the 18th century and reflect the agricultural nature of the area. Wanborough was also a point on the Ridgeway where the Welsh drovers stopped to rest and drink in the local pubs. There are still six pubs in this village.

Harrow Inn on Ermin Street, Wanborough

Exit the meadow into the village of Wanborough, near The Brewers Arms at the junction of Ermin Way and Rotten Row, close to the bus stop.

The name Rotten Row was a common medieval place name describing a row of tumbledown cottages. However, the Rotten Row in Hyde Park, London, derives from Route de Roi (Road of the King).

Turn right onto Ermin Way (SE) to pass the Harrow Inn and start climbing Callas Hill (originally called Gallows Hill due to the gibbet at the top of the slope).

Access Point: Wanborough, 3.5 miles. Shop, pubs, telephone. GR 210835 (junction of Rotten Row and Ermin Way).

Continue climbing the hill, part of the scarp slope of the chalk Wiltshire Downs (a continuation of the Berkshire Downs) towards the end of the village. Just beyond the speed limit sign, past a house called 'Silver Springs', there is a metal pole indicating a narrow footpath leading to the left (NE). Turn onto the footpath and continue walking in the same direction to climb the gentle slope (NE, 60°) of a small field to reach a stile on a field bank, right of the hedge. Go over another stile to walk along the uphill (right) side of the next field boundary (NE), following the contours, to turn sharply right (uphill) in the corner.

Halfway up the hill, at a black waymark post (GR 218833) turn sharp left (E) across the open field, keeping to the contours of the slope (84°) towards the buildings of Home Farm on the outskirts of **Hinton Parva**. There are amazing views of the flat flood plain of the River Cole to the north. Cross two stiles in a small copse, then keep along the uphill (right) edge of the next field to walk beside a black painted, corrugated iron barn. Leave the field via a stile in the far left corner down to the lane below. Turn right to join a minor road, then left (NE) at the road. Pass Icknield Cottage on the left with its fine thatched roof which has a straw owl and four ducks modelled on the ridge.

Shortcut at Hinton Parva

Next to a house called 'The Banks', there is a footpath to the right (SE) GR 224833. Follow the path down to the brook, then up the hill, to turn left in the lane at the restriction sign. Walk 350 yards to the village hall. This saves half a mile.

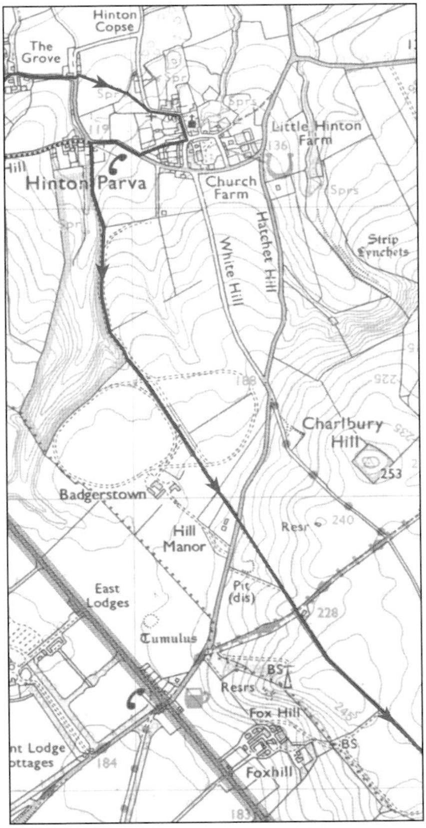

St. Swithun's Church

This church is 1,000 years old. The tower is probably Saxon and the aisles have Norman pillars and arches dating to before 1100. The shallow arched wooden roof is 15th century with clerestory windows. Immediately to the left, inside the church, is a wooden bier that is still used to transport coffins from people's homes into the church. The font is late Saxon, with mysterious carvings including a snake. Nearby is the grave slab of a former Civil War soldier who died in 1653.

The Royal Coat of Arms dated 1789 on the west wall commemorates King George III's recovery from his first attack of madness. In the south wall is a Whistler engraved window celebrating Gerald Manley Hopkins' poem 'Glory be to God for Dappled Things'. (See Day 9). The beautiful stained-glass east windows are by Kempe, whose hallmark was to make angels' wings look like peacock feathers. His emblem of a tiny golden wheatsheaf can be seen in the bottom left-hand corner of the windows. There are four bells, the first of which is from the Aldbourne foundry dated c1730.

Follow the narrow lane to a bend. West Hinton House on the right, built in 1727, is a good example of a house made of Malmstone blocks (cut from hard greenish-white chalk). Continue on for 350 yards then, just as the road turns sharp right (S) take the footpath opposite at 'City Corner'. This surprising name is a corruption of Smithy Corner, since the garage to the left (N) of the footpath is on the site of the former blacksmith's forge. Continue straight ahead (SE) on a path along the right side of a wooden fence. Join the road, bear right (SE) past a chapel and along a raised path past the entrance to the Manor House towards the church.

Hinton Parva Manor has an interesting history. During the Civil War, it is believed to have been a Parliamentarian house and used as one of their headquarters by the Cromwellians preparing for the Battle of Newbury (see Day 11). The manor wall is also built of a mixture of different stones.

To visit the church, turn left up the stone steps into the churchyard and enter the building by its Norman south door. To leave the churchyard, go out by the south gate and turn right, down onto the village street.

Take a narrow footpath opposite, along the left side of a house called 'Greystones'. At the end of the path, turn right (W) to walk for 250 yards to the village hall.

Access Point: Hinton Parva village hall, 5 miles. Telephone. GR 228832.

Turn left (S) through a wooden gate onto a bridleway. Enter the National Trust land of 'The Coombes' and walk up the track for 300 yards along the left side of the valley.

The Coombes is a rare surviving example of unimproved chalk grassland. It is a dry valley cut during the Ice Age. In July the slopes were full of the lilac-coloured field scabious, yellow rock roses and lady's bedstraw, dark purple knapweed and white yarrow. There were marbled white, comma and peacock butterflies. Along its sides are a series of terraces. These are strip lynchets.

Marbled White butterfly

Keep uphill alongside the fence near the track beside the valley. Go through a metal gate to leave the National Trust land and continue on the track (SE) across the gallops, passing Badgerstown stables on the right. Liddington Castle Hill can be seen to the right (SW). Charlbury Hill with its trig point is to the left (E). Continue (SE) with the fence on the right into a narrow enclosed path between trees, cross a minor road with care and then on up the bridleway on the right side of a fence. Leave this field via a metal gate, to turn left and continue uphill (SE, 144°). Cross the Ridgeway.

We saw native grey partridge running across the ploughed fields in October.

Strip lynchets and soil creep

The terraces on the right (W) slope were formed in the early Middle Ages when population pressures increased and farmers were forced to cultivate the steep slopes. Their ploughs cut into the hillside forming a series of terraces along the contours, known as lynchets.

The narrower and smaller ridges on the left side of the valley are an example of soil creep. This is where the soil begins to slide down the slope under its own weight. Sheep then walk along the ridges so formed. They are naturally-made ridges, in contrast to the man-made lynchets.

Strip lynchets, The Coombes, Hinton Parva

The Ridgeway is an ancient track used by prehistoric man that stretches for 80 miles between Ivinghoe in Buckinghamshire and Avebury in Wiltshire. It was more like a broad zone of communication than a road and keeps to the high ground. Along it flocks and herds were driven, and it continues in use for walkers to enjoy the tremendous views across the Vale of White Horse or southward across the downland.

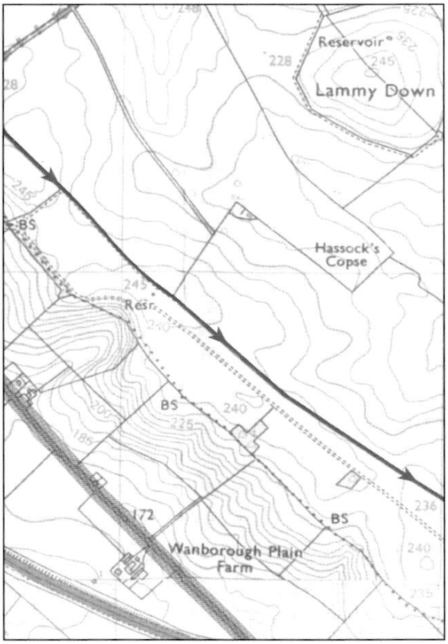

Walk on in the same direction (SE) for about 600 yards. By a stout wooden pole near the notice about the beetle banks, and 50 yards before the round concrete reservoir on the right (243 metres high, GR 239811), it is sometimes possible to see by looking diagonally left (NE, 70°), and three miles distant, the gleaming white building of Ashdown House (GR 282820).

This house was built by the Earl of Warwick for Elizabeth, Queen of Bohemia (The Winter Queen), who lost her throne in 1620. It is a National Trust property.

From here, a 1.5 mile steady descent starts down towards the bridge over the M4 with **Aldbourne** visible to the south of it.

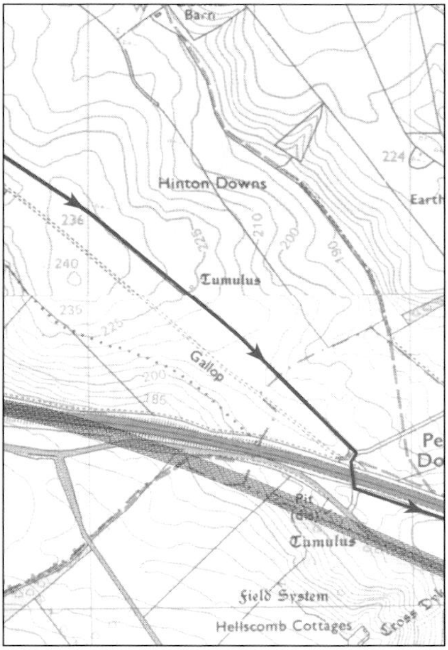

This is an open landscape of large arable fields though we did see small herds of roe deer with their distinctive small horns, and yellowhammers singing in the stunted hawthorn bushes beside the bridleway. As the motorway comes in sight, there is a Bronze Age tumulus just by the track to the left west of Peak Downs. The Roman road was excavated in 1969 before the M4 was built. This work revealed that the agger was 22 feet wide laid on a 35 feet wide bedding of clay and crushed chalk.

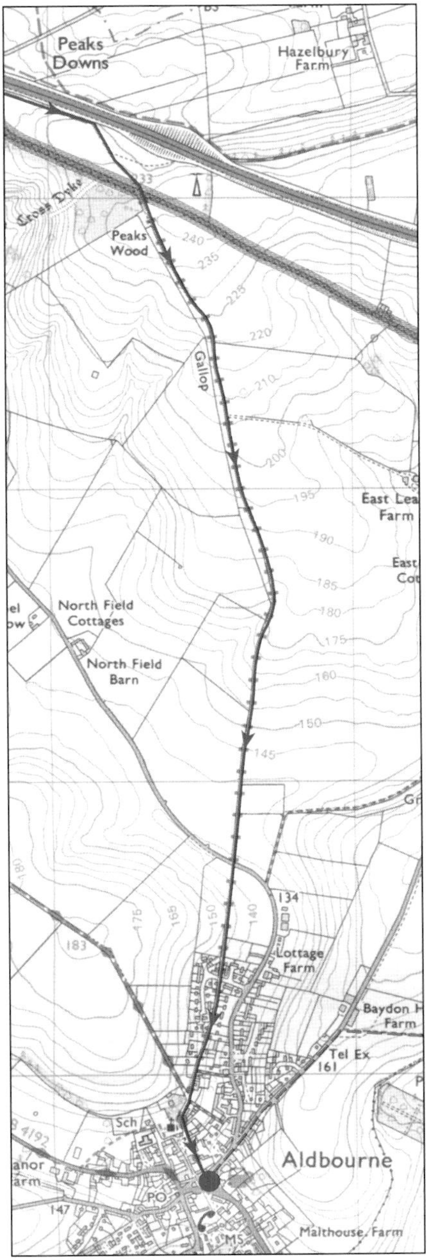

Turn right before some oil drums to cross the motorway bridge. Immediately after the motorway, turn left through a metal gate into a field to walk beside the motorway for 375 yards. Here, at GR 261792, in a dip, bear right (SE, 148°) uphill towards a small wooden gate beside the road. Cross this road with great care (this is the Roman Ermin Way).

The cross dyke marked on the map is a rare example of a territorial boundary used by the Anglo-Saxons, but we could see no sign of it. From the road enter a byway through Peaks Wood and make a 2.25 mile descent to Aldbourne on the left side of a chalkland dry valley.

Deep purple coloured knapweed and field scabious were still flowering here in early autumn.

Cross a minor road then walk along behind the houses to enter a lane and on towards the village green and the church to the right. There is an ancient preaching cross on the green.

There are several houses of diaper (lozenge-shaped) brickwork with the shiny vitrified (fired) bricks alongside the green. Pass the Blue Boar Inn to the right to reach the village pond. The houses are built mainly of sarsen, coarse sandstone and some flint. Cross over the Aldbourne stream to reach the car parking in South Street.

St. Michael's, Aldbourne

This church's origins are Norman, but much has been restored by the eminent Victorian architect, William Butterfield. The two ancient fire pumps housed in the church were purchased in 1778, the larger named Adam, the smaller one Eve, in response to a number of fires in Aldbourne. The fires spread rapidly between the thatched roofs. As the notice describes, there was another serious fire in 1817, which in spite of the engines, destroyed fifteen cottages, three barns, two malt houses, a carpenter's shop, a smithy and a large quantity of grain to the value of £4,000. Thatched roofs were often forbidden in cities for this reason. The churchyard is a wildlife haven for flowers and lichens.

'Adam', fire pump, Aldbourne

The Aldbourne (OE old stream) is a winter bourne typical of chalk valleys. It usually starts flowing in November and stops in June due to the drop in water levels of the chalk aquifer in the slopes above the village.

Village pond, Aldbourne

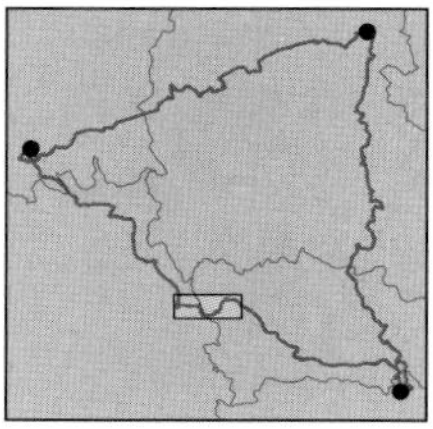

Day 9

Aldbourne to East Garston

Aldbourne GR SU 265756 to East Garston GR SU 365767

A day high on the chalk North Wessex Downs, passing through a huge Iron Age hill fort. We cross from Wiltshire into Berkshire to meet and walk along part of the east/west route of the Roman Ermin Way. We then turn north over the watershed and down into the Lambourn Valley, where there is a fine Whistler window in Eastbury church.

Distance: 9.3 miles (15km).

Maps: Explorer 157 – Marlborough & Savernake Forest.
Explorer 158 – Newbury & Hungerford.
Landranger 174 – Newbury & Wantage.

Transport: Buses
- Aldbourne/Swindon, 46.
- Newbury/Lambourn/Eastbury/East Garston/Great Shefford, 4.
- Lambourn/Eastbury/East Garston/Great Shefford/Shefford-Woodlands/Hungerford. Call-a-Bus, 99. Tel: 01189 753070.
  Traveline – Tel: 0871 200 2233. www.traveline.org.uk

Taxis: Ramsbury (near Aldbourne)
- Ramsbury Taxi Service. Tel: 07836 268869.

Lambourn
- Pottingers Taxis. Tel: 01488 71482 or 07885 136424.
- Ray's Taxis. Tel: 01488 71819.

Car Parking: Aldbourne – By the village pond or near the Old Forge in South Street, north of the pond.
East Garston – At the corner of Humphrey's Lane and Back Street, in the village hall car park. (Please contact Wendy Money (01488 649691) in advance to check availability).

Accommodation/Public Houses/Refreshments:

Upper Lambourn
- The Malt Shovel PH, B&B and Restaurant. Tel: 01488 71623. (3 miles from route)

Eastbury
- Plough Inn. Tel: 01488 71312.

East Garston
- Queens Arms Hotel. Tel: 01488 648757. www.queensarmshotel.co.uk
- B&B, shop, post office

Shefford Woodlands
- Fishers Farm B&B. Tel: 01488 648466. (2.75 miles from East Garston)
- Pheasant Inn Guest Rooms. Tel: 01672 541036. (3 miles from East Garston)

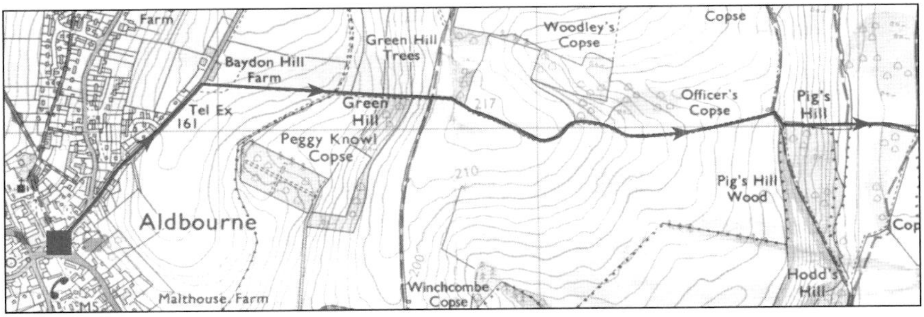

From the Old Forge in South Street walk (NE) past the Co-op shop, which is near the site of the former workhouse (1802). At the next fork, keep on the Oxford Road marked to Baydon.

A number of the houses on the right are built of broken-up sarsen stones, though many have now been painted. The long line of cottages, on the right, called Prospect Buildings, were built in 1850 and are of chalk blocks with brick quoins. Windmill House, near the top of the hill on the left, is a reminder that there was a windmill here: there are records from the early 20th century that the miller used to stop the mill wheel at 11.59pm on Saturday nights in order to observe the Sabbath.

After nearly half a mile on this road, turn right (E) at the waymark post under a big, old ash tree and before Baydon Hill Grange. Cross the gravel track (E) to go through an avenue of beech trees and over a stile. From the stile, continue east down the hill, bearing left (90°), to aim towards the middle of the fences beside the gallops in the bottom of the valley. There is a field boundary bank leading up to the left side of a wood.

At the base of the valley cross the track, go under the gallops fences to go over a wooden stile. This is before the wide metal gate in the field nearby. After the stile, turn left (E) to follow the right side of the fence, up the steep side of Green Hill. Keep between the right side of the wire fence and the wood to the right.

Among the trees on the edge of the wood we saw what we thought was a dormouse's nest: a small round ball of moss about four feet above the ground. The coppiced hazel provides a ready food supply of nuts and the twigs provide a nesting-place safe from predators. It was near the top, on a Sunday morning, that we heard the delightful combination of the singing of skylarks in the blue sky above with the peal of church bells from the village below.

Continue ascending the hill to meet the bridleway that crosses north/south. Dog-leg left and right to walk across an open field in the same easterly direction (E, 92°) to walk along the south side of a wood. At the end of this wood, follow an ancient hedgerow on the left, which has large oak trees with hawthorn, holly, coppiced hazel, ivy, ash and wild privet. This is an old route and has a typically meandering course. The hollow of the previous older track can be seen within the hedgerow. Follow the bridleway as it descends through a plantation of young mixed woodland, past the wood called Officer's Copse to the clay-lined pond in the base of the valley.

We saw a red kite here circling above with prey in its talons, trying to defend it from another kite.

Clay-lined ponds

In this chalky landscape where surface water is scarce, ponds are an important source of water. Clay was used to line the ponds; being impervious, it acts like cement on top of the porous chalk. Now that metal troughs for sheep and cattle have replaced ponds, they are becoming increasingly rare, but they are a precious resource for birds and aquatic wildlife.

At the bottom of the valley, turn right (SE) then, after only 50 yards turn left (E) uphill, through a gap in the hedge to enter a field. Turn right (E) to climb Pig's Hill beside the wood (do not enter the wood). At the top, go through a gap in the fence to turn left to continue in the same direction (E) beside the fence where there are more large standard oak trees.

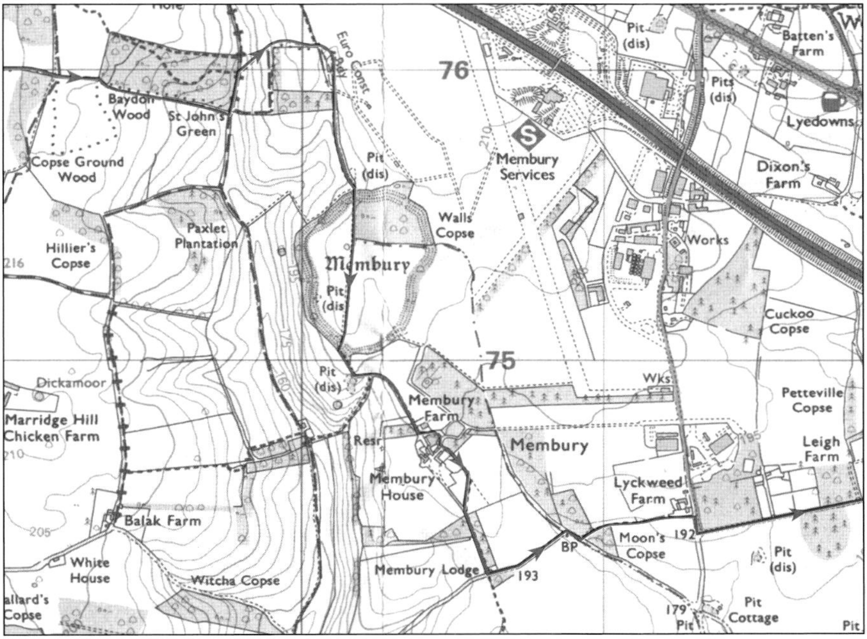

Cross an open field (E) then go beside Baydon Wood and down to St. John's Green. This dry valley is particularly beautiful with formal clumps of beech trees along it. At the bottom of the slope, turn left (N) onto a byway into an ancient piece of woodland. Only 150 yards further on, where a footpath through the wood joins the byway from the left (there is no waymark), turn right up a bank by an oak tree and through the hedge to bear diagonally left (NE, 58°) up across the slope towards the left-hand end of the hedgerow leading from the wood on top of the hill.

The noise of the M4 motorway increases, whilst the ploughed field was full of interest when we walked uphill in January. There were rounded pebbles, probably glacial outwash, and large lumps of chalk and flint that had split. The type of stone changed, too, as we climbed the slope and at the top there were pieces of limestone in the soil.

At the corner, change direction (E) to walk along the edge by the hedge, turn right along the concrete track (S) to the beginning of a wood on the right.

We are on the edge of the site of the World War II Membury airfield, of which the Nissen hut to the left is a surviving relic. For more information, go to www.ramsburyatwar.com. We met a man flying his model aeroplane on the wide flat surface.

This track marks the county boundary, with Wiltshire on the right (W) and Berkshire on the left (E) and, as is often typical of the boundary, crosses the high point of the hill fort. Although the main track diverges to the left, our route turns right soon after the bend, at the waymark, down into the woodland over a stile. Go under the cupressus trees and walk south (180°) within the wood even though the map shows the path as being on the edge. Leave the wood to walk along the left (E) of a beech 'hanger' (a clump of trees on the edge of downland) and join a track, which goes through the entrance of Membury hill fort between its thirty foot high double ramparts.

Walk south across the large enclosure, past a pond on the right, then bear right through another entrance with double ramparts then bear left keeping along the track (SE). Go through the double metal gates, ignoring the track going downhill to the right and keep on the track uphill (E). Enter the yard of Membury Farm, bear left around the edge of a timber barn, ignore the drive to the left, and bear right by the entrance to the farm with its prominent clock tower, to go along the main entrance drive to Membury House with its avenue of pollarded lime trees.

In March, we saw a flock of fieldfares that often congregate in the very tops of trees.

Membury hill fort in the Iron Age (reconstruction)

Ramparts, Membury hill fort

At the lodge gates, ignore the footpath ahead, turning left (NE) into a winding lane with wonderful old oak trees. The road turns sharp right (SE) and is again the county boundary with Wiltshire to the right (S) and Berkshire to the left (N). There was no sign of the boundary post (BP) which is marked on the map, though a prominent woodland bank still exists. A hundred yards past the corner, turn left (E) over the stile into Berkshire.

Go through Moon's Copse, keeping the wire fence to the left. Once out of the wood, turn right to follow the right side of the field and then cross it (80°) to Lyckweed Farm. This building has tile-hung walls with black header-bricks on its front (roadside) façade. Turn right (S) at the road, then after 100 yards, turn left (NE) along the south side of a wood.

There were turkey oaks on the right side of the road. These trees have larger leaves than the native oak and a mossy cup surrounds the acorn.

Walk for nearly a mile past the junction of Half Mile Road and the entrance to Leigh Farm where there are two more large turkey oaks.

We saw hares in the fields here.

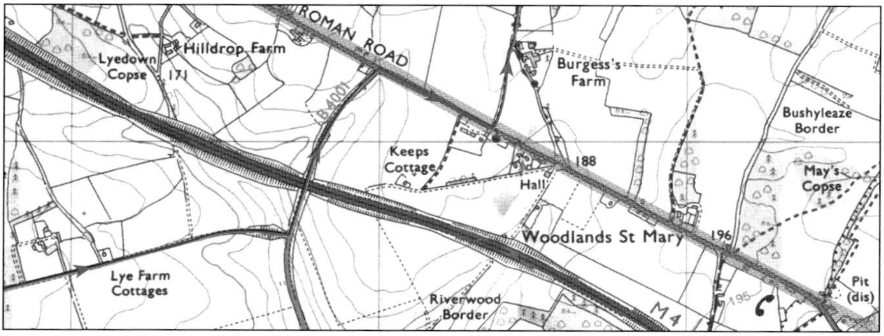

Woodlands St. Mary Church is a 25 yard diversion further SE along the Ermin Way. It is built of the local knapped flint with an octagonal belfry. It is closed but cared for by The Churches Conservation Trust. We enjoyed a picnic lunch in the south porch looking at the graveyard carpeted with snowdrops in February. There is a water tap by the gate.

Continue in the direction of the motorway; where a track leads left, we get a first glimpse of the Ermin Way, which is now the B4000. It runs parallel with the motorway on the far side. At the next road junction, turn left (N) onto the B4001 signed to **Woodlands St. Mary**. Go under the motorway bridge, to turn right to walk on the route of the Roman road. It is advisable for safety, to keep to the verges, partly due to the speed of the traffic and also due to a dangerous blind summit. After 450 yards turn left (N) at the footpath sign opposite the Coach House.

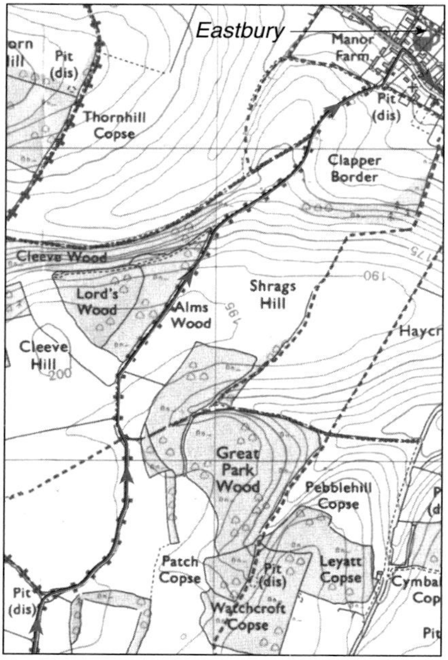

Follow the left (W) side of the hedge (although on the map the footpath is marked on the east side of the hedge). Continue north to go through the hedge at the first gap and by turning left go along the other side (N) on the byway. Where the track divides go right (NE). This is an ancient path with a typically sinuous course and a mixture of tree species in the hedges. Ignore the crossing footpath to continue along the byway.

Around Lord's Wood on the left there is a distinctive woodland boundary bank, a relic of the former need to keep the deer away from the young shoots of the coppiced woodland.

Continue down the byway ignoring a footpath to the right; and continue to descend the stony track towards **Eastbury**. From here, it is possible to see a small black and white thatched cottage 'Ploughley' where Oliver Cromwell is reputed to have stayed.

Before crossing the stream, there is a small lane by Spicers Farm running parallel to the main street. Turn right onto this beside the River Lambourn, a stream fed by the chalk aquifers.

When we walked by in December 2005, it was dry, but in spate with water over the banks twelve months later. The big willows beside the brook indicate the dampness of the soil.

By going across the small footbridge opposite the church, it is possible to read the plaque on the wall of Cross House. It tells how the village lamps in Eastbury were erected in 1897 and paid for "by public subscription to celebrate the Diamond Jubilee of the reign of Her Most Gracious Majesty, Queen Victoria". Nearby are the remains of an ancient preaching cross.

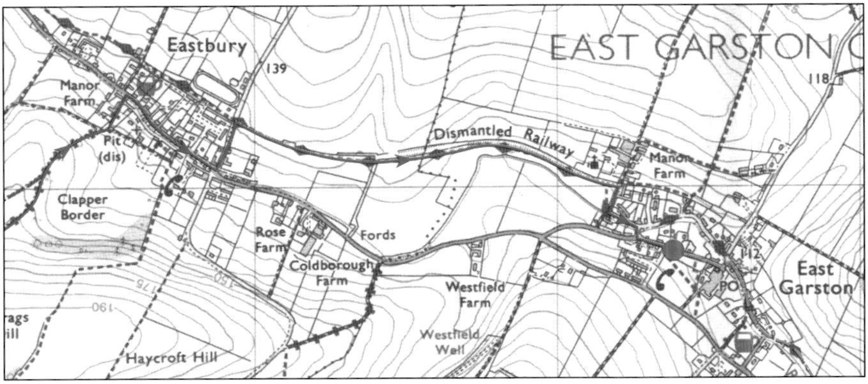

Whistler window, Eastbury church

Eastbury village history

The route beside the stream reveals some of the history and activities of the village. The church of St. James the Great, built of flint and Bath stone, is to the right. It has a beautiful window engraved by Laurence Whistler commemorating the lives of the poet Edward Thomas and his wife, Helen, who lived in Eastbury in her old age. *Key available.*

Thatched cottage beside the River Lambourn

Back on the small lane, pass two footpath signs, the Old Forge and Garden Cottage, with its bread oven protruding from the wall, and go past the stables on the right. Turn left, across the stream and over the main road. Turn uphill (NE) beside the large, dark, elm-boarded barn on the corner.

Access point: Eastbury. Downs Close, 100 yards left (W) of the corner barn. Limited parking, telephone, buses. 7.75 miles. GR 348771.

Go uphill, past a large octagonal flint and brick dovecote on the left. Turn right to climb up steep concrete steps out of the lane, to join the Lambourn Valley Way, a 20-mile-long footpath from Whitehorse Hill near Uffington to Newbury. Continue on the footpath with a hedge on the left, over a stile and walk along the line of the now-dismantled Lambourn Valley Railway towards the church tower of **East Garston**.

The railway was used for transporting passengers and milk churns. There were banks of primroses when we walked here in February. The name East Garston is a corruption of Esgarestun meaning the settlement of an 11th century Dane called Esgar, which is why there is no West Garston!

At the edge of the village, turn right (SW) down Station Road, to reach a row of cottages, including Haymaker's Cottage, built in 1708. Here, turn left and first right across the river, then left past the war memorial. Turn left into Back Street and continue for 100 yards to just beyond Humphrey's Lane where, on the right, is the dark-green wooden boarded Social Club, and Village Hall with its car park.

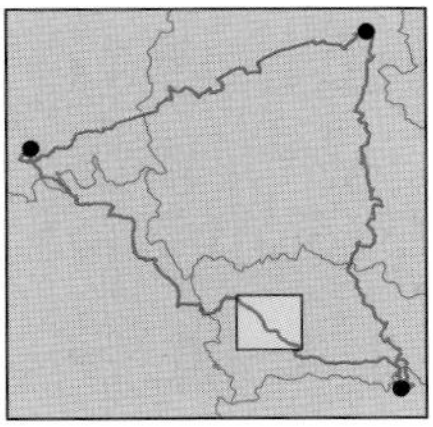

Day 10

East Garston to Donnington

East Garston GR SU 365767 to Donnington Castle GR SU 461690

In this section, we continue the south-easterly direction of Ermin Way, but, much as the Anglo-Saxons might have done to escape thieves on the Roman road, we follow the safety of the quiet settlements along the valley of the River Lambourn a few miles to the north. Most of the route follows the clear waters of the chalk stream, but ends by arriving at the strategic hill-top position of Donnington Castle.

Distance:	8.75 miles (14 km).	
Maps:	Explorer 158 – Newbury & Hungerford. Landranger 174 – Newbury & Hungerford.	
Transport:	Buses	• Newbury/Lambourn/Eastbury/East Garston/ Great Shefford, 4. • Lambourn/Eastbury/East Garston/Great Shefford/ Shefford-Woodlands/Hungerford. Call-a-Bus, 99. Tel: 01189 753070. • Donnington (Castle Inn)/Newbury, 6A. Traveline – Tel: 0871 200 2233. www.traveline.org.uk
Taxis:	Newbury	• Broadway Cars. Tel: 01635 847784. • Dolphin Cars. Tel: 01635 44444. • Kenikabs. Tel: 01635 41405.
Car parking:	East Garston – At the corner of Humphrey's Lane and Back Street, in the village hall car park. (Please contact Wendy Money (01488 649691) in advance to check availability). Donnington Castle – English Heritage car park. (N.B. open only from 9.30am–6.30pm).	

Accommodation/Public Houses/Refreshments:

East Garston – www.east-garston.com	
Great Shefford	• Swan Inn. Tel: 01488 648271.
Southfields	• The Bell Inn, B&B. Tel: 01488 608721 (GR 428715, 400 yards from route at Boxford)
Bagnor	• The Blackbird PH. Tel: 01635 40638.
Donnington	• The Three Horseshoes PH, Castle Road. Tel: 01635 41366.
	• The Pilgrims Guest House. Tel: 01635 40694/44873.
	• The Castle at Donnington. Accommodation and Restaurant. Tel: 01635 40615. www.thecastleatdonnington.com
Newbury	• Newbury Tourist Information Centre, The Wharf, Newbury. Tel: 01635 30267. www.visitwestberkshire.org.uk

Turn right (E) out of the car park to walk along Back Street past the village stores and post office. Turn left over the River Lambourn, then right (SE) along the main village street.

When we passed through in January 2006, there were only pools of water and no flow in the river here, whereas in March 2007, the river was in spate.

Continue along the road ignoring a footpath sign to the right, past East Garston house, then an ancient gable-end cottage with wooden beams on the left. Where the road turns right (S), start on a track straight ahead to continue walking south-east along the Lambourn Valley Way. Follow the left (N) bank of the River Lambourn, which is a clear chalk stream with watercress growing in it.

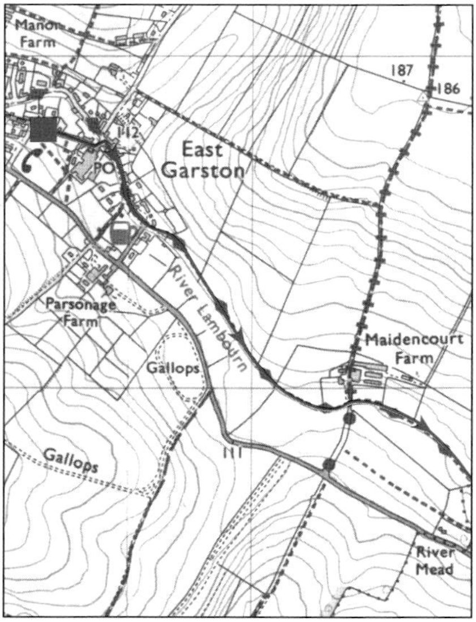

When we reached Maidencourt Farm, the river was flowing continuously even when it was dry at East Garston.

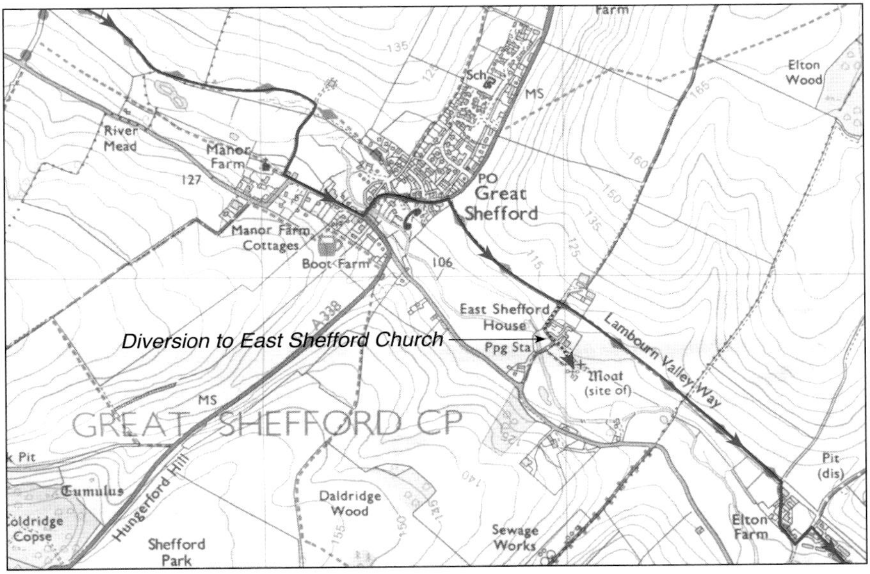

Great Shefford church (OE sceapford - sheep ford) is one of only two churches in Berkshire with a circular tower, and to reach it, we need to leave the Lambourn Valley Way for a while. So at the farm track, turn right (S) across the river, then after 150 yards, turn left (SE) to walk across the field (126°) to the tall fir trees to the left of the black and white timbered house. Go along the enclosed footpath behind the garden. Cross the next field to a stile and along the path towards the church.

St. Mary's Church, Great Shefford

Great Shefford church has Norman capitals and chevron stonework around the south doorway arch. The interior contains beautiful glass and inscriptions from the Oxford Movement, which was associated with Christ Church College in Oxford, and had the aim of restoring High Church standards and practices within the Church of England. Some of its members emigrated to New Zealand where they established the city of Christchurch on South Island. In the bell tower, the original bobscratches remain. This set of numbers shows the order in which the bells are to be rung. Interestingly, the bell ropes are tensioned, so they need to be plucked rather than pulled.

The conservation riverside meadow area lies below where we saw herons standing motionless fishing. There were peacock and red admiral butterflies feeding on the late-flowering ivy in November.

Exit the footpath via the wooden kissing gate, turn right up the track beneath an avenue of lime trees and into the churchyard.

Leave the churchyard to walk (SE) along the main village street. At the Swan Inn, turn left onto the A338, over the River Lambourn and at Station Road, for the sake of safety, cross the road to the left (W) side where there is a wide pavement. The memorial stone by the village seat is sarsen and has '2001 AD (population 808)' carved on it.

Access Point: Great Shefford, Station Road, 1.75 miles. Pub, shops, telephone. GR 384752.

St. Thomas' Church, East Shefford

This is one of the churches featured in Simon Jenkins' book *England's Thousand Best Churches*. It stands close to the site of an old moated manor house of the Fettiplace family, which was destroyed in 1870 but part of the moat can still be seen where the reeds are, south-east of the church. The plan of the church (excluding the porches and side chapel) is probably of original Norman design. The font is early Norman and a consecration cross can be seen on the lower stone of the north pier. There is a beautiful alabaster altar tomb of Sir Thomas and Lady Beatrice Fettiplace. His armour is typical of the reign of King Henry VI: he has a lion at his feet, symbolising allegiance to the throne, and his head rests on his tourney helm (the helmet that he wore for jousting matches). Lady Beatrice wears a mantle of state over her shoulders and has a small dog at her feet. There is a fine 16th century Purbeck marble tomb to John Fettiplace. The Fettiplace family held large tracts of land: Adam Fettiplace was Mayor of Oxford in 1245 and nine times subsequently. In the sanctuary is a replica of a rare salade (a helmet) denoting the military calling of one of the family.

Sir Thomas and Lady Fettiplace, East Shefford church

Walk east and after the garage turn right (SE) along the tarmac track to East Shefford Farm. On reaching a large farm complex, 600 yards from the road, we recommend a 0.5 mile diversion to see a delightful, isolated church. To reach it, turn right (SW) down the bridleway towards East Shefford House. Go through the automatic gates and down the drive towards the river. Do not cross it, but turn left (SE) along the footpath towards the cottage and small church of East Shefford.

Retrace the route back to the Lambourn Valley Way.

Here, we saw a remarkable sight: poppies and cornflowers flowering in November, the remains of a wildflower meadow.

Turn right to cross the field (SE) and through a green lane hedged with brambles. At the waymark sign, immediately after a gate at the end of the green lane, turn right to go through the yard of Elton Farm.

Here is an interesting series of farm buildings: first, the oak-beam shelter sheds, now roofed with corrugated iron, then more buildings of knapped flint with brick quoins and jambs since this is an area short of building stone. The fine 18th century farmhouse is built completely of brick. The small half-hipped brick granary nearby is raised on staddle stones, but now supported by breeze blocks.

Elton Farm granary

Leave the farmyard and turn left uphill on a track, turn right (SE) after only 50 yards in front of some new buildings to follow the Lambourn Valley Way past the Elton House Hotel. Go beside an old hedgerow with mature spindle trees in it, and into a field. Bear right to the first footbridge near a ford across the now strongly-flowing River Lambourn and on towards the hamlet of **Weston**.

Ragged robin, a plant typical of water meadows, grows here.

Mistletoe, Weston

In this field are two poplar trees with large 'balls' of mistletoe, and there are several more on the approach to Weston. Mistletoe is especially interesting botanically since it is a hemiparasite (a partial parasite). It grows mostly on the branches or trunks of apple, oak and poplar trees and sends out roots that penetrate the tree to take up its nutrients. However, mistletoe is also capable of photosynthesis, producing its own nutrients through its green leaves – hence, its hemiparasitic status. There are male and female plants, but only the females bear the familiar white berries.

The folklore of mistletoe is rich. The origin of its common name comes from an ancient belief that mistletoe started where birds left their droppings. Since there was a widespread belief that life could start from dung, mistletoe meant 'dung-on-a-twig', from 'mistel', the Anglo-Saxon word for dung, and 'tan' for twig. In fact, mistletoe seeds are spread by birds. The continuing belief that it bestowes life and fertility explains the tradition of kissing under the mistletoe at Christmas. Farmers also give a Christmas bunch of mistletoe to the first cow to calve in the New Year as a good-luck token to the entire herd.

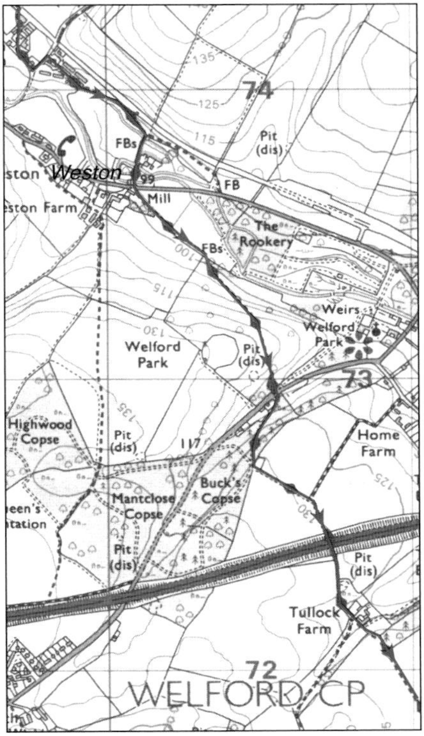

Cross another footbridge over the braided River Lambourn, well-stocked with trout, to pass the former Primitive Methodist Chapel, built in 1864. Go past Weston mill, a former flour mill, to cross the road with care. Go beside the former chapel house and continue along the river valley (SE) beside ancient pollarded willow trees, over a stile and to a wooden kissing gate.

Here bear right uphill (140°) following the line of square concrete slabs in the ground. Near the top it is possible to see Welford Park House with its church down below on the left, and on higher ground beyond, Welford Airfield, a World War II satellite in case the nearby Membury airfield (see Day 9) was destroyed. At the summit, continue following the concrete slabs to descend (S, 164°) to the wooden gate and cross a minor road.

From the information board behind a cottage, climb uphill through the woods, then bear left (SE) across a field. At the junction of the tracks, turn right over the motorway bridge and along the track to Tullock Farm. Follow the right side of a large barn, and up the right side of a hedge in the same direction as the track (SE, 142°), to follow along the right side of an old hedgerow with standards in it.

Cross the road, then bear left (112°) to walk across the field corner to join a hedgerow. Where a track and footpath go right, continue in the same direction (104°) along the right side of the hedge to the gap. Cross to the left side of a wood and continue walking (E) across a field, then descend Rood Hill (OE: the hill with a cross or gallows on it) to follow the line of the hedge.

On approaching the village of **Boxford**, go through a small gap in the hedge, right of a house, taking great care when stepping down into the road. We noticed that each of the three gables of Rood House is a 'Berkshire hip' (a half-hipped roof). Turn right, then after 50 yards, go left

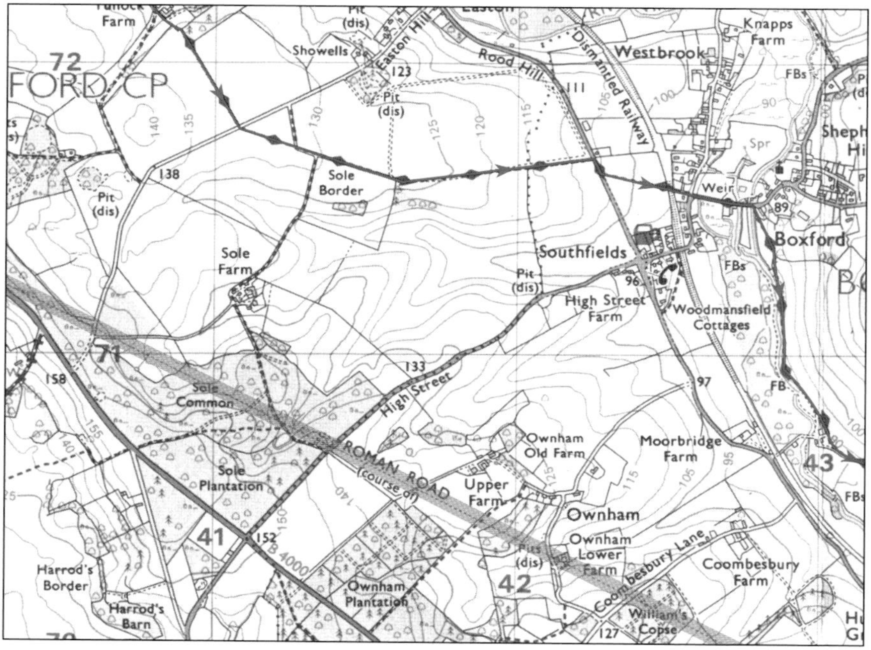

through the wooden kissing gate beside metal farm gates. Cross the field (SE) and descend via wooden steps into the village and go along the road in the same easterly direction.

In the field we saw what we thought was a rough-legged buzzard wheeling overhead. This bird is a winter visitor and is distinguished by the black band at the end of its tail.

At the road junction there is a nearby pub at Southfields to the right (S). Continue on along the main village street past the water meadows of the River Lambourn and over the bridge, then just after the mill, built of blueish industrial bricks and with its sack hoist still remaining, turn right (S) along the left (E) bank of the river.

There was a Roman villa nearby where a pot containing 800 coins was found in 1825. Only the unusual 4th century red ware bottle that contained the hoard remains and can be seen at the museum in Newbury (see Day 11, page 124). There are signs here that the Romans cut a way through the forest to Speen.

Access Point: Boxford church (200 yards from route), 6 miles. Pub, telephone, accommodation. GR 428716.

Continue along the river bank for 1.5 miles (SE), past the woodland edge where there are large poplar trees with more mistletoe.

Here we saw a mistle thrush high up in the branches. It was characteristically alone, and bigger than a song thrush with distinctive bold spots across its pale breast. The coppiced hazel trees had catkins in January.

A Roman road atlas

South of the junction of the tracks in Jannaways wood, near Woodspeen Farm (GR 437685), was the Roman settlement of Spinis ('at the thorn bushes') which gives its name to Speen. The exact site has not been found, but there is a wide scatter of Roman finds in the area. This was the junction of two major Roman roads and was a sufficiently noteworthy stopping place to be documented in the Antonine Itinerary, a 3rd century compilation of routes throughout the Roman Empire.

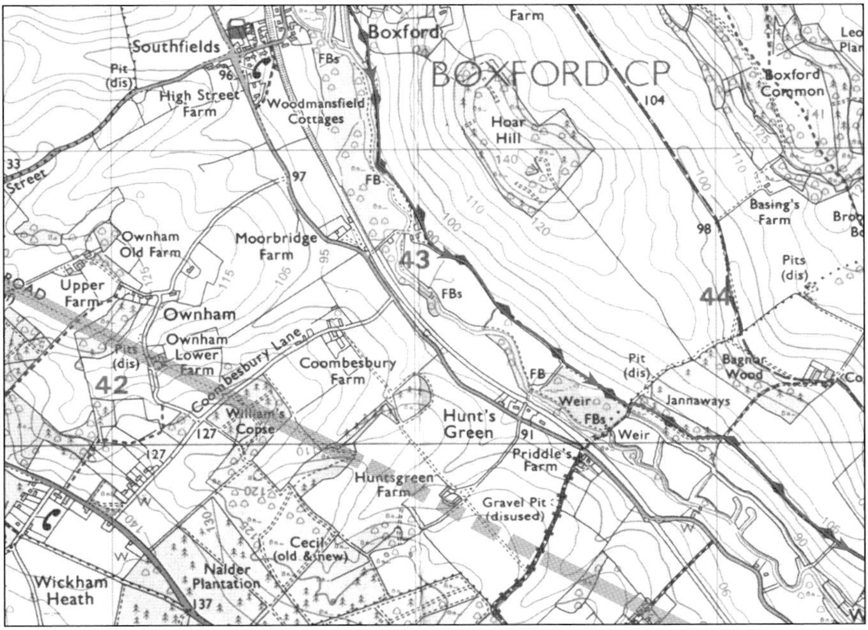

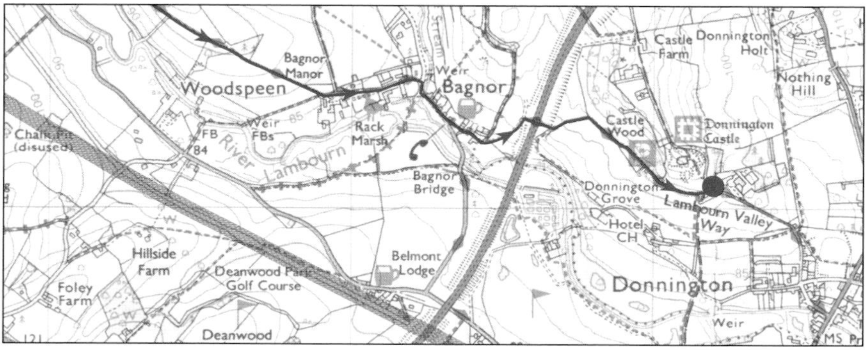

At the end of the hedge, bear left (SE) for 0.6 miles along the path through the wood called 'Jannaways' and on down the green lane between hedges.

Pass a wood with big larch trees where we heard the high-pitched call of goldcrests, and on towards the farm buildings and dovecote of Bagnor Manor. Bear left (E) here, and follow the track beside the Watermill Theatre car park into the village of **Bagnor**. At the minor road, turn right, then left over the bridge.

Rack Marsh

On the right are water meadows and Rack Marsh, so named because the mill was originally a cloth-mill and the marsh was an area of waste ground where the cloth was dried. It is now a nature reserve with a rich variety of marshland flower species, and the rare and tiny (2mm) Desmoulin's whorl snail that threatened to hold up the building of the Newbury bypass in 1996. The reserve is a Site of Special Scientific Interest (SSSI) and is owned by the Berkshire, Buckinghamshire & Oxfordshire Wildlife Trust (BBOWT). Tel: 01865 775476. www.bbowt.org.uk

Access Point: Bagnor, 8 miles. Pub, telephone. GR 453693.

The cottages in Bagnor on the left include another house built of the blueish industrial bricks. At the pub, bear left along the path signed to **Donnington** and go through a wooden gate on the left. Start ascending, turn right (E) over the Newbury bypass, then up beside the golf course.

At the junction of the tracks, turn sharp right (SE) following the Lambourn Valley Way signs through the woods following the contours of the hill along the bottom of Castle Wood with its ancient woodland bank and ditch, to arrive at Donnington Castle car park.

Donnington Castle

Donnington Castle is managed by English Heritage. There is a twin-towered gatehouse of a 14th century castle. Richard II granted a licence to Richard de Abberbury in 1386 allowing him to build "new and fortified with stone, a certain castle on his land at Donyngton". Being in a strategic position controlling the junction of two important north/south and east/west roads, the castle was seized by the Royalists in the Civil War. They built the impressive star-shaped earthworks around the castle for additional defence. The castle was then besieged by the Parliamentarians in 1644, but held out for 20 months in one of the longest sieges of the Civil War.

On our Roman Way route, we now have reached nearly 100 miles (99.1). This 100 mile mark is passed on Day 11 in the nearby village of Speen.

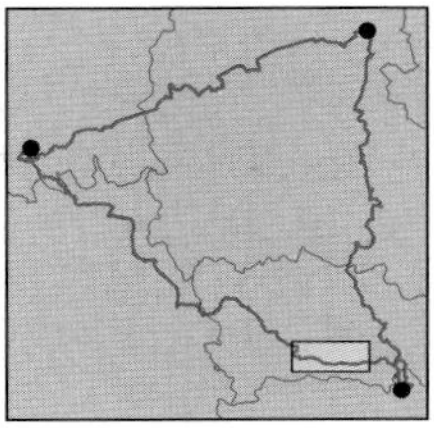

Day 11

Donnington Castle to Woolhampton

Donnington Castle GR SU 461690 to Woolhampton GR SU 572664

From the low-lying land where Cromwell's troops were camped during the siege of Donnington Castle, we cross over the watershed from the valley of the River Lambourn into the valley of the River Kennet. We pass a Roman well in Speen, through the canal-side town of Newbury, then along quiet meadows. It was here that some of the richest finds from Mesolithic man were found. Then, there were wild pig and red deer; today this marshy land is inhabited with bird life in the Thatcham reedbeds. East of Thatcham, the Ermin Way crosses the meandering River Kennet.

Distance: 9.5 miles (15.2 km).

Maps: Explorer 158 – Newbury & Hungerford.
Landranger 174 – Newbury, Wantage & surrounding area.

Transport:
Buses
- Newbury/Woolhampton, 1.
  Traveline – Tel: 0871 200 2233. www.traveline.org.uk

Trains
- Newbury/Thatcham. Tel: 08457 484950.
  www.nationalrail.co.uk

Taxis:
Newbury
- Broadway Cars. Tel: 01635 847784.
- Dolphin Cars. Tel: 01635 44444.
- Kenikabs. Tel: 01635 41405.

Thatcham
- A1 Abacus Taxis. Tel: 01635 86665.

Car Parking: Donnington Castle – English Heritage car park. (N.B. open only from 9.30am–6.30pm).
Woolhampton – Rowbarge Inn car park.

Accommodation/Public Houses/Refreshments:

Speen
- The Hare and Hounds Hotel, B&B. Tel: 01635 521152.

Newbury
- Newbury Tourist Information Centre, The Wharf, Newbury. Tel: 01635 30267.
  www.visitwestberkshire.org.uk

Newbury	• Kennet and Avon Canal Trust Tearooms (includes exhibition of canal history). Tel: 01635 522609.
Thatcham	• One Church Lane, B&B. Tel: 01635 869098.
	• J.E. Baldwin, Green Lane, B&B. Tel: 01635 863116.
Midgham	• Premier Inn. Tel: 0118 971 4114.
Woolhampton	• Rowbarge Inn. Tel: 0118 971 2213.
	• Angel Inn. Tel: 0118 971 3307.

Turn to face west towards the point where we entered the car park on Day 10. Leave the car park by turning immediately left (S) down a path along the right side of a hedgerow. Where two paths cross, continue down the drive (S) with the large Donnington Country Club on the right. Cross the lake and a double bridge over the River Lambourn. Bear right to start ascending a well-defined stony path across the park. On nearing the houses, ignore the wooden gate and turn right (W) and follow the path inside the park. It is worth turning to look right (N) to see a splendid view of Donnington Castle.

This low-lying meadow was the area where Cromwell's troops were camped for weeks during the siege of Donnington Castle (see Day 10).

Leave the park via a gate, to turn right and almost immediately left (S) along Station Road to the village of **Speen** and the A4 road. At the road junction, turn right past the Hare and Hounds Hotel and Cromwell Terrace on the right (named after the Battle of Newbury) to cross into Speen Lane at the war memorial.

There is an interesting building in the cul-de-sac of Kimbers Drive. It is a brick-built granary store on staddle stones in typical juxtaposition for security's sake to Rectory Dene, the former farm on the left side of the road (see also Elton Farm on Day 10).

Access Point: Speen Lane, 1 mile. Pub. GR 454681.

Fifty yards after Kimbers Drive, bear right along the Lambourn Valley Way on a footpath. At a bench on the right, there is a short path leading down to the Ladywell.

Continue down the main path to the lych gate of Speen church, then bear left through the graveyard to meet a lane. Turn left, then right past the entrance of Elmore Abbey and right through the church car park, then due south down the slope on the headland between fields.

When we walked here in February, we could see the snow-covered hills of Walbury Hill and Combe (SW).

At the end of the field, go through a kissing gate and turn left (E) along the path, still the Lambourn Valley Way. Go under the dismantled railway, ignoring the footpath sign to the left, and continue along the track. At the park, turn right along the road to turn (E) beside the left side of the Northcroft Leisure Centre. Before a big iron gate, there is a view ahead (E) of the four pinnacles of St. Nicholas' Church in **Newbury**. By looking left (N) Goldwell House can be seen in the upper corner of the park.

The Ladywell, Speen
The Ladywell may date back to Roman times when Speen (Spinis) was an important Roman road junction (see Day 10).

Goldwell House is appropriately named as it was built for the person who owned all the shares in the Kennet and Avon Canal and commands a good view of it!

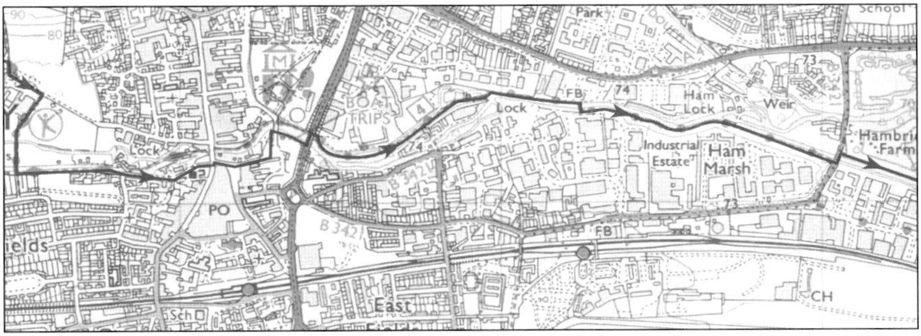

Turn right (S) through the car park of the Leisure Centre to cross the bridge over the River Kennet with willow and alder trees on its banks. On approaching the Kennet and Avon Canal, a concrete pillbox (see Day 12) can be seen to the right. Turn left (E) to walk beside the canal with its barges and narrow boats.

'Pillbox' beside bridge, Newbury

Go past West Mills and Club House with its fire insurance badge. On reaching Town Mills, do not cross to the north side as the Lambourn Valley Way does, but continue along the right (S) side to reach the centre of Newbury. Cross Bartholomew Street into Mansion House Street. There is a cast iron notice near the base of the Mansion House wall on the right that says "The use of Traction Engines in Market St. is Prohibited". Follow Wharf Street ahead.

It is worth making a short diversion (right) to see the market place with its Corn Exchange (erected 1861). The heraldic arms of Newbury on both the Corn Exchange and the West Berkshire Museum are of three domed towers representing the former Norman (Newbury) Castle.

Continue (E) along Wharf Street to pass the West Berkshire Museum which occupies the Cloth Hall (1627) restored in 1902. It is a fine half-timbered building.

Access Point: Newbury canal basin, 2.7 miles. Pubs, accommodation, shops, telephone, toilets, car park. GR 472671.
West Berkshire Museum. For opening times, telephone 01635 519562.
www.westberkshiremuseum.org.uk
In the museum there are finds from the Mesolithic period (see Box on page 126).

Newbury Wharf and Cloth Hall

The large car park was once part of a busy inland canal port, with a long low wooden granary on the right-hand side. Subsequently, it was used as a weights and measures office and part of it now forms the Tourist Information Centre.

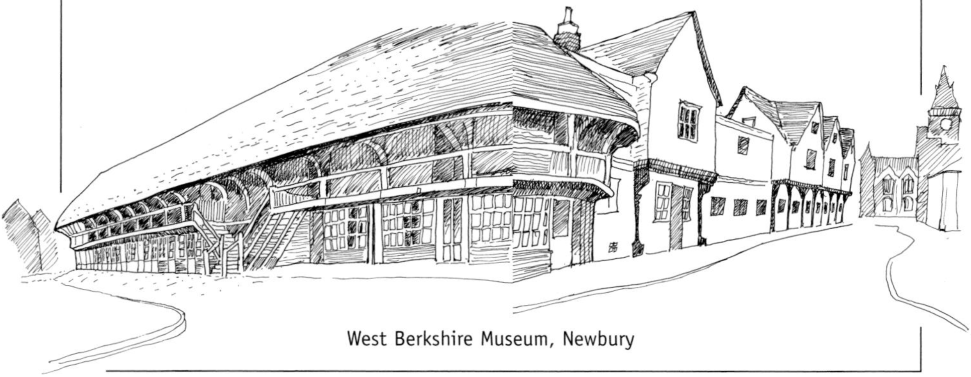

West Berkshire Museum, Newbury

Cross the car park to the canal, turn right (E) along the right (S) side of the canal to pass a stone building, a former corn store, with its sack hoists still in place. This is the Kennet and Avon Canal Trust Tearooms and souvenir shop. Pass an early 19th century crane used for loading barges and on reaching the road bridge, climb the stone steps, turn left and go over the bridge on the left (N) side and down the steps on the same side so removing any need to cross the busy road. Turn left at the bottom to go through a small wooden gate to cross a weir and follow the towpath (E).

Continue on the same side of the canal to a wooden footbridge just before the Narrow Boat pub sign. Cross the bridge to walk along on the right (S) side. An overflow ditch runs alongside to the south; at a much lower level than the canal, it carries excess water when the river is in flood. Continue on past Ham Lock and to the bridge just south of Ham Bridge Farm. Here go up the slope to cross the road bridge near the Ericsson buildings, then on the other side double back to walk (E) on the left (N) side of the canal.

Ham Bridge Farm has a half-hipped roof and is built of flint and brick.

After half a mile, the River Lambourn joins the canal on the northern side at Bull's Lock where the railway line crosses the river and the canal. Pass Lower Farm on the right side of the river.

This place name, along with Ham Marsh (OE Ham = meadow by river-bed) indicates that the whole area is low-lying. Common reed grows in the damp ground. Near here a Mesolithic summer hunting camp was located.

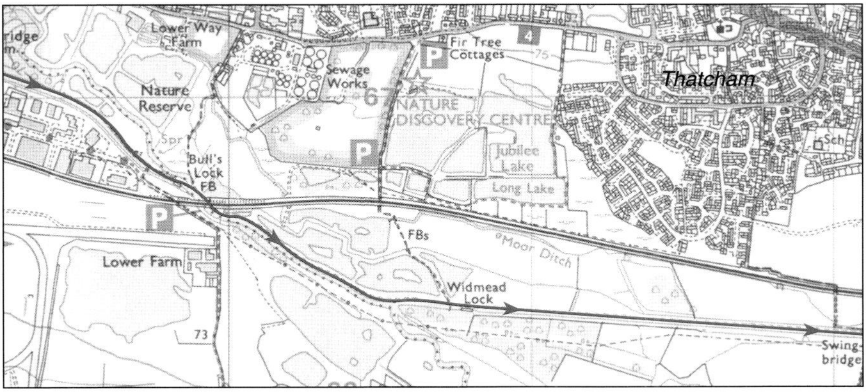

Mesolithic Man in the Kennet Valley
In later Mesolithic times (the Middle Stone Age, 7,000–4,000 BC) the River Kennet was a wide, braided river bordered by woodland. Animals such as oxen, wild pig and red deer came down to feed on the plentiful vegetation by the river. Mesolithic man developed a series of tools, such as saws and spearheads made of bone and antler, which have been preserved beneath the overlying layer of peat. They also hunted the animals with flint-tipped arrows shot from bows. Many microliths, or small trapezoidal slivers of flint originally set into arrow shafts, have been found in this area.

Continue for half a mile to where the River Kennet leaves the combined waterway via a weir (SW). Just after this point, and before a straight canal cut lined with poplar trees, is a wooden stile and a noticeboard on the left just before Widmead Lock (GR 507663).

It was here that we saw some canoeists practising for the International Devizes (in Wiltshire) to Westminster canoe marathon, which takes place every Easter. This 125-mile non-stop endurance test, involving porterage around 56 locks, has an average duration of 17.25 hours.

Access Point: Thatcham Nature Discovery Centre. Tel: 01635 874381. www.westberks.gov.uk, 6 miles (diversion of 0.6 miles from route). Information centre, café, toilets, car park. GR 506670.

Thatcham Reedbed Nature Reserve
Here there is an opportunity to visit the Nature Discovery Centre in the Thatcham Reedbed Nature Reserve by making a 1.25 mile diversion (NW). As the information board says, the reedbeds are one of the few wild places in this vicinity. The Reserve is made up of a mosaic of different habitats of lakes, damp woodlands, river and canal. It provides an important breeding place for birds, such as grebe, sedge warblers, nightingales, cuckoos and the rare Cetti's warbler. There are plentiful insects and snails, including the scarlet tiger moth and the rare Desmoulin's whorl snail (see also Day 10). Within the reserve a number of sluices have been installed to create deep lagoons to encourage hobbies and bitterns. The whole area is a Site of Special Scientific Interest (SSSI) and also of great archaeological interest due to the Mesolithic finds. There is an interesting information centre using renewable energy on the north side of the reserve.

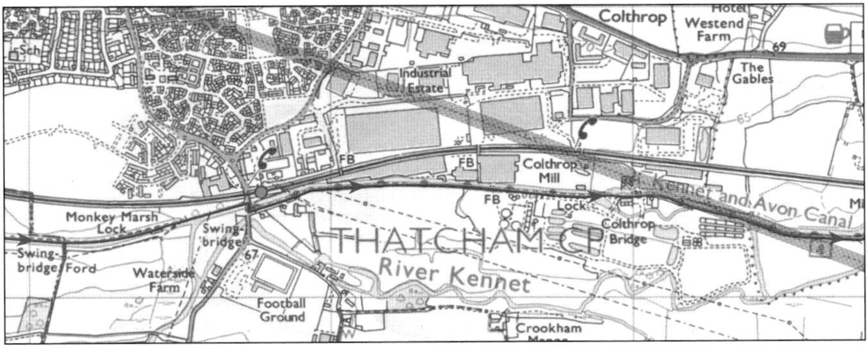

Continue the route along the canal where it is now high above the reed beds and the River Kennet. There is a swing bridge on the canal, which is near a ford of a tributary of the River Kennet. The weir just before Monkey Marsh Lock still has its original sloping turf sides. Moor Ditch joins from the left where watercress grows. Beyond the lock there is a weir linking to the River Kennet. At the bridge near Thatcham station, cross over the river to reach the south bank.

Access Point: Thatcham Station, 6.5 miles. Telephone, car park. GR 527663.

Go east past the industrial buildings of Colthrop (Colthrop which was famous for the manufacture of cardboard) to Colthrop Lock. Pass Gardiner's Bridge, now an iron bailey bridge. Continue along the towpath for 400 yards past the bridge, over a weir leading to the River Kennet on the south side.

Here, at GR 546662, just before an old ash tree near fishing lot 47, is the point where a Roman bridge crossed the River Kennet. The Roman road continued in a south-easterly direction towards Brimpton village, but we could find no sign of it now.

The History of Thatcham

According to the Guinness Book of Records, Thatcham claims to be the oldest continuously inhabited place in England. The Roman road is believed to have crossed the River Kennet near Thatcham (see above) using a bridge rather than the normal ford. The terrain was difficult for transport, being very boggy, and remains of chariot wheels have been found.

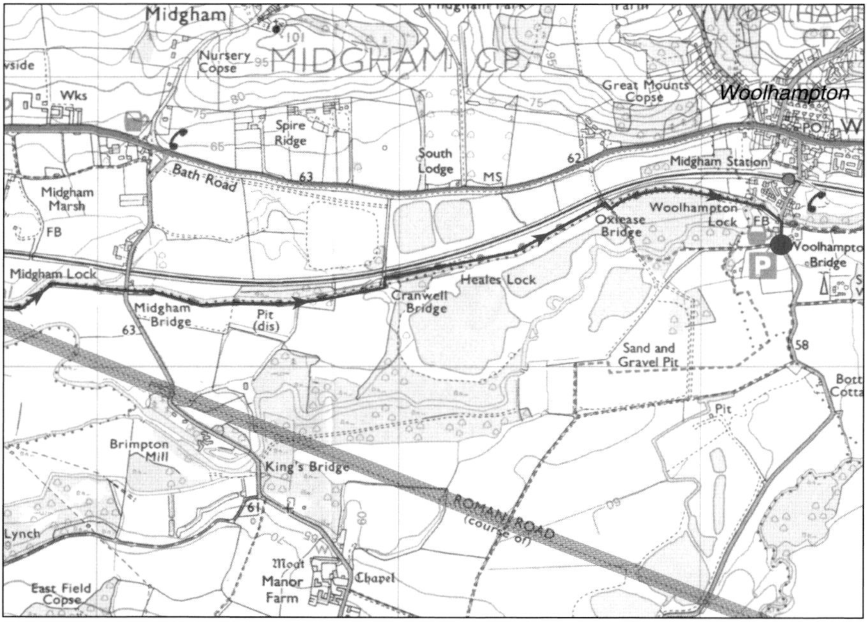

At Midgham Bridge, the spire of Midgham church can be seen up on the hill to the left (N). Continue through this open canal landscape.

We saw woodpeckers, wrens, moorhens and swans. There are crack willow and alder trees, and we saw the yellow flowers and heart-shaped leaves of the greater celandine here.

Canal History

At Woolhampton Lock, there is a noticeboard describing the 18th century navigation between Reading and Newbury. In its heyday, the waterway here was busy with heavily laden barges and narrow-boats carrying coal, grain, stone, timber and food products. The meandering River Kennet was streamlined by John Hore's 'cutting-edge' 18th century engineering solution that completed 11 miles of artificial channel with 20 locks, sluices and weirs. All the locks were originally turf-sided, consisting of low retaining walls and grass banks.
For more information, see: www.britishwaterways.co.uk *and the Kennet and Avon Canal Trust:* www.katrust.org

Turning bridge, west of Woolhampton

At the swing bridge (Cranwell Bridge), cross the canal to the left (N) side. Go on past Heales Lock with its winding hole where barges were able to turn (see Day 6) to reach another swing bridge at Oxlease.

Cross the swing bridge to the right (S) bank to continue (E) to Woolhampton Lock where the River Kennet rejoins the canal from the south. Pass the information board on the left to turn right at the road. Walk for 50 yards to the Rowbarge Inn, named after the 19th century passenger boats that travelled up and down this waterway, to the car park beyond it.

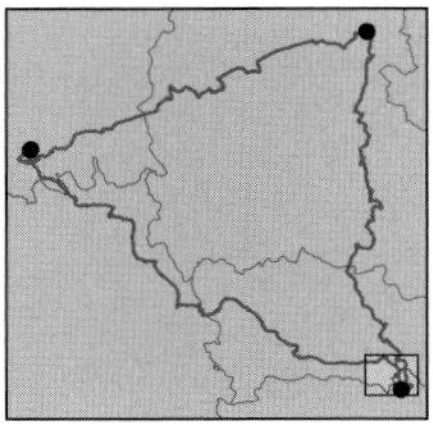

Day 12

Woolhampton to Silchester

Woolhampton GR SU 572664 to Silchester GR SU 636629

This day's walk is shaped by the geology of the area. First, we follow the gravel filling the Kennet valley, then up above its southern slopes, we walk on the sandy soils where heathland flora thrive. Pine forests have been planted in the light soils. At the end of the day, we arrive at the Roman town of Calleva Atrebatum, near Silchester, with its massive flint walls and impressive amphitheatre to visit.

Distance: 9.7 miles (15.6 km).

Maps: Explorer 159 – Reading, Wokingham & Pangbourne.
Landranger 175 – Reading & Windsor.

Transport:

Buses
- Thatcham/Brimpton Common, 3.
- Brimpton Common/Tadley (1.75 miles from route), 3.
  Traveline – Tel: 0871 200 2233. www.traveline.org.uk

Trains
- Midgham/Aldermaston or Mortimer stations.
  Tel: 08457 484950. www.nationalrail.co.uk

Taxis:

Woolhampton
- Broadway Cars. Tel: 01635 847784.
- Kenikabs. Tel: 01635 41405.

Tadley (near Silchester)
- 1st Call. Tel: 0118 981 6840.
- D&I Cars. Tel: 0118 981 2812.

Car Parking: Woolhampton – Rowbarge Inn car park.
Silchester (Calleva Atrebatum) – English Heritage car park.

Accommodation/Public Houses/ Refreshments:

Aldermaston Wharf
- Kennet and Avon Canal Visitor and Information Centre.
  Tel: 0118 971 2868

Silchester
- The Calleva Arms PH. Tel: 0118 970 0305.
- The Romans Country House Hotel. Tel: 0118 970 0421.
  www.romanshotel.co.uk

Pamber Green	• Pond House B&B. Tel: 01256 850797. (2.5 miles from Silchester village centre – GR 608596)
Pamber Heath	• Pelican Inn. Tel: 0118 9700286.
Tadley Heath	• The Broom Esquire Hotel. Tel: 0118 9814857. (1.75 miles from Silchester village centre)
Reading	• Visitor information. Tel: 0118 900 1624. www.livingreading.co.uk

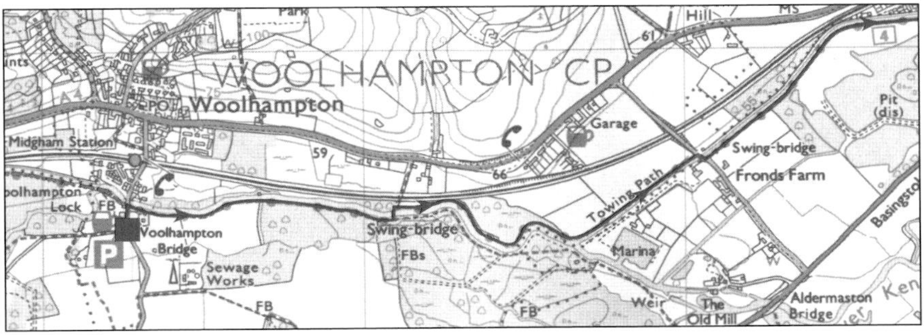

Leave the car park to walk past a concrete pillbox and the Rowbarge Inn. Turn right at the swing bridge and follow the south side of the canal towpath. About 400 yards along there are brick-built pillboxes near the towpath. This was part of the Blue Line of defence.

Walk beside the poplars and alder trees until crossing the canal via another wooden swing bridge to continue walking east on the north side. At the bridge near Fronds Farm Nursery, cross back to the south side where there is another concrete pillbox hidden in The Anglers' car park beside the bridge. Continue walking on the south side of the canal as far as **Aldermaston Wharf**.

Pillboxes and World War II

Between May and September 1940, a series of anti-invasion measures were built south from Edinburgh along the east coast. The defensive line then skirted around London inland towards Aldershot and along the Kennet and Avon canal westwards to Bristol. This was known as the Blue Line.

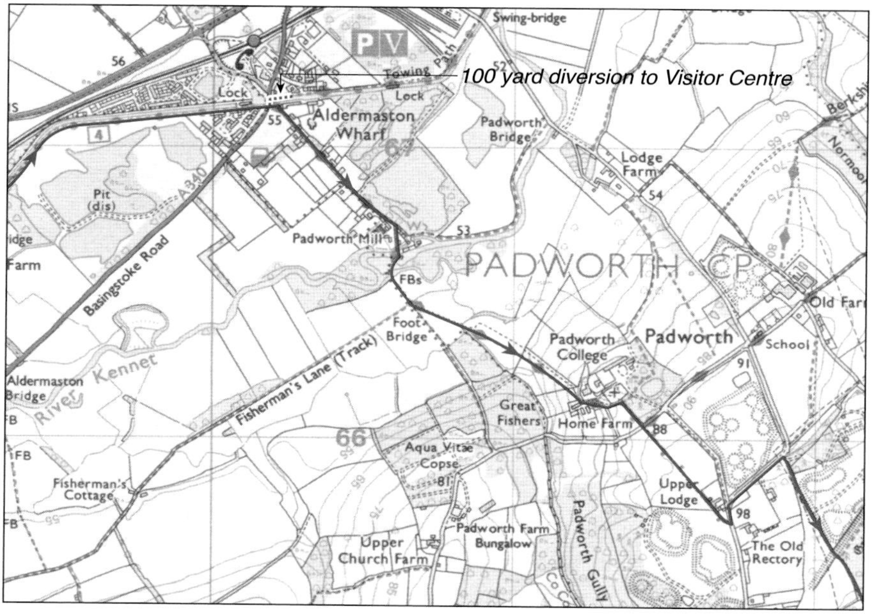

Access Point: Kennet and Avon Canal Visitor and Information Centre car park, 2.25 miles. Shop, railway station, car park, toilets (a brick building on north bank), telephone, buses. GR 602671.

Go past a winding hole for turning barges (see Day 6), then turn left to cross the blue-painted swing bridge, which was originally made of timber, to turn right (E) along the north bank towards the visitor centre which has more information on the canal, together with a café and toilets. This centre is housed in a former lengthman's house (see Day 6). It has a separate brick-built wash-house and kitchen with a tall chimney and range inside.

Retrace your steps across the swing bridge to bear left (SE) and then right in front of Alder Bridge School and past the red brick house with tile-hung walls. Continue walking along Mill Lane past former canal workers' cottages, which were built of dark bricks in 1864 and 1876. At a waymark by a large old chestnut tree on the right, there is an opportunity to make a short diversion by continuing along Mill Lane for a further 100 yards to see the elm-boarded Padworth Mill with its sack hoist and weir.

The Kennet and Avon Canal
The noticeboard explains that the Kennet and Avon canal stretches from Hanham, near the River Avon, just inland from Bristol, through Wiltshire to Reading where it joins the Thames. The original name of this lock was Brewhouse Lock because the Strangers Brewery stood beside it. The river was a busy inland waterway before the Kennet and Avon canal was established in the early 19th century. The river had wharves in Newbury, Reading and Aldermaston. Huge horse-drawn barges carrying up to 100 tonnes at a time, loaded and off-loaded cargoes of coal, timber, grain, beer, gravel and wood products such as barrel hoops, tool handles and brooms, along with basket weaving materials. They were like modern motorways.

Return to the footpath sign to bear right (S) along a narrow footpath with a high wooden fence to the right and a wire fence to the left. Pass over the weirs of the River Kennet where, by looking left, it is possible to see the brick-built back of Padworth Mill. Further on, the information board indicates that this weir has a salmon pass situated just beyond the double wooden gates (the fish ladder is below the metal cladding over the weir).

Cross over another two weirs of a tributary of the River Kennet past an ancient gas lamp, to turn immediately left over a stile into the fields of the alluvial flood plain of the River Kennet. Go straight across the first field and footbridge then bear diagonally left (120°) across the field aiming right of Padworth College up on the valley slope. Go over another foot-bridge still walking south-east (120°).

At the corner of the wood, we heard a woodpecker drumming, saw a nuthatch and heard a buzzard mewing.

Salmon on the River Thames
The life cycle of a salmon begins by hatching in freshwater, after which the young fish must journey to the Atlantic Ocean, before returning to the same stream to breed and die. The salmon encounter a problem with weirs, as they cannot swim around them and most cannot swim over them. Provision of a fish ladder enables the fish to move up and down the river. This example is part of a millennium project that has established seventeen fish ladders in the hope of re-establishing the salmon population on the River Thames and its tributaries. Some of the salmon tagged and released in London have made it to the River Kennet, hopefully to breed.

Gas lamp and sluice gate, Oxliers bridge

Climb the slope to arrive at the splendid curved brick wall of Padworth College, formerly Padworth House. It is worth looking back to view the Kennet valley. Join the drive to walk past the riding stables of Home Farm, but then leave it after 50 yards at the waymarked post to turn left onto the path towards Padworth church.

Face away from the church beside the war memorial. Ignore the footpath to the left, but go up the gravel track opposite (SE, 140°). Cross over a minor road, through a wrought iron kissing gate (part of the original Padworth House estate).

It has an iron gadget on it to enable horse riders to open it without dismounting (see illustration in Day 5). This one does not have the small drain in the ironwork cup!

Continue in the same direction between barbed wire fences.

Padworth Church

The church of St. John the Baptist is a 12th century Norman building with Saxon influence. The churchyard contains a 350-year-old yew tree surrounded by a bench inscribed 'Work while 'tis day, then rest awhile and pray, 1907'. The north and south doorways are unaltered and the church has a semi-circular apse, the design which developed from the Roman basilica. It is well worth a visit to see the beautiful, tall Norman chancel arch with its intricate carving and the ancient consecration crosses scratched into the walls. Roman bricks in the flint walls were probably taken from the ruins at Silchester.

Church keys are available. Tel: 0118 983 2203. To collect, go up Church Drive from Home Farm for 150 yards, turn right onto the road to reach the first cottage on the left, called Culmer.

Greenham Common fuel depots

The green mounds on either side of the path and beside the road to the south, represented by the curious features on the OS map, are underground fuel reservoirs. They were originally built to pipe fuel to the US Air Force nuclear bombers based at Greenham Common. They still contain fuel.

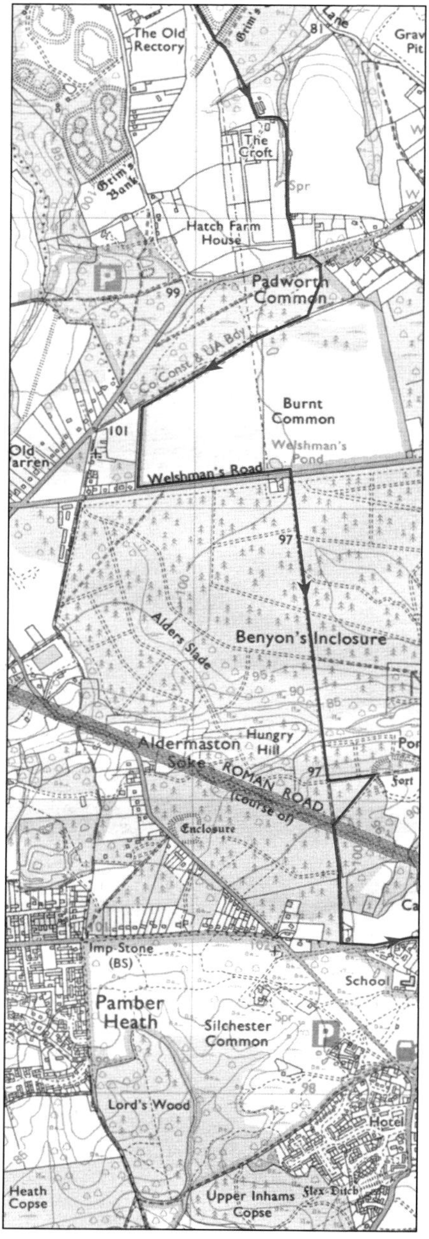

Pass through another metal gate (with another opening gadget for horsemen). The gazebo with its carved wooden cupola and its ornate weather vane belongs to Upper Lodge, part of the former estate of Padworth House. Turn left at a minor road to pass the lodge and the sign to Upper Lodge Farm. Walk for 300 yards (NE) past the day nursery and, before a sharp left-hand corner, turn sharp right (SE) along a bridleway. Cross the earthworks of Grim's Bank just before a junction of footpaths.

Grim's Bank

These entrenchments may have been dug at some time around AD 400 and were probably additional fortifications built by the inhabitants of Silchester as a measure against being attacked by early Germanic settlers from Dorchester-on-Thames. Grim was a Welsh king, but the name originates from the Saxon, since the Saxons thought that anything unusual was the work of their pagan god, Grim, or Woden as he was called. Many embankments or ditches of this type can also be called Devil's ditches. Sometimes they were just a boundary, but this one was a fortification.

Continue on along the bridleway (SE, 150°) past some coppiced oak trees and a woodland bank on the right that indicate the antiquity of the wood. Cross a damp hollow in the wood and continue on the path past Croft Cottage on the right. Continue along a drive for 200 yards to pass Yew Tree Cottage on the left with its thatched roof, tile-hung walls and tall chimney stack, which are all typical local features.

At the road bordering Padworth Common, turn left and walk for just 20 yards, then cross this busy road with care, and turn right onto a path beside the road to continue walking east to the corner of a garden wire fence. Bear away right (S, 160°) and follow the waymarks, ignoring crossing paths.

These heathlands are a rare treasure as the soil here is poor in nutrients, since it lies above sandy rock. This geology produces an acidic soil where birches, pines, bracken, gorse, sedge, tall grass, bell heather, ling heather and mosses grow.

Turn sharp right to take another path and follow the waymarks (SSW) across the heathland. Cross a footbridge (SW, 238°) through pine trees. Leave the wood to walk along the side of Burnt Common on the county boundary between Berkshire (N) and Hampshire (S).

The gorse was out in flower in February that reminded us of the proverb "No kissing when gorse is missing", i.e. hardly ever as gorse blooms most of the year! Grass cutting has been used as part of a heathland management programme to prevent encroachment by the gorse. We saw a ruddy darter (a rusty-coloured dragonfly!) feeding on the gorse flowers.

Walk south to a waymark sign on a post. Keep right of it and enter a narrow path between gorse bushes. N.B. this footpath has been diverted due to the creation of gravel extraction pits. Turn left under the transmission pylon lines beside a newly-planted wood, to meet the road. Here turn left along a narrow footpath between a wire fence on the left and a belt of trees on the right. At the first stile on the right, by a holly bush, go over a footbridge, through the trees and cross Welshman's Road with great care.

Drove Roads
Welshman's Road used to be a drove road for the cattle driven overland from Wales to the London markets. Sometimes they were driven as far as Kent, where they were fattened up after their long journey and then sent to market. Along the drove roads there were watering holes both for the cattle, as in Welshman's Pond indicated on the map, or for humans, such as the numerous pubs called Drovers Arms. The drove roads died out in the 19th century as improved transport, particularly the coming of the railways, made them redundant.

On the other side of the road, go through the line of trees and turn left onto a wide track, part of the permissive network of forestry paths. Walk around the electricity sub-station to meet a wide north/south track. Turn right to follow the wide footpath (S) through Benyon's Inclosure, where the majority of the trees are Scots pines, grown for timber production, and across another heathland. Cross an east/west path to descend the slope, then go up the other side. This path is a permissive one created by the Forestry Commission.

In August we saw bilberries growing along the edge of the path and in October identified six different fungi.

At the top of the slope by a notice board and at a crossroad of paths (GR 634631), turn left (E) for 200 yards to reach the ramparts of a large circular Iron Age fort. At the edge of the ramparts, turn sharp right to walk diagonally back (SW, 222°) returning to the main path. The footpath meets the main path at the point where the Roman road from Corinium (Ermin Way) crosses (GR 625629). We could see no sign of it, although there is a bank.

Bilberries
Bilberries are low-growing shrubs from the same family as the blue-berry and thrive on the damp acidic heathland soils.

We stood in the quiet wood and imagined the sharp contrast of the noise and clatter of Roman soldiers.

Turn left to continue to walk (S) to the road. Turn left (E) to pass brick cottages built with diaperwork platbands. Follow the road (E) for 400 yards into the outskirts of the village of **Silchester**.

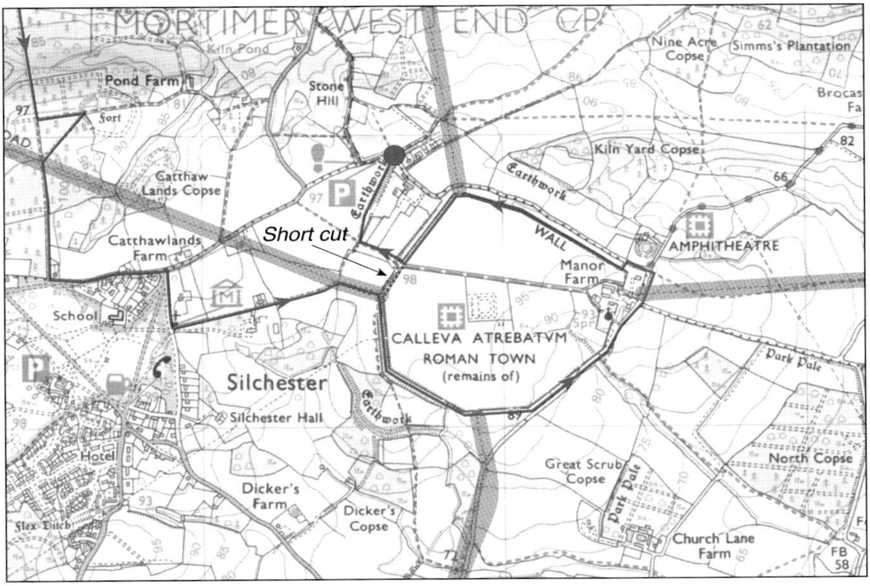

Calleva Atrebatum

The Iron Age town or oppidum of Calleva (town in the wood) was founded less than a hundred years before the Roman invasion of AD 43. The Roman city was called Calleva Atrebatum, as it was the capital and administrative centre of the Atrebates, a tribe controlling territories stretching from Wiltshire to Surrey and from south Oxfordshire to central Hampshire. Silchester was a thriving and important town for about 400 years and lay at the hub of the Roman road network in the area: east leading to London, north to Dorchester-on-Thames, west to Cirencester (Corinium) and Bath, and south to Winchester and Chichester. To see many of the objects excavated from the site, a visit to Reading Museum is recommended. Tel: 0118 9399800. www.readingmuseum.org.uk Guide books to the Roman site are usually available from the Calleva Arms pub or the Romans Hotel in Silchester.

At the road junction, turn right (S) into Little London Road and then immediately left onto Bramley Road. After 125 yards along this road, just past the green-painted, wooden-boarded Mission church and former museum, turn left (E) along the bridleway and through the metal gates. The point where the path turns right is where the Roman road joins it from the north west.

Arrive at the West Gate in the external wall of the Roman town. From here it is possible to make a 1.5 mile circuit on the Roman Town Trail. In places, the Roman walls are 15 feet high (near to their original height) and are a really remarkable survival. The short-cut to the car park is made by turning left (NE) at the West Gate, then left again (NW) to the car park (650 yards). To make a circuit of the site, start by walking right (S) along the base of the southern wall to see the mixture of flint and stone used by the Romans.

The flints are huge and limestone was used for the bonding courses. This stone came from as far away as Bath (50 miles). The lime mortar looks as fresh as it must have been when new.

Soon the South Gate is reached, which controlled access from all the principal routes into the town from Chichester and Winchester.

Access point: Silchester church, 8.8 miles. Limited parking. GR 643623.

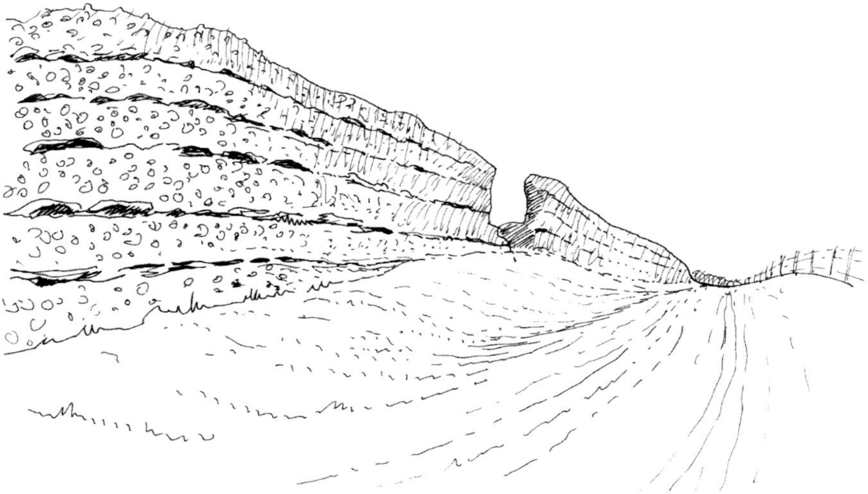

South Gate and Roman walls, Silchester

St. Mary the Virgin Church, Silchester

From the South Gate, follow the road to the church, which is on the former site of a Roman temple. Inside the churchyard is a yew tree which is over 250 years old. The church dates from the 12th century, but has recent wooden shingles on the belfry. Pieces of Roman stone and bricks retrieved from the town were used in building the walls. Inside the church, the floral motif of red roses in the window splays symbolises Mary Rosa Mundi (Virgin Mary, Rose or Soul of the World). In front of the altar is an oak screen dated to the time of Henry VIII's marriage to Catherine of Aragon, showing their badges: a Tudor rose and pomegranate. It would originally have been brightly painted.

Roman amphitheatre, Silchester

The Roman amphitheatre was built between c. AD 55 and 75 on the eastern edge of the town. Typically, it was used for executions or public entertainments such as gladiatorial combats or wild beast fights. The seating capacity is estimated at around 3,000 or perhaps up to twice that number if the audience was standing. Around the arena were two apsidal chambers which can still be seen on the edge of the arena. Their function is unclear, but they might have been used as shrines or as waiting areas or refuges for combatants. The amphitheatre was abandoned in the 4th century.

Leave the churchyard to turn left (NE) onto the road passing Manor House Farm towards the post box. Turn left along Wall Lane where a wooden gate on the right leads to the Roman amphitheatre.

To leave the amphitheatre, bear right to the gate onto the road and over a stile opposite, and onto the Roman Town Trail again. Turn right (NW) to walk below the walls in what would originally have been a ditch. The next gate is the North Gate which guarded the route towards Dorchester-on-Thames (N), the route which we will be following in the next stages.

The North Gate was originally built of timber in AD 200 but was sufficiently important to be replaced by masonry structures even before the town wall was added to the ramparts. A gate would have hung in the entrance, and it is still possible to see the recess for its threshold. Near this gate, two human skulls were found that had been thrown into the ditch. It was likely that they had originally been displayed as severed heads on poles over the gateway. The road was again a single track, just four metres wide.

Roman Town Defences

An earthen bank or rampart made of clay still survives as a grassy bank below the wall. The bank served to heighten the wall and as an extra defence with two parallel ditches dug outside to provide the material for the ramparts. It would have taken 300 people about 120 days to complete these walls, then the earthen ditches were back-filled. An estimated 45,000 wagon loads of bonding stone and 105,000 loads of flint were used to build the wall. It probably took about ten years to complete and was built in sections. The irregular breaks in the stone courses indicate the length of these building phases. (Source: English Heritage).

Walk on to the second interpretation board about the town wall defences near the North Gate. Walk (SW) either on top or to the left of the wall for about 400 yards to turn right (NW) through a gap in the wall, then left through a small gate beside a wooden fence on the left (NE) to follow the path to the car park beside the road.

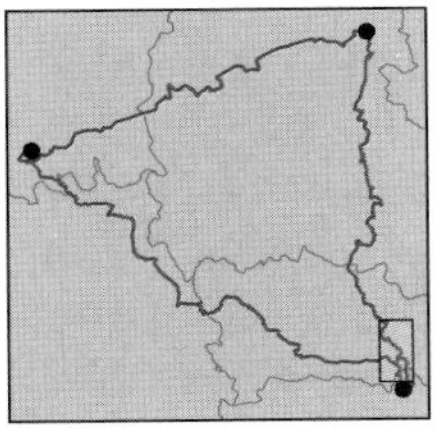

Day 13

Silchester to Bradfield

Silchester GR SU 636629 to Bradfield GR SU 606728

From Calleva Atrebatum, the former Roman town, we head north, parallel to the route of the Roman road from the town gate. All evidence of this northerly road is lost in the extensive pine forest of the Englefield Estate, but there is a chance to enjoy the very different flora of this heathland and woodland environment. We pass the elegant Elizabethan manor house of Ufton Court, descend and ascend across the River Kennet valley to arrive at the distinctive architecture of Bradfield College.

Distance: 10.3 miles (16.5 km).

Maps: OS Explorer 159 – Reading, Wokingham & Pangbourne.
Landranger 175 – Reading, Windsor & surrounding area.
Landranger 174 – Newbury & Wantage.

Transport: Buses
- Newbury/Thatcham/Southend/Bradfield/Reading, 101/105.
- Thatcham/Brimpton Common, 3.
- Brimpton Common/Tadley (1.75 miles from start), 3.
  Traveline – Tel: 0871 200 2233. www.traveline.org.uk

Taxis: Tadley (near Silchester)
- 1st Call. Tel: 0118 981 6840.
- D&I Cars. Tel: 0118 981 2812.

Theale
- Theale Taxis. Tel: 0118 930 2345.

Upper Basildon
- Pangbourne Taxi Service. 01491 671979.

Car Parking: Silchester (Calleva Atrebatum) – English Heritage car park.
Bradfield College Sports Complex car park. (Ask permission to park in this private car park. Tel: 0118 964 4600. www.bradfieldcollege.org.uk)

Accommodation/Public Houses/Refreshments:

Mortimer West End
- The Red Lion PH. Tel: 0118 970 0169.

Beenham/Lower Padworth	
	• The Winning Hand PH, B&B, Restaurant. Tel: 0118 930 2472.
Bradfield	• The Queen's Head. Tel: 0118 974 4332.
Stanford Dingley	
	• The Old Boot Inn. Tel: 0118 974 5213. (2.5 miles from route)
Pangbourne	• Wier View House B&B. Tel: 0118 984 2120. (4.5 miles from route)
Tidmarsh	• The Tithe Barn, B&B. Tel: 0118 984 2829. (3 miles from route)

Leave the car park by the vehicle entrance to cross the road onto a byway going north. This byway is a sunken way, due to hundreds of years of use.

This byway is bordered by splendid old oak trees and has all the hallmarks of antiquity: a winding course, widely-spaced woodland banks on either side showing its original width, a mixture of deciduous tree species and plant indicators of ancient woodland, such as bluebells and dog's mercury.

At the end of the byway, turn right onto the road before the Red Lion and almost immediately right (NE) along the track past The Elms farm.

There are more old oak trees, and when we walked along in April, the verges were full of wild flowers such as greater stitchwort, ground ivy, comfrey, celandine, dead nettle and dandelions. There were swallows wheeling overhead.

Ignore the first footpath sign on the left, and instead walk to a junction of the tracks by the entrance to Lovegrove Farm. N.B. the route of the Roman road goes north from West End Farm 100 yards to the east; there is however, no agger to be seen, just the straight lane crossing the road.

Turn left (NW) along a path beside an old hedgerow on the right side of a field. Turn right along Church Road to cross Chapel Road with care. This is a continuation of Welshman's Road walked on Day 12. Go into the forestry plantation via the footpath entrance, but once through the gate, dog-leg right and left. For 500 yards, follow the wide, straight bridleway (N) that leads to track eight. Do not take the footpath going north-west. Walk through Stockwell's Piece on a permissive pathway created by the Forestry Authority. On the gatepost is a blue badge with a picture of Englefield House on it.

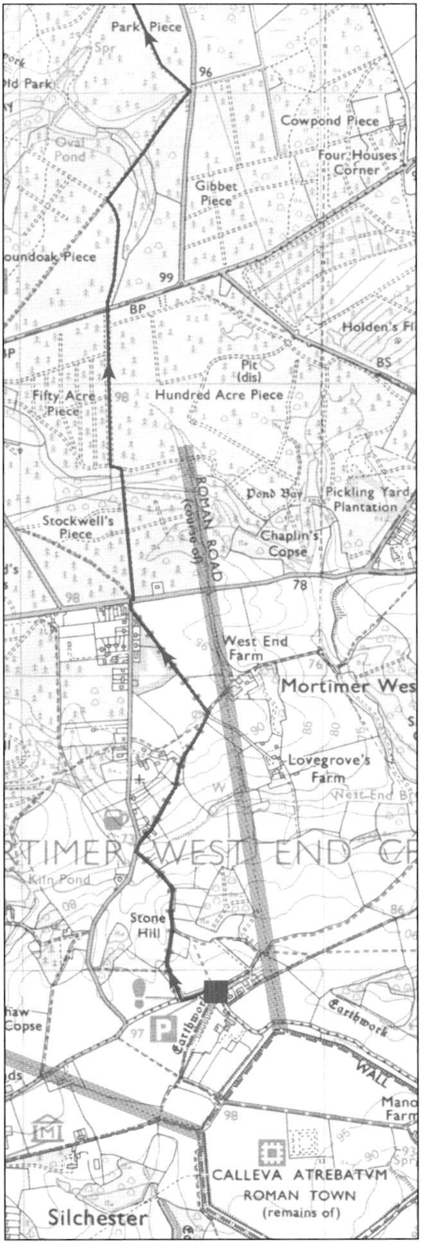

The Englefield House and Estate
Englefield is the site of an English battle against the Danes in 871, won by Æthelwulf, ealdorman (an Anglo Saxon sheriff) of Berkshire. The large estate includes this extensive area of woodland (15,000 acres) with conservation areas of native woodland species. Englefield House is Tudor in origin and can be seen later in the walk (see page 147). In the wood there is a wealth of fauna and flora: we saw roe deer, a jay, tiny goldcrests, several wood ants' nests, speckled wood and brown ringlet butterflies, as well as gorse, bracken and silver birch in the woodland clearings.

Speckled wood butterfly

Throughout these woods there is the smell of pine. Other plants typical of a heathland habitat were growing, such as bilberry, ling and bell heather, hard fern and common rush. The underlying gravel plateau (the Bagshot Sands) produces a low-nutrient, acid soil which accounts for the strikingly different flora of this area.

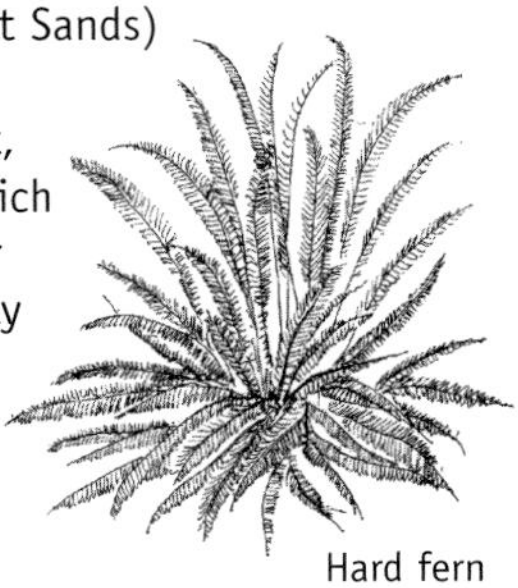
Hard fern

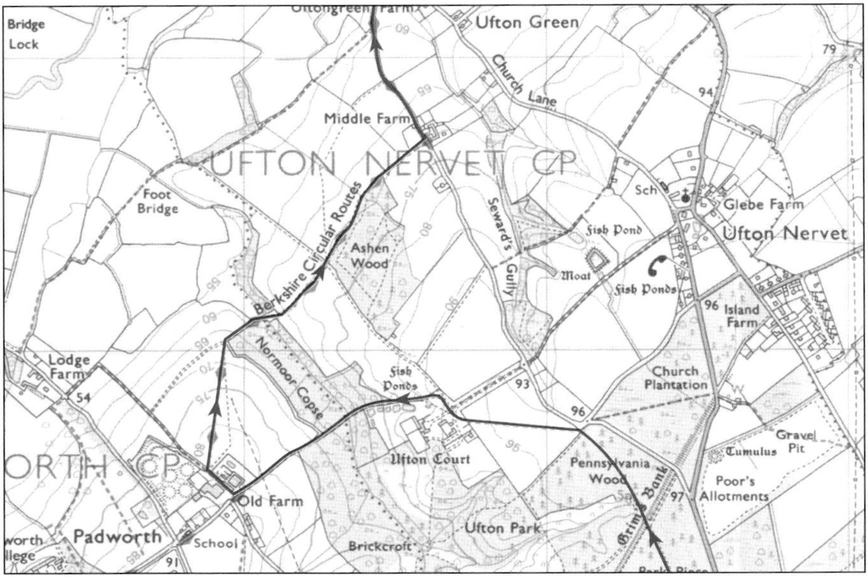

Go up a steep slope to meet a track, and turn left at a T-junction. The track swings right and continues north. Go on to the wooden barrier, then cross the road (the county boundary between Hampshire and Berkshire) and go straight ahead through gate 15. Nearly 500 yards further on, GR 633656, there is a wide public footpath crossing at right angles (NE/SW). Turn right (NE) here to the road and gate 17. N.B. It is only marked on the road side. Do not go through gate 17, but instead keep left and follow the forest path (NW).

Beside this path we saw candlewick fungi, so called because it looks just like a grey candlewick bedspread!

Go through Park Piece for nearly 500 yards to a junction of tracks. Grim's Bank (see Day 12) can be seen as a ditch running NE/SW. Cross the ditch, continuing on the track to take the middle of the three paths on the other side. This is a grassy track bearing right (NW, 342°), though it is not marked on the Ordnance Survey map.

Continue walking through Pennsylvania Wood (NW) to the edge of the trees. Turn right (NE) along a track to a metal barrier just before the road. Turn immediately sharp left through a wooden kissing gate to cross a field (W, 274°) towards the estate buildings of Ufton Court

Ufton Court

Ufton Court is referred to in Domesday Book (1086) as Offetone "with land for five ploughs, forty acres of meadow and wood for one hog". It was the home of Lord Lovell (see also Day 3) who was one of the inner circle of King Richard III, but fell from favour after the Battle of Bosworth in 1485. He was accused of high treason by Henry VII and the house was confiscated by the Crown. The current timber-framed building dates from 1575 and is designed, as many Elizabethan houses were, in the shape of an 'E' to demonstrate allegiance to the throne.

behind the trees on the far side. Emerge onto a lawn and turn right along the edge of it on the footpath crossing the oak tree avenue in front of Ufton Court.

At the far (N) side of the drive, beside the entrance to a private farm track, is an old oak tree that dates back to Elizabethan times. Turn left (W) to take a footpath which descends through the woodland and past a remarkable series of medieval fishponds.

These ponds would have supplied the house with fresh fish. There are five in all, each created by a dam placed lengthwise across the sloping hill-side. There is a woodland bank on the right of the copse, which would have provided timber for the estate.

Follow the footpath to Old Farm then at GR 620665, turn sharp right (NW) along the side of a large milking shed to join the Berkshire Circular Route footpath. At the first field entrance on the right, cross the field diagonally right (N, 006°) descending the slope of the valley of the River Kennet ahead and aiming for the metal gate by the left corner (W) of Normoor Copse. The large grey stone building, Englefield House, can be seen by looking (N) across to the other slope of the valley. Leave the field via the gate and turn right along the footpath.

This northern end of the copse has a woodland ditch as a boundary inside which indicators of ancient woodland such as foxgloves, bluebells and dog's mercury are present. Willow warblers and a blackcap were singing.

Continue along this footpath (NE) past Ashen Wood to meet the road at Middle Farm. This is a brick-built, lobby entrance house with a typical half-hipped roof (known locally as 'Berkshire hips'), two barns and a wooden-boarded granary on staddle stones (see Day 5), again positioned 'under the farmer's nose'.

Turn left (NW) down the lane descending the gravel river terrace of the Kennet valley to the road junction near Uftongreen Farm. It is sometimes possible to see the narrow boats moored on the Kennet and Avon Canal below. All that remains of Ufton church (accessible by a 100-yard walk along the road to the right (E)) is a solitary ivy-covered flint wall. Turn left (NW) along Church Lane on the flat flood plain of the river. Cross over two tributaries of the river and pass West Meadow Woods.

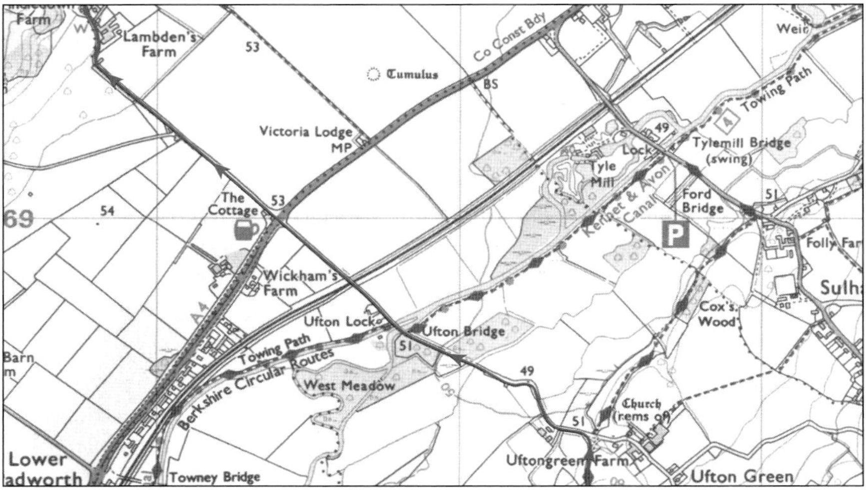

Here we heard, in January, a mistle thrush singing, a buzzard 'mewing', and on 24th April a cuckoo calling. It is the male cuckoo that calls to attract a female. There is no bonding since the female has no nest to build but simply lays her egg in another, usually smaller, bird's nest and abandons responsibility for rearing the young. We saw a kingfisher fishing beside the Kennet here and a grey wagtail (called grey yet its most distinctive colour is the bright lemon yellow of its belly).

Cross Ufton Bridge with WWII pillboxes defending it, one on the right and one on the island to the left. Go over the swing bridge at the canal then cross the railway and arrive at the A4 road.

We noticed that Lock Cottage beside the canal was built of dark industrial brick. A 'header bond' building method had been used in which the narrow end of the brick is exposed on the surface, rather than the length or 'stretcher', which is currently the commonest method.

Cross the A4 with great care and pass the pub and restaurant on the left. There is limited parking for customers only, so it is not suitable for an access point at 6 miles. Continue to walk (NW) along Admoor Lane. This is another curving, narrow road edged by old oak trees. Pass Lambden's Farm, which is again brick-built, with tile-hung gables, a half-hipped roof and a timber-boarded granary on staddle stones next to the farmhouse. Climb the steep slope, which is the gravel river terrace through woods.

Here there were plants such as sun spurge, arum lilies (commonly called 'lords and ladies') and garlic mustard growing. We picked some of the mustard to make garlic-flavoured cheese sandwiches for lunch!

Pass Lambden's Hill Cottages to continue to descend the hill, then turn sharp left (SW) along Webbs Lane for 500 yards towards Beenham. Pass the drive on the left to Trindledown Farm. Continue past another ancient wood where it was striking that the bluebells finished abruptly on the line of the woodland bank.

Much newer woodland has spread towards the road. There was laurel in flower, horse chestnut trees coming into leaf, and coppiced hazel within the old wood.

At a metal gate opposite the entrance to Park Farm (GR 601697) turn right (NW) onto the bridleway to descend through Peartree Copse and across The Bourne. Climb towards the village of **Southend**. The presumed route of the Roman road follows a parallel course (NW) to ours to the east.

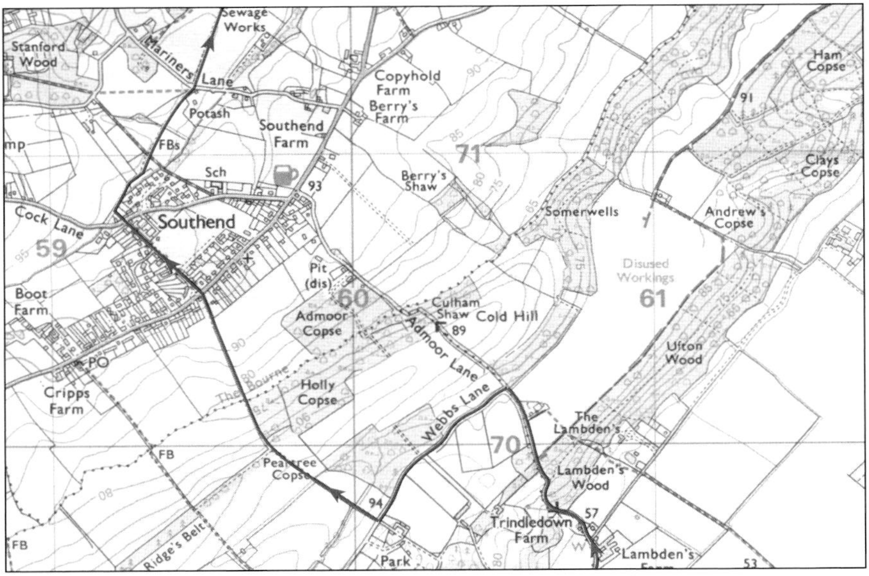

Access Point: Southend, 7.2 miles. Pub, telephone, buses 101 to Newbury, Thatcham and Bucklebury/Reading. GR 595705.

Cross the road and go along Heath Road (NW). There are some mature Scots pine trees as the only reminders that this area was heathland before the house building. Cross the lane to arrive at Holly Tree Cottage with its wooden dog-tooth carved porchways. Enter the narrow footpath where, on the stump of an old horse chestnut tree, we noticed huge bracket fungi. Follow the footpath behind the houses (NE) and across three fields to meet Mariners Lane (named after the house called 'Mariners').

Here we heard a song thrush singing its song twice over. "Lest you should think he never could recapture the first fine careless rapture!" (Robert Browning).

Cross Mariners Lane and continue along a fenced path across a field and through two more fields (NE). Cross a lane leading to Horse Leas house, then dog-leg left and right along the footpath beside the golf course to walk under an oak and horse chestnut tree avenue (NE) along the top of the hill. Continue over two stiles in a wood. Immediately after crossing the third stile which leads into dense woodland, turn sharp left (GR 601721) to descend the slope by the wire fence.

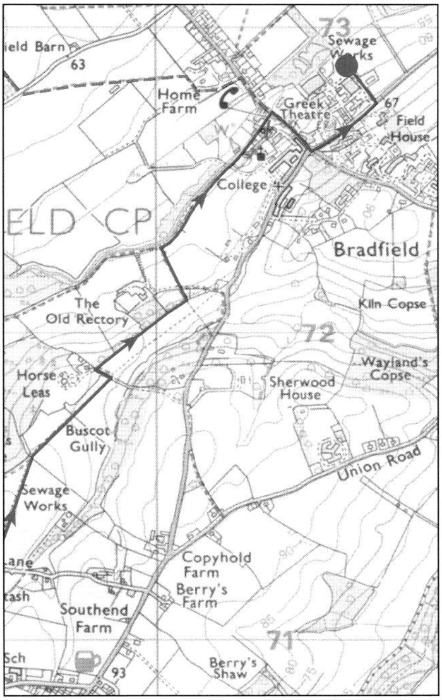

Cross the small road and go down some steps onto Bradfield College's large playing field. Walk across the field (NW, 340°) to an opening in the trees opposite. To the right (NE) are some of the fine buildings of the College, a public school, educating boys and girls from all over the world. Descend the steps to the River Pang.

Turn right and walk beside this stream, past a bridge and sluice gates to the end of the footpath, then bear right up towards St. Andrew's Church, which dates from the Norman Conquest. The church would have been much smaller then. Its present successor is flint-built since building brick was previously in short supply. Continue past a former mill and the art school on the left with its fine diaper brickwork and tall chimneys.

Bradfield College Art School

Turn right (SE) at the road and pass Forge Cottage, The Old Smithy and on towards the main school building. This is a fine piece of architecture, with decorative tilework and a circular stair turret. There is a visitors' centre just right (SW) of the crossroads. Turn left (NE) towards the Sports Complex passing the modern Greek Theatre on the slope below. Just before the de-restriction sign, turn left down to the car park.

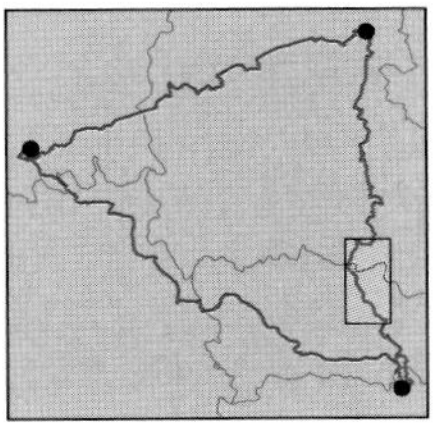

Day 14

Bradfield to Aston Upthorpe

Bradfield GR SU 606728 to Aston Upthorpe GR SU 553861

We head north-west across the undulating, wooded landscape of Berkshire with its dispersed settlements. We find some of the best-preserved English medieval wall paintings in Ashampstead church and, at Aldworth, stone carvings of 'giants'. Climbing steadily, we reach the high, open downland near the site of a Roman temple, then descend to the spring-line village of Aston Upthorpe.

Distance: 11.5 miles (18.4 km).

Maps: Explorer 159 – Reading, Wokingham & Pangbourne.
Explorer 170 – Abingdon, Wantage & Vale of White Horse.
Landranger 175 – Reading, Windsor & surrounding area.
Landranger 174 – Newbury, Wantage & surrounding area.

Transport: Buses
- Newbury/Thatcham/Southend/Bradfield/Reading, 101/105.
- Aldworth/Reading/Newbury, 99/99A.
- Aston Upthorpe/Didcot, 95.

Traveline – Tel: 0871 200 2233. www.traveline.org.uk

Taxis:

Theale
- Theale Taxis. Tel: 0118 930 2345.

Goring
- Chrissie's Cabs. Tel: 01491 682412 or 07808 162985.
- Murdock's Taxis. Tel: 01491 872029/875875.
- M&S Taxis. Tel: 01491 873253.

Car Parking: Bradfield College Sports Complex car park. (Ask permission to park in this private car park. Tel: 0118 964 4600. www.BradfieldCollege.org.uk)
Astons – Village hall car park. (Contact the bookings secretary to check availability of spaces. Tel: 01235 851324.)

Accommodation/Public Houses/Refreshments:

Aldworth
- Four Points Inn, B&B. Tel: 01635 578367. (0.4 miles from route)
- The Bell PH. Tel: 01635 578272. (Closed on Mondays)
- Fieldview Cottage B&B. Tel: 01635 578964.

Aston Tirrold • The Sweet Olive Restaurant at The Chequers Inn. Tel: 01235 851272. (N.B. both closed on Wednesdays and Sunday evenings)

Aston Upthorpe • Middle Fell B&B. Tel: 01235 850207.

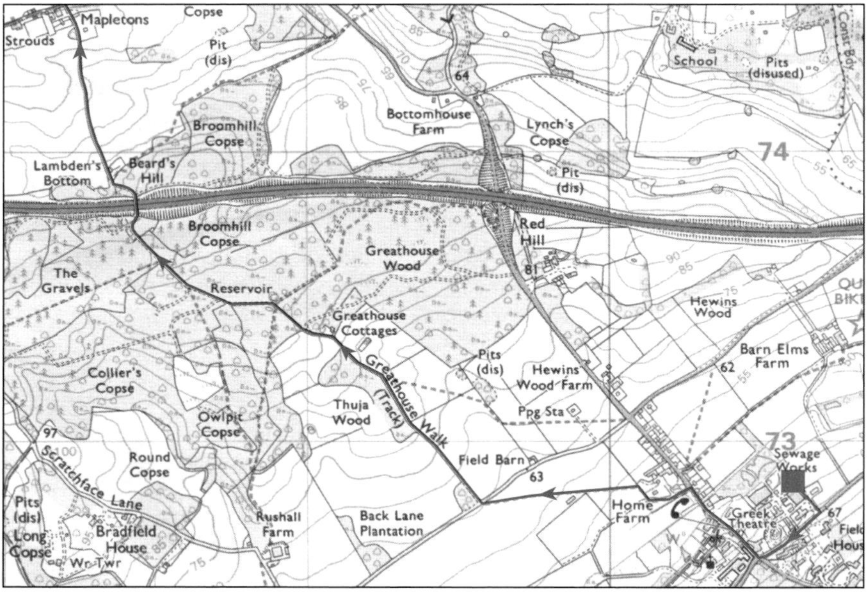

From the car park, go up to the main road and turn right (SW) to the crossroads then turn right again (NW) to retrace steps of Day 13. Cross the mill leat, then the River Pang to cross left over the road opposite Holme Cottage onto a footpath. Take the path left of the Old Gas House (so called since it housed the coal-fired gas works for the village). At the end of its boundary hedge, turn right along the field edge. Bear diagonally left (W, 268°) from the footpath sign across the field, passing near to a projecting corner on the left, to a double stile in a hedge. Cross this to a metal field gate on the far side. Cross Back Lane onto a wide bridleway, which is Greathouse Walk.

This name refers to a now-demolished large mansion house, once occupied by Elias Ashmole, founder of the renowned Ashmolean Museum in Oxford. This is an ancient way, which winds through the woodland. We heard the high-pitched call of goldcrests in the conifer trees, and buzzards mewing overhead.

At Great House Cottage (with tile-hung eaves in the local tradition), continue along the track and at the junction of the paths continue half-left (270°) along the bridleway towards the motorway crossing.

There was a variety of woodland grasses here with brome grass and hard ferns. Violets and dark-blue ground ivy were growing, and in May we saw an orange tip butterfly on the cranesbill flowers beside the track.

Cross over the M4 and along the concrete track, to rejoin this ancient winding lane with big standard oak trees, coppiced beech, guelder rose, honeysuckle, blackthorn and elder in its hedges to arrive at the tile-hung buildings at Mapletons. These are brick-built buildings with fine diaper work and wash houses at the rear of the house. Continue across the byway (NW) to enter a narrow enclosed path bordered by wild cherry, field maple, holly, hazel and a huge old oak tree. Cross another byway and ascend to the beech hanger above. The path leads through the wood (NW). Ignore crossing tracks.

This is part of Ashampstead Common, an ancient wood-pasture. The blue-bells, yellow archangel, wood spurge and yellow balsam, a four petalled yellow flower, are flowers that thrive in this kind of habitat.

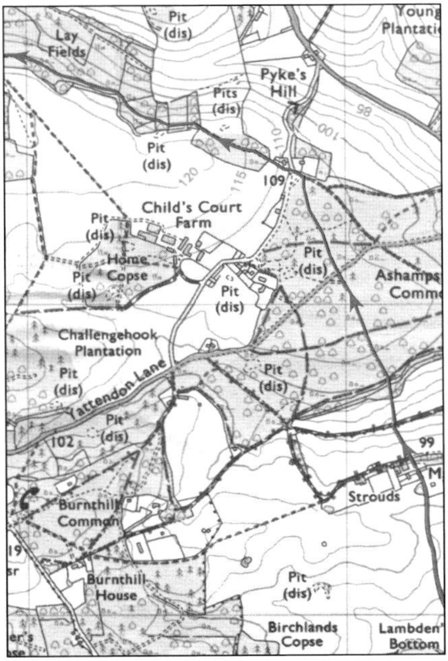

Yellow archangel

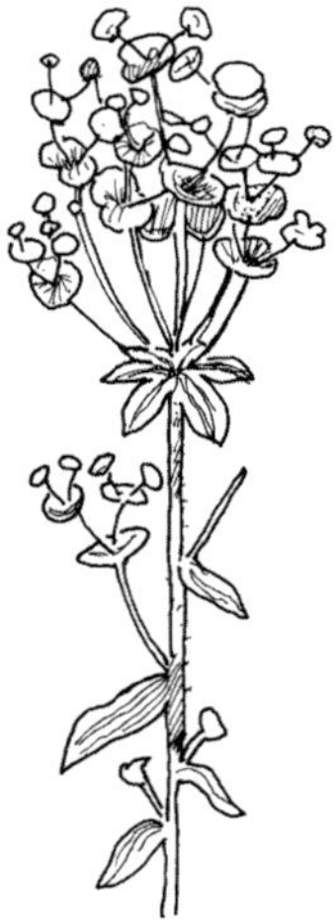
Wood spurge

Cross a minor road and continue along the bridleway (NW). Another bridleway crosses, but continue (NW) for 200 yards. At the drive of a house, turn left to cross the road and take the footpath left of the cottages (NW). Follow the garden fence to walk through more woodland in the same direction.

Buzzards were mewing in the tall trees, and below we saw wood brown butterflies.

Following the bridleway signs, continue through the beech wood (NW). Immediately after a bridleway sign, before an open field, (GR 568758), go sharp left (S) through the hedge and not across the field, then immediately right (W) onto an ancient, sunken footpath.

At the junction of tracks, turn left, then, after 100 yards, at another junction of tracks, turn right (NW). Ahead is a large pit that is known locally as 'Dead Horse Pit'.

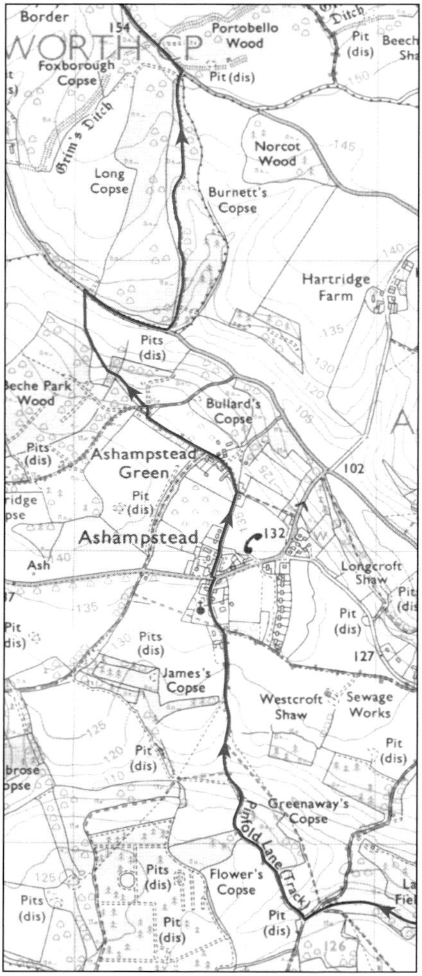

We were unable to find out whether dead horses were thrown in here or not, but it was originally dug to excavate clay for the tile-making industry in Tilehurst.

By turning right (NW), we enter another sunken way called Pinfold Lane (a pinfold was a pound or enclosure for stray cattle). When we walked along in May, it was bordered by cow parsley. Continue on the lane to ascend the slope arriving at Woodway Cottages on the edge of **Ashampstead**, with its weather-boarded church to the left. From the church, turn left (N) past the village houses.

St. Clement's Church, Ashampstead

Although this church does not look ancient from the outside, it was built in about 1150. The wooden bell turret may date from the 15th century when English parishes were rich from the wool trade and could afford bells to summon parishioners to church. Inside, the magnificent medieval wall paintings are a wonderful surprise and are some of the finest in England. The colours have remained remarkably bright with the yellow and red ochre still strong colours. The ochre may have come from the rich source at Wheatley, near Oxford. Scenes on the chancel wall from left to right represent the Annunciation, Visitation, Nativity and the Appearance of the Angels to the Shepherds. Above the chancel arch in the apex of the roof, a Doom, or Last Judgement is painted. Saint Michael is shown with his scales weighing souls, while Christ sits in judgement raising the souls worthy of going to Heaven. From the left, an angel leads three souls away, and on the right, a Devil directs the damned towards Hell.

Medieval wall paintings, Ashampstead

Access Point: Ashampstead village green (50 yards right (E) of the crossroads), 4.4 miles. Telephone. GR 565769.

At the crossroads, cross the road into Chapel Lane (N) to arrive at Ashampstead Green and chapel. The lane swings left, but continue on the track ahead (NW) between woodland banks with coppiced hazel bushes.

Ashampstead cottages
The cottages beyond the church are built of the local flint and brick, due to a lack of local building stone. Many of the village buildings have half-hipped roofs since shorter beams were cheaper: they have intricate diaperwork patterns in the brick. There are several houses with their original iron garden railings that were not melted down in World War II. On the wall of Vine Cottage to the right is an 18th century fire insurance plaque for the Norwich Union Society. In those days if there were no sign indicating that you had paid insurance, the fire brigade would not put out the fire!

Fire insurance plaque

Where the tracks divide and at a crossroads of paths, take the narrow woodland footpath straight ahead (NW, 318°) to descend through a beech wood.

More buzzards, this time six of them, riding the thermals on fixed wings, circled above us.

Bear right to join a track across an open field up to a belt of trees and turn right onto a minor road. This is a narrow, dangerous road, so walk with care. Continue for 300 yards along this road beside a steep chalk bank. It is possible to join a track that runs parallel above the road to the left, but be careful not to turn left onto the first footpath. Otherwise, walk along the road to climb the steep wooden steps, then turn right for 10 yards to pass a waymark post. Turn left (N) through mixed woodland.

There were yew trees festooned with white clematis or 'Old Man's Beard', so called due to its fluffy, silvery seed heads.

Keep parallel to the edge of the wood. At the minor road (GR 563786), turn left (NW). 100 yards further on, before a farm track enters from the right there is a distinctive bank and hollow crossing the road at an angle. This is Grim's Ditch, to be seen again later in the day on the Berkshire Downs. From here, it is possible to walk for 200 yards beneath the beech trees on the right side of the road. Watch out for the Byway sign leaving the road left (NW). At the end of this byway, turn left onto a minor road. Follow it with great care as this road has fast traffic and no verges. Bear right at the small triangular green and go towards the church.

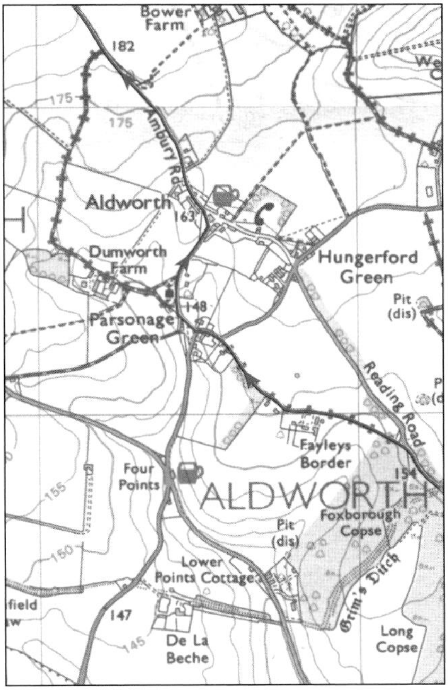

Good deed of the day

When we passed along this road in May, there was a set-aside field with skylarks singing and a kestrel hovering while hunting for small mammals. We came across a freshly-killed rabbit, a victim of the road and a tempting meal for the buzzards and red kites above. We overcame our squeamishness to pick it up by the ears and throw it over the hedge, thus saving the raptors the same fate.

Aldworth Church

The Saxon origin of the name Aldworth means 'old enclosure'. In the Norman church, there are nine effigies of the de la Beche family, who were so tall that they were known locally as the Aldworth giants. Sir Philip de la Beche is thought to have been seven feet tall, a very unusual height in the 14th century. When in court, he was accompanied by a dwarf in order to show off his height to the best advantage. He is portrayed with a mantle over his embossed leather armour to signify that he was a valet to King Edward II. A notice in the church describes how William, Duke of Normandy, crossed the Thames at Wallingford and marched on to London. In the years following the invasion, many of the Conqueror's sympathisers and supporters crossed the English Channel in order to gain lands and favours in the new Norman kingdom in England. The de la Beche family were knights from Flanders, and were granted land to build the manor house at Aldworth. Also displayed in the church is a delightful millennium tapestry showing village activities. Outside in the churchyard is a very ancient yew tree thought to be 1,000 years old. Its main trunk fell down in 1976, but it is still alive. The de la Beche manor to the south of the village is on the site of the original house.

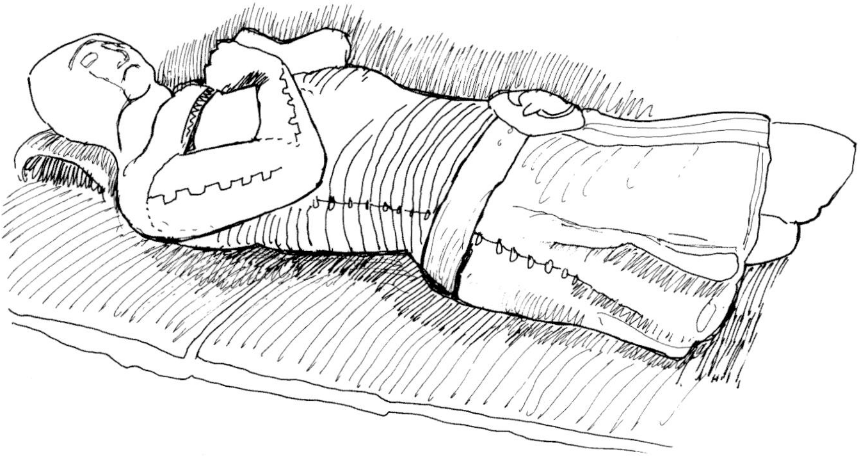

Aldworth 'giant' – Sir Nicholas de la Beche

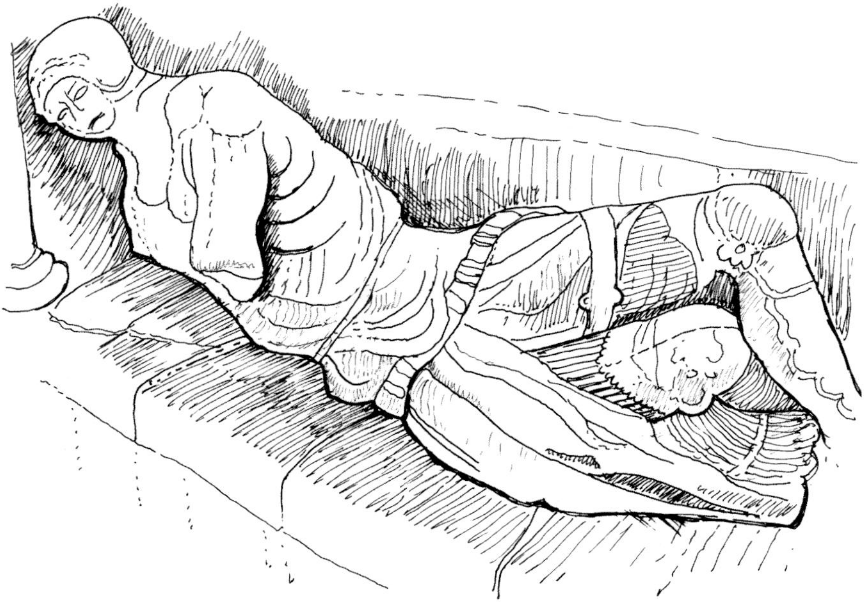

Aldworth 'giant' – Sir Philip de la Beche, lying cross-legged and cramped under a canopy

Turn left (N) out of the churchyard, towards the centre of the village. At the road junction on the right is the former shop front of McQuhae's Baker and Grocer's shop. Bear right to the well, which was sunk in 1868 by monies raised from the parish. At 372 feet deep, it is one of the deepest in England.

The Bell Inn is a former five-bay cruck manor hall, most likely part of the de la Beche estate, and dates from about 1340. It has been owned by the same family for five generations and has twice been awarded 'Pub of the Year' by CAMRA.

Access Point: Aldworth, The Bell Inn, 6.75 miles. Telephone, pubs, car park, buses, B&B. GR 555796.

At the Bell Inn, turn left (NW) passing the Ebenezer Primitive Methodist Chapel built in 1861 on the left. Go along Ambury Road to pass Bower Farm with its tile-hung gable and original timber beams. Continue NW past the sign to Warren Farm with views to the Ridgeway and on towards Starveall Barn.

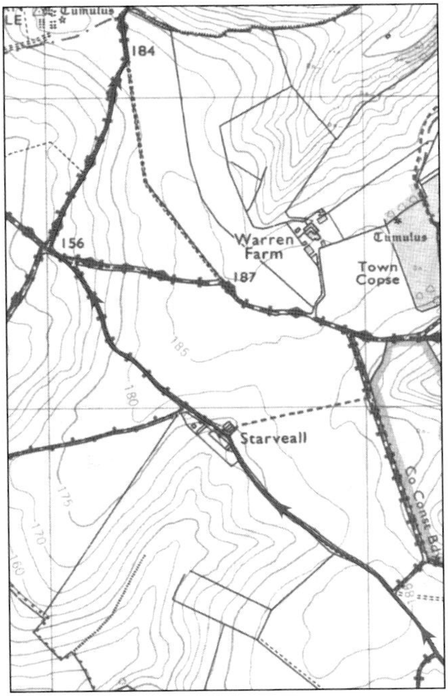

Place Names and the Battle of Ashdown

The unusual name 'Starveall' originates from a derogatory name for unproductive land. Other names for poor land range from 'Hopeless', 'Lousy Leaze', 'Sodom Lane' (near Ashampstead) to simply 'Starve' (Gelling, M. *Place Names of Oxfordshire*, 1974). It is recorded that on the night of January 7th AD 871, the invading Danes camped overnight at Starveall while the Saxons led by King Ethelred, made a camp at the track junction with the Ridgeway (see page 162). In the battle on the following day, the Danes were defeated.

Continue along the wide track (NW) past a junction.

As we walked between the hedges in May there were blackcap, goldfinches and yellow hammers singing, with grey partridge running for cover. The flowers of dark blue speedwell, Jack-by-the-hedge, cow parsley and dead nettle made this a delightful path.

The Ridgeway (see Day 8) joins from the right (GR 540815). Cross it, then leave it to follow the right-hand of two tracks, a byway (NE) and continue along it for nearly half a mile. Near the summit, a footpath (part of the *Seven Shires Way*, see Day 4) joins from the right. Bear left (N), crossing the county boundary, to enter Oxfordshire near the summit of Lowbury Hill. Leave the main track to turn left to a metal field gate for a short diversion, if wished, to visit the summit.

Grey partridge

Descend along the right side (E) from the summit of the hill on a flinty track with a blackthorn hedge, then coppiced beech trees on the right side.

Here, on a dark January afternoon, we saw a short-eared owl hunting from a fence post. Short-eared owls are distinguishable by their conspicuously long wings and the fact that they hunt in daylight on open downs such as these.

Continue descending (NE) to where The Fair Mile joins from the right. The Fair Mile simply means a fine, long straight road (there is also a Fair Mile leading down to Henley-on-Thames).

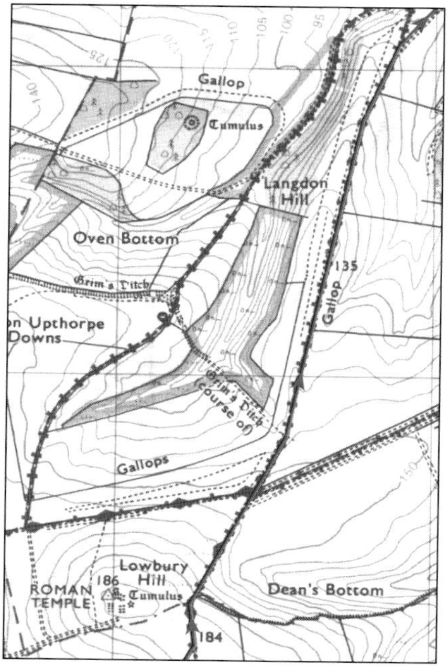

Lowbury Hill
Lowbury Hill is an ancient ritual site with a Romano-British shrine on its summit. The field in which the Roman temple was sited is on an area of Open Access; it is, however, an environmentally sensitive area, so dogs need to be controlled. At this lofty setting, it is easy to imagine the Romans worshipping their gods, Mercury and Mars (such as at Wanborough, Day 8). On a more earthly level, oyster-shell remains can be found; a reminder that the Romans ate oysters which were rapidly transported from their beds on the Essex coastline. To the north-west, the buildings of the Harwell International Business Centre (formerly AERE Harwell) can be seen, and Didcot power station is visible ahead (N).

Cross the track to continue descending the Downs in the same direction (NE, 026°). There are wonderful views from here down to the Thames Valley.

Here on the chalk downs are flowers typical of calcareous grasslands, an increasingly rare habitat in England: sapphire-blue milkwort, common vetch, speedwell, forget-me-not, salad burnet and cowslips were all growing in May. Skylarks were singing high above, and there were corn buntings in the hedge and lapwing calling from the set-aside field to the east. In the hedges were shrubs such as wild apple, hawthorn, blackthorn, wild privet and elder, and out on the downs were scattered juniper bushes.

Continue the gradual descent for 0.9 miles, to the second wide gap in the hedge (with former gateposts) on the right. Bear right here (NE) down Chalk Hill Bottom keeping to the left side of the hedge. (If you miss the gap in the hedge and arrive at a barn, you will need to retrace your steps to get back on the route).

Grim's Ditch
200 yards (NW) from the junction, Grim's Ditch can be seen on the map. On the ground, it is where the fence on the left comes up the side of the steep valley. On the far side, signs of the ditch can be seen. This prehistoric boundary continues west along the base of the Downs from north of Streatley to south-east of Wantage.

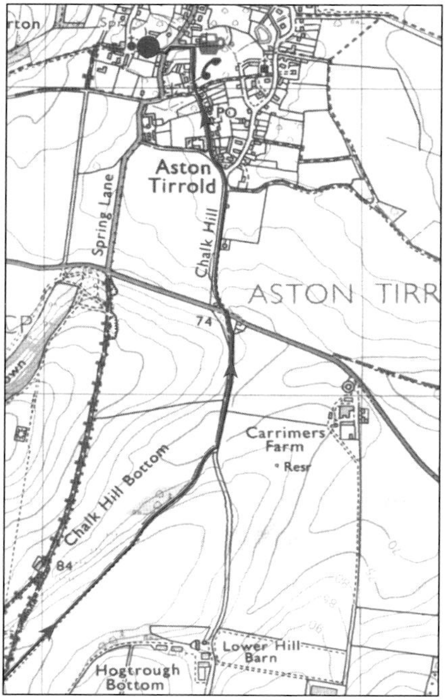

Continue on the footpath keeping to the left side of the hedge, mined with rabbit holes, to enter a mixed woodland where we saw blackthorn in flower in January 2007. Beyond it, take the open track (N), bear right and left between the hedgerows to continue (N) along the concrete track with Carrimers Farm to the right.

Cross the A417 with care to descend via the narrow Chalk Hill Lane to **Aston Tirrold**. Walk beside the sports field with ancient banks and ditches on either side of the lane, with a huge coppiced sycamore to the left. Go along Baker Street. Ignore the footpath on the left and continue on past Rose Cottage, the Old Bakehouse and Keepers Cottage. Cross the culverted brook near Springfield Cottage to arrive at the Chequers Inn in Baker Street. Beware of the traffic from the left that has right of way.

Springline villages

Springline villages develop where the permeable layer of chalk meets the impermeable clay at the base of an escarpment: here, the Berkshire Downs. From Saxon times, a constant water supply was vital for an agricultural community.

Turn left past the Thames Travel bus stop, then right along Thorpe Street past the large sarsen stone on the street corner, to arrive at the village hall of **Aston Upthorpe** on the left side and the Norman St. Michael's Church at the end of the lane.

Fulling Mills

Fullers Road originates from a surname that was common in medieval times. From about the 13th century fulling became an industrial process powered by water-driven mills. The hammers of the fulling mills pounded woollen cloth with fuller's earth, a kind of clay that removed the natural grease so that the cloth felted, making it much denser and so warmer to wear. Such early industrialisation made it possible to dispense with the very unpleasant task of the 'walkers', men who trod down the cloth in large troughs of cold water. Hence, another common surname – Walker.

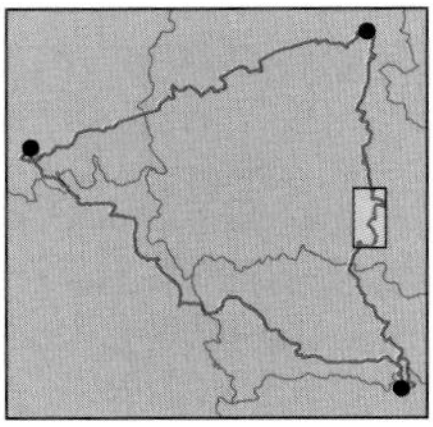

Day 15

Aston Upthorpe to Dorchester

Aston Upthorpe GR SU 553861 to Dorchester-on-Thames GR SU 578940

A day travelling north, part of it parallel to, and part of it actually on, the route of the Roman road. We cross the valley of the River Thames passing through villages that were previously 'islands' in the surrounding marsh and streams. One ancient Roman crossing of the River Thames is reached west of Shillingford. The route passes through the remarkable Dyke Hills to arrive at Dorchester-on-Thames. This was a Roman town, one of the centres converted to early Christianity by Saint Birinus. It has both a magnificent medieval abbey and plentiful 21st century hospitality.

Distance: 11.5 miles (18.5 km).

Maps: Explorer 170 – Abingdon, Wantage & Vale of White Horse.
Landranger 174 – Newbury, Wantage & Surrounding Area.

Transport: Buses
- Aston Upthorpe/Didcot, 95.
- Oxford/Dorchester bypass/Wallingford/Reading, X15/X39/X40.

Traveline – Tel: 0871 200 2233. www.traveline.org.uk

Taxis:
- Goring • Murdock's Taxis. Tel: 01491 872029/875875.
- Didcot • Pryors Cars. Tel: 01235 812345.
- Abingdon • Dazbus (minibus). Tel: 01235 553796.
- Wallingford • Busher's Taxis. Tel: 01491 826161.

Car parking: Astons – Village hall car park. (Contact the bookings secretary to check availability of spaces. Tel: 01235 851324.)
Dorchester – Public car park by the river bridge.

Accommodation/Public Houses/Refreshments:

Cholsey
- Red Lion. Tel: 01491 651295.
- Morning Star. Tel: 01491 651413.

Brightwell-cum-Sotwell
- Old Dairy House. Tel: 01491 824229. (1.25 miles from route)
- Red Lion PH. Tel: 01491 837373.
- Nunsacre B&B. Tel: 01491 836746.

Shillingford
- Marsh House, Courts Drive B&B. Tel: 01865 858496.
- Shillingford Bridge Hotel and Restaurant. Tel: 01865 858567.
- Bridge House. Brigid's Kitchen Tea Rooms, B&B, camping. Tel: 01865 858540. www.bridge-house.org.uk

Dorchester
- Fleur de Lys Hotel. Tel: 01865 340502.
- George Hotel. Tel: 01865 340404.
- Plough Inn. Tel 01865 340012.
- White Hart Hotel. Tel: 01865 347044.
- Buena Vista B&B. Tel: 01865 340903.
- Dorchester Abbey Tea Rooms. 01865 340054. Wed–Sun, 3–5.15pm. www.dorchester-on-thames.co.uk

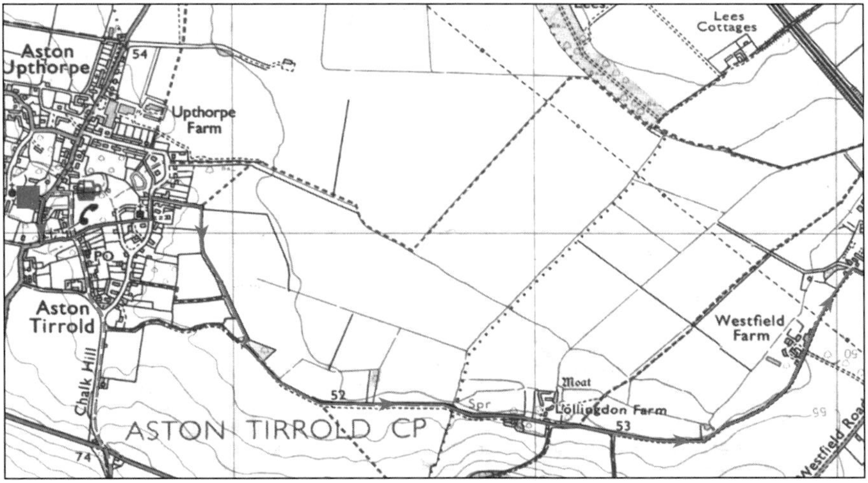

Turn right (E) out of the car park along Thorpe Street to turn right (S) into Spring Lane. Pass the United Reform Church then, just as the road turns sharply to the right, turn left (E) along the footpath just beyond the church car park. Go under a large lime tree to follow a narrow footpath beside an ancient coppiced sweet chestnut tree. Cross the village road and continue in the same direction along the path to the church.

Aston Tirrold church has a Norman doorway. Inside, some of the stones in the doorway from the north aisle into the vestry are even older, being Anglo-Saxon workmanship. On the south side of the chancel arch is the head of a painted 'green man', a pagan vegetation spirit.

Leave the churchyard and turn left (N) along the road for 100 yards. At a fine elm-planked barn, turn right (E) to follow a concrete track to a pair of metal field gates. Do not take the path ahead, but turn right to go round a metal gate (S) and into a green lane. At the T-junction of two paths (GR 560856), turn left (SE) between the hedgerow and field.

On the map, this track shows the characteristics of a former woodland boundary in that it is sinuous in course; it also has a multi-species hedgerow. We found elm suckers, wild cherry, elder, black poplar, ash, hawthorn, spindle tree, guelder rose, hazel, wayfaring tree, dogwood, ivy, rose and blackthorn.

Continue past Lollingdon Farm with its timber granary raised on cast-iron staddle stones, and its wrought-iron door hinges and three-dimensional weathervane. Lollingdon Farm was originally moated and there are still banks and a large pond as a reminder. Pass a fine barn with its huge wagon porch.

We saw swallows that fly mainly low over the fields, swifts that fly high, and house martins that are mainly to be found flying around buildings where they nest under the eaves.

How to date a hedge

Although considered a controversial theory, these are the guidelines:

Each species counts for a hundred years of age.

Take a sample length of 30 yards and count the number of flowering shrub species and trees. Leave out brambles and woody climbers (e.g. ivy and honeysuckle). Include alder, apple (including crab), ash, beech, blackthorn, briar, broom, buckthorn, cherry, dogwood, elder, elm, gorse, guelder rose, hawthorn, hazel, holly, hornbeam, lime, maple, oak, pine, plum, poplar, privet (wild), rowan, sallow, service tree, spindle, sycamore, wayfaring tree, whitebeam, willow and yew.

Count the species in 3 or more stretches, measured by taking 30 long strides (approximately 1 yard each), mark the length, then walk back to count the species. Calculate the average number of species per stretch.

Hedges with 2–3 species are likely to date from after the 18th century Enclosure Acts; those with 4–6 species are 16th–17th century, and those with 7–10 species are medieval. The oldest are likely to be parish or county boundary hedges.

(Source: *Hedges*, Pollard, Hooper and Moore; 1974).

Continue along this track until it turns right. Leave it to continue along the bridleway (E) to pass Westfield Farm and along the fenced footpath.

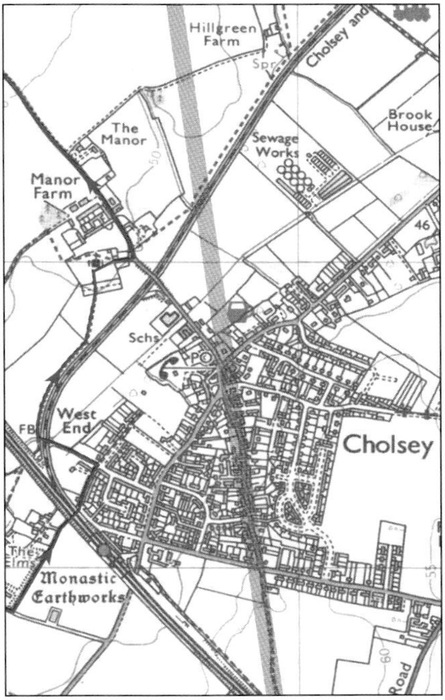

At the road, turn right, then left at the end of the wooden fence towards the London–Oxford railway line. The railway runs in the same direction as the course of the Roman road, though there is no trace of it.

Go under the railway bridge to turn left along West End beside a housing estate, then turn left opposite the entrance of Sandy Lane into a narrow footpath (NW). Keep to the footpath's course as it curves left past footbridges to go under the railway bridge (the Cholsey to Wallingford line). Immediately after the bridge, turn right (NW) to follow the path alongside the branch railway's track.

The railway bank forms a wildlife corridor with mare's tail, blue meadow cranesbill and hawthorn bushes.

Cholsey church tower comes into view. Go over the footbridge and through the metal hand gate to bear left towards the churchyard.

Access Point: Cholsey Church, 3.25 miles. Cholsey village (600 yards from route), shops, PO, telephone, B&B. GR 583870.

Leave the churchyard via the main (E) entrance gate to turn left (NW) onto the road opposite the entrance of 'The Hazels'. Pass the buildings of Manor Farm including its brick-built half-hipped granaries and buildings made of brick and flint.

There are some particularly fine implement sheds on the right together with a barn, again with huge wagon porches. Interestingly, the Manor House is separated from all the farmyard activity on the east side of the road.

Agatha Christie

Cholsey Church is a Norman cruciform building of flint and stone. Agatha Christie, the author and playwright, and her archaeologist husband are buried here in the NW corner of the graveyard. Her tombstone is tall and has cherubs carved on it. On her grave is engraved:

> "Sleepe after toyle, port after stormie seas
> Ease after war, death after life does greatly please."

Cholsey benefited from its slightly higher position in this low-lying land; Ceol's island means dry ground in a marsh and 'ey' is the Anglo Saxon for island.

Keys available from Dot Chapman, telephone 01491 651414 or Nick Hammond, telephone 01491 652136.

The Great Barn

It is worth walking to the north side of the churchyard to see the long barn of Manor Farm. It is on the site of what was once an even larger barn and the largest in England. Built in the late 12th or early 13th century, it was 303 feet long, 154 feet wide and 51 feet high. As the outer walls were only 8 feet high and the central stone pillars 35 feet high, it made the "expanse of roof tremendous" (Pevsner). The barn was so spacious that a coach and four could turn around in it. Sadly, it was pulled down in 1815.

The Great Barn, c.1200, Cholsey

Manor Farm barns

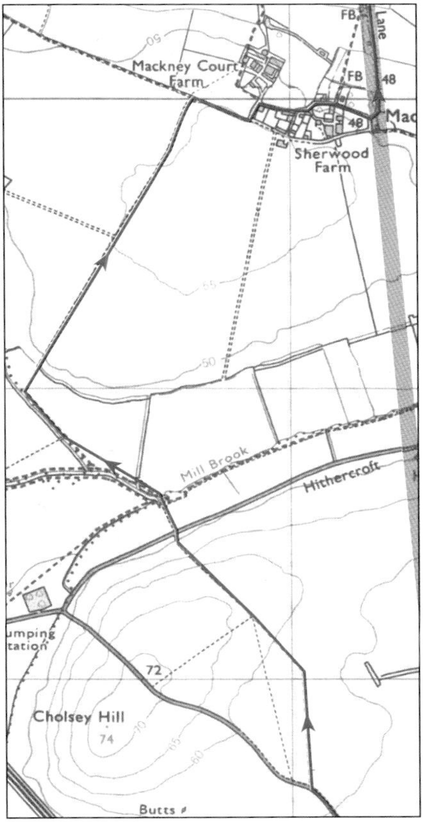

Follow the road for nearly half a mile, walking along the verge with care as traffic travels fast here. At the waymark, bear right to leave the road to cross a large open field, walking first due north (0°) then, at the tall signpost in the centre of the field, turn half left (NW, 320°).

It is possible to see the silhouette of the tree-topped hills (NW) of Wittenham Clumps or, as it was known locally, 'Mother Dunch's Buttocks' (the Dunch family are buried at Little Wittenham Church). In this field, we heard the call of yellowhammers and corn buntings and, on a cold day in March, saw dozens of golden plover feeding on the ploughed land.

Cross the road and the stile to follow the left side of a hedgerow 100 yards to turn right (NE) onto a narrow path to cross a footbridge. If you reach a footbridge straight ahead of you, you have gone too far! On the other side of Mill Brook, turn left (NW) to follow the north-east side of the brook. Follow this for 30 yards, turn left, crossing a tributary via a wooden footbridge with metal railings to continue to follow the bank (NW) of the Mill Brook. Before the next footbridge, at GR 573887 and the waymark signed 'Mackney, North Moreton', turn right (NW) to follow beside Kibble Ditch.

Follow Kibble Ditch for 375 yards, then at GR 571890, turn right (NE) across a field and onto a track for 0.75 miles running parallel to the course of the Roman road to the east.

This track was remarkable in June for its borders of wild flowers that included purple mallow, white yarrow, lilac-blue scabious, milk parsley, scentless mayweed, groundsel and blue viper's bugloss with its distinctive flower heads that unfold like a scorpion's tail.

Wetland habitats
We saw purple and cream comfrey flowers in the ditch, bryony, flag iris and milk parsley. There was a young swallow on the wire fence calling for food: a rare sight to see a swallow not in the air. There was also a pair of reed buntings with their striking streaked plumage. They are the most common victims of cuckoos laying their eggs in their tiny nests.

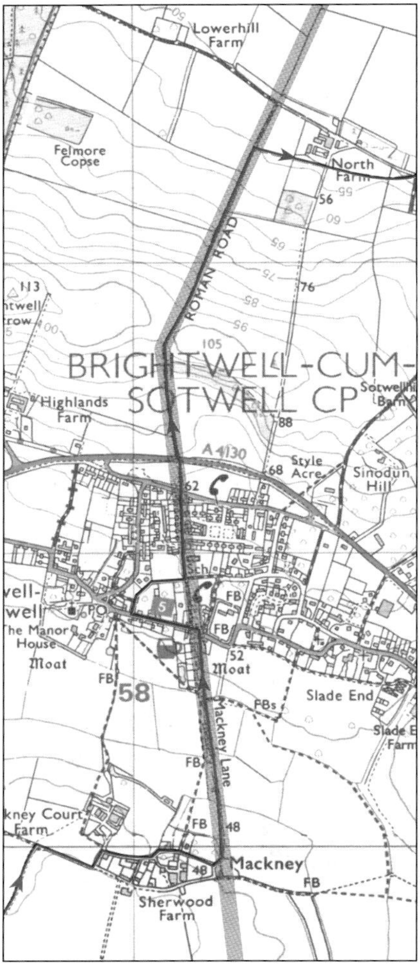

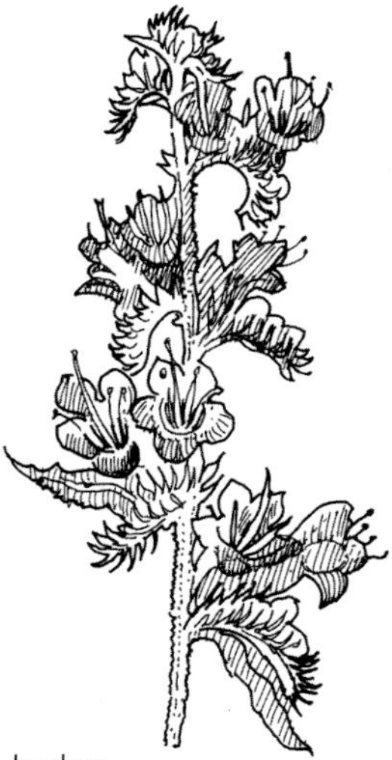

Viper's bugloss

At the T-junction, turn right (SE) towards the hamlet of **Mackney** (OE, Macca's island, a drier part above the stream made by the 175 feet contour south-west of the village), and Small's barn, a fine building of Malmstone (a sandy rock) with a tiled and thatched roof. Turn left by the barn, then right along the road (NE) and around Small's House, built of clunch with its delightful yew topiary faces.

Topiary, Mackney

Walk (E) through Mackney village passing Sherwood Farm yard on the right, with its timber granary and staddle stones. Turn left (NW) with the Malt House Cottages to the right. It is here, at the beginning of Mackney Lane, that we begin to walk on the route of the Roman road as it joins the lane from Cholsey to the south. Approach the village of **Brightwell-cum-Sotwell**, passing some brick cottages on the left. Ignore footpath signs to the left and right.

At the village crossroads, the Red Lion pub is on the left. Turn left here to follow the main street past the delightful diversity of houses and cottage gardens. To enjoy the village, continue left (NW) along the street for 200 yards where High Barn House on the right has a thatched catslide roof with a straw cat on the ridge.

Should you wish to follow the course of the Roman road directly north, then turn left (NW) for just 50 yards, then right (GR 582907) between houses to rejoin the Roman Way by the school at GR 581909, 200 yards further north.

On reaching the war memorial, bear left (W) through the tall brick gate piers and wrought-iron gates into St. Agatha's churchyard. The church dates from Norman times and was originally within the Brightwell Castle enclosure. To the right (W) of the church, there is an ancient yew tree and a young one planted for the millennium.

Catslide roof

A catslide roof is a long gently sloping roof built to cover an outshut (outbuilding); it often nearly reaches the ground so that a cat could slide down it, though that is not its principal purpose!

There are Georgian houses, thatched cottages including one that was obviously the former bakery – 'S.J. Kew' – and a former pub 'The Woodman', of which only the faint sign on the wall remains.

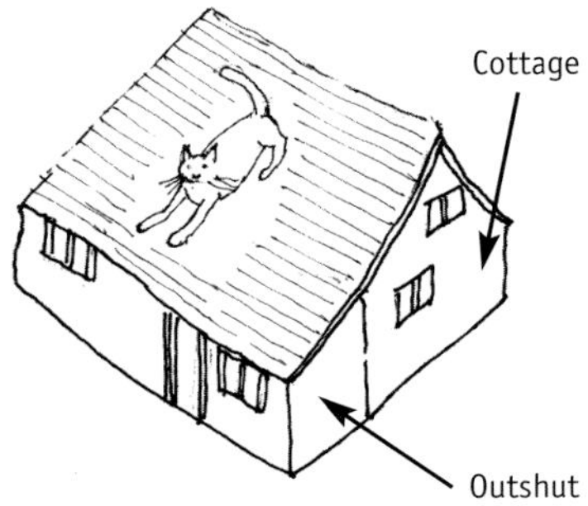

Cob walls

(See also illustration of cob wall in Dorchester-on-Thames, Day 16, page 182)

In the churchyard on the right is an example of a cob wall. The noticeboard explains that such walls were once extensively used in villages for buildings and boundaries. They were made on a clunch (hard chalk), flint or brick base, and thatched. The body of the walls was made of cheap local materials such as clay, gravel, flint, manure, bone, straw, lime and water. "Give a cob a good pair of shoes and a good hat, and he will last you for many a year".

Access Point: Brightwell-cum-Sotwell war memorial, 7 miles. Limited car parking in the main street. Buses to Wallingford, telephone, pub. GR 582907.

Return to the war memorial in 'The Square' to go diagonally right (NE) past the triangular green leading into Church Lane. The tall Gothic tower of the village hall is to the left (W). After only 50 yards and opposite a thatched cottage, turn right (E) along a narrow alley. Pass a sports field on the left, then at a metal barrier, turn left (N) to join the north/south footpath (GR 582909) on the course of the Roman road.

Pass the school on the right-hand side. This path, bordered by old oak, hawthorn and ash trees was known as 'The Old Street' a 10th century Saxon charter and forms the parish boundary between Brightwell to the left (W) and Sotwell to the right (E). We follow it almost to the River Thames. Continue along the footpath north through a housing estate in the same direction, and by the Green Lane flats.

Cross a minor road, passing a thatched cottage and continue along the bridleway. Start to ascend and cross the A4130 Didcot/Wallingford road with care. Climb the slope beside a multi-specied hedge to the summit walking along the embankment or agger of the Roman road. Margary (1973, see introduction) describes this part of the Roman road as having "a distinct low agger of about 15 feet wide".

We enjoyed this open downland on a gloriously sunny October day, with the hedgerow fruits shining scarlet and crimson, and the slate-blue sheen of the sloe berries. To the left (W), there is a clump of trees marking Brightwell Barrow, a prehistoric tumulus; to the south, the Berkshire Downs are visible and to the north the tower and long roof of Dorchester Abbey can be seen.

Go down the slope beside damson trees, then near the bottom at a bridleway sign, turn right (E) to make a diversion in order to cross the Thames at **Shillingford**. Follow the path along the south side of North Farm buildings. Continue along the farm track, to cross North Farm's drive, and go (E) under an avenue of elm, ash, sycamore, oak and crack willow.

Go through a gate, and turn left to the river, right over a wooden footbridge, to walk alongside the River Thames to reach the grass lawn of Shillingford Bridge Hotel and Restaurant. Turn left (N) over the bridge, then left again (NW) opposite Ferry House, following the Thames Path past Brigid's Kitchen Tea Rooms.

Just before the small road turns sharp left, at the gates of High Trees, bear half-right following the route of the Thames Path through a kissing gate, to follow an enclosed path. Turn left after 200 yards round a metal barrier to reach the river on the opposite bank.

At the house beside the old wharf where coal, steel and beer were landed, there is a plaque on the side of the wall showing historic flood levels. The highest was in 1809, the most recent one in January 1947. Interestingly, the 2007 level was only up to the first course of bricks of the house, since the river is now much better managed by locks. There is a resting spot here, where we watched swans with their cygnets, coots, and house martins catching insects over the water.

Turn right (N) to pass the house on the right called 'Old Wharf' and Shillingford Farm on the left with brick on the front ('posh side') and Malmstone behind. On the left is Wisteria Cottage with an enormous fifty-year-old wisteria plant trained along its wall. Turn left at the Kingfisher pub to walk for 700 yards beside the busy A4074 road. At the large brown and white road sign, cross to join a footpath.

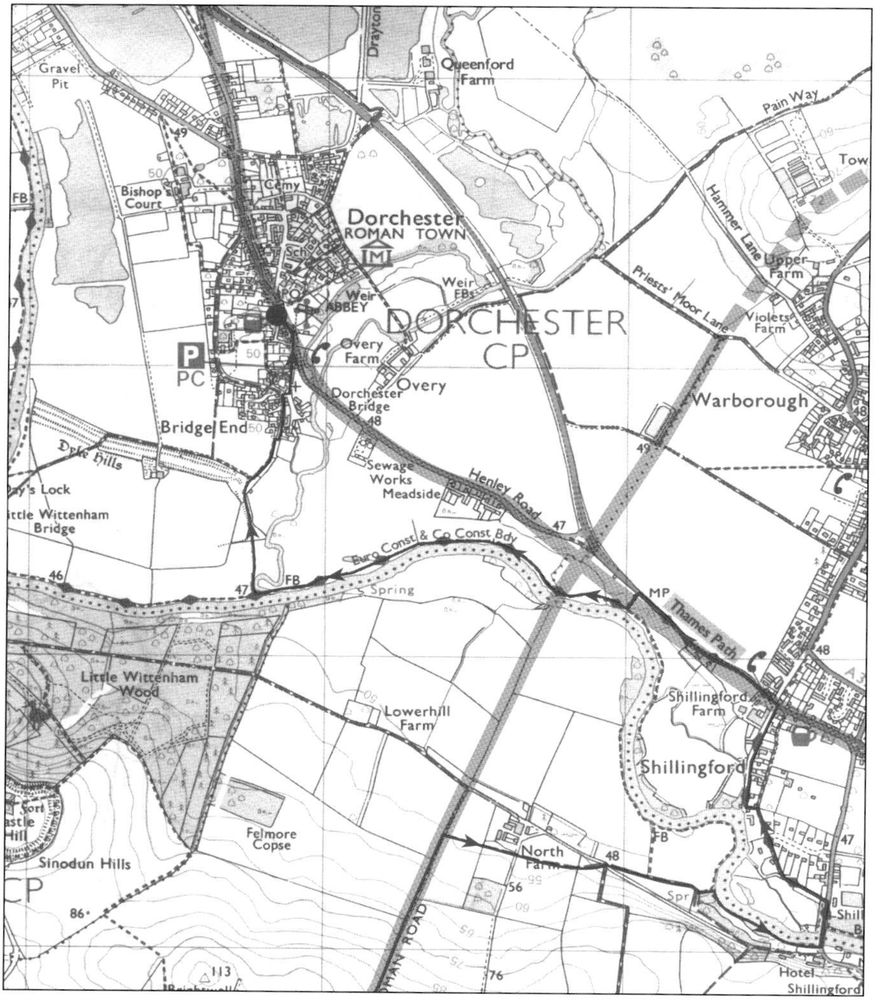

Across the road, on the other side of the hedge, a brick pillbox can be seen on the right. Like the others seen on this route, it was built to guard the River Thames in World War II. At the river, turn right across two fields, only divided by ditches, to 25 yards beyond the second field boundary where there is a ditch and a line of willow trees joining the Thames at an angle.

Roman crossing, River Thames
The low riverside bank is what was known as 'Old Street Ford' in the 10th century and was one of the Roman crossings of the river at GR 588932 identified by G.B. Grundy, the other one being at Streatley (OE: a clearing on the Roman road) 7.7 miles to the south, where the Romans used the much older prehistoric Ridgeway crossing.

Follow the river bank on its north side to cross a wooden bridge over the River Thame joining the River Thames. Turn immediately right to follow the footpath (N) towards the houses of **Dorchester** (known locally as **Dorchester-on-Thames**). Go through a metal kissing gate, pass the Dyke Hills earthworks to the left and another pillbox on the right.

Follow the footpath to a minor road at the edge of the village. Bear right, past 'The Thatched Cottage', then at the road junction, bear left, past Vine Cottage on the left, the Chequers Inn and the Catholic Church on the right (a carved statue of St. Birinus is set in a niche on the wall) to arrive at the car park where there are toilets.

Dyke Hills

The long linear banks are the remains of a heavily-occupied Iron Age oppidum (a fortified village) where the remains of gullies, pits, hut circles and enclosure ditches show there were dozens of round houses. The site was particularly safe, being protected by the loop in the River Thames which created a barrier on two sides.

Dorchester was a good crossing-place of the River Thame as well as the River Thames. Roman bridge piles have been found for the crossing of the River Thame. To see this spot at GR 579938, divert from the main route near Vine Cottage by turning sharp right (SE). Go along the road to 'The Green'. Bear left to go beside the cottages, then left in front of 12 Riverside and down the path to the river bank. Today it is a quiet corner where yellow water lilies, bulrushes and willow trees grow.

Dorchester Abbey and lych gate
Romans often chose low-lying places on which to site their towns. Dorchester Abbey is one of the earliest Christian sites in Britain. In AD 635 Bishop Birinus was sent from Rome to convert the people of Wessex. He preached to King Cynegils on a hill south-west of Dorchester at Churn Knob on the top of the Blewbury Downs (GR 522847). The king was converted to Christianity and granted land to build a cathedral probably comprising a simple wooden building on the site of the present Abbey.
In Saxon times, the diocese of Dorchester was of such importance that it stretched from the River Thames north to modern-day Kingston-on-Hull on the River Humber. In the museum there is a map of some of the Roman roads that converged on Dorchester-on-Thames due to its strategic river crossing site. These are vividly described by F.J. Malpas in VCH, Berks, i, 214.

Dorchester Abbey Museum is open May to September inclusive Tues–Fri, 1–5pm; Sat, 11am–5pm; Sun, 2–5pm. Tea Rooms.

Dorchester Abbey and Toll house

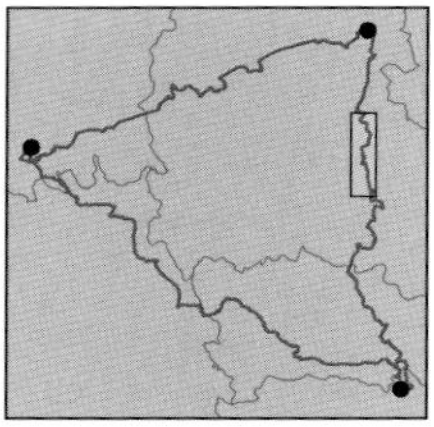

Day 16

Dorchester to Oxford

Dorchester GR SU 579940 to Oxford GR SP 567074

We follow the route of the Roman road for much of the day as we 'march' northwards. In places, signs of the agger are still visible. There is a short diversion to see a rare survival of one of England's largest village greens at Marsh Baldon, but we are back on the Roman route as we approach Oxford. We take the rural Green Belt route through the villages of Garsington and Horspath. The walk ends near C.S. Lewis' inspiration for Narnia.

Distance: 12 miles (19.2 km).

Maps: Explorer 170 – Abingdon, Wantage & Vale of White Horse.
Explorer 180 – Oxford, Witney & Woodstock.
Landranger 164 – Oxford.

Transport: Buses
- Oxford/Dorchester bypass/Wallingford/Reading, X15/X39/X40.
- Thornhill Park & Ride/Oxford city centre.
  Traveline – Tel: 0871 200 2233. www.traveline.org.uk

Taxis:

Abingdon
- Dazbus (minibus). Tel: 01235 553796.
- Phil's Taxi Service. Tel: 01235 522555.
- Premier Taxi Services Ltd. Tel: 01235 555455.

Oxford
- ABC Taxis. Tel: 01865 770077/775577.
- 001 Taxis, Tel: 01865 240000.

Car Parking: Dorchester – Public car park by the river bridge.
Oxford – Thornhill Park & Ride on the east side of the city, south of the A40 (free parking), toilets available.

Accommodation/Public Houses/Refreshments:

Berinsfield
- Village Inn PH. Tel: 01865 340340.

Marsh Baldon
- Seven Stars PH. Tel: 01865 343255.

Toot Baldon	• The Mole Inn. Tel: 01865 340001.
Horspath	• The Chequers Inn PH. Tel: 01865 872401.
	• Taste of India Restaurant. Tel: 01865 874800/876767.
Oxford (Risinghurst)	
	• Lewis Lodge B&B. Tel: 01865 762285.
Oxford (Headington)	
	• Pickwicks Guest House. Tel: 01865 750487.
	• The Conifers Guest House. Tel: 01865 763055.

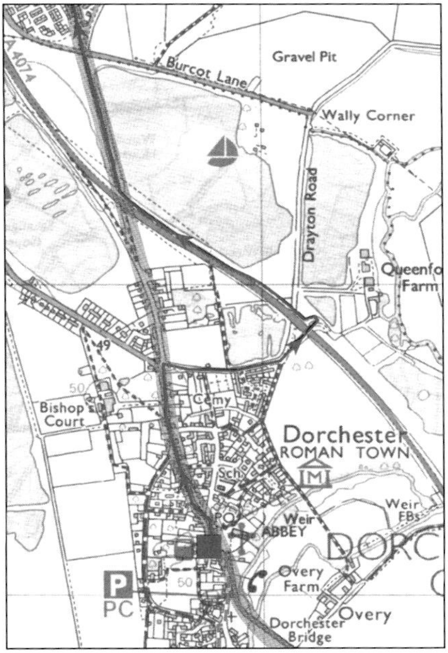

From the bridge car park, turn left (NW) by the Fleur de Lys Hotel along the High Street on the course of the Roman road, past the George Hotel on the left and the White Hart Hotel (built 1691) on the right.

This High Street shows a wide range of different vernacular architecture with bow windows, jettied houses (55 on the left dated 1610 on an upright beam and inscribed 'IH') and herring-bone brickwork (30 on the right). When we walked past the white-painted Willoughby House on the left in July, it had numerous house martins' nests under its eaves.

Walk to the end of the High Street, where it becomes Oxford Road. Turn right along Drayton Road under an avenue of horse chestnut and lime trees, with celandine and white violets flowering in April. Go past the footpath and lake on the left and the cul-de-sac, Page Furlong, on the right to the bridge over the busy A4074. This deviation from the Roman road avoids a dangerous road crossing.

Cob wall, Dorchester (*See also, Day 15 at Brightwell-cum-Sotwell*)

Turn immediately left (N) on the far side, down concrete steps to walk (NW) for 750 yards on the bridleway beside the road, then by the flooded gravel pits to bear right away from the road onto a green lane. At the concrete bollards to the left, we resume the course of the Roman road (NW).

We saw a bright pink male bullfinch in the bushes and large purple dog violets when we walked through in April.

On the outskirts of **Berinsfield**, cross the road (Fane Drive) to bear half-left (350°) across a green onto a concreted enclosed path between houses. Continue (N) to cross the edge of a green and onto the right side of a sports field. It is very obvious that we are walking on the raised agger (bank) of the Roman road.

Access Point: Berinsfield, Fane Drive, 2.25 miles. Post Office, shops, telephone, pub all 450 yards to the left (SW). GR 572966. Ample parking available outside the small row of shops. GR 570964.

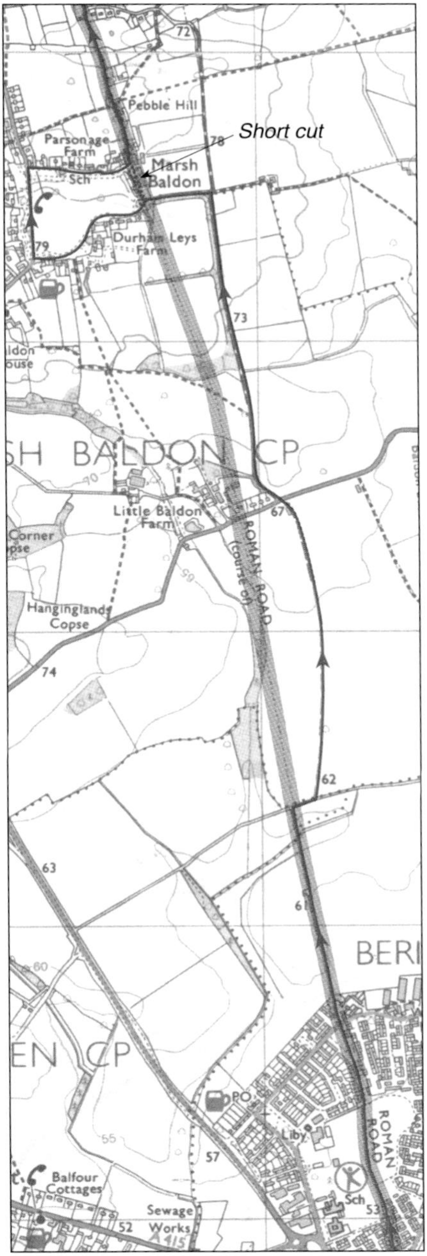

The village of Berinsfield derives its name from Saint Birinus, mentioned in Day 15. It was built to house the airmen's families from the nearby airfield.

Continue (N) on a narrow road to the right of a play area to reach Fane Drive again. Cross this road into Roman road (N). Continue (NW) along Roman road to go across a big field. Where a track crosses east/west, turn right. After 100 yards, turn left through a gap in the hedge to continue north parallel to the course of the Roman road on the left and towards the corrugated iron Dutch barn.

In this large field, it is still possible to see the distinctive bank of the agger. This is flat, open country, which explains why this site was formerly used as an airfield.

Red kites were flying overhead, skylarks singing and swallows catching insects high in the sky in early April. In October we saw a wheatear, an unusual bird, distinctive because of its white rump. A rich mixture of wild flowers was growing along the path in July, such as pale violet-coloured scabious, deep-purple greater knapweed, red clover, storksbill, white campion, yarrow and yellow lady's bed-straw, agrimony and hawkbit. Bumblebees and hedge brown butterflies were feeding on the nectar in the flowers.

Agger of Roman road, Berinsfield, looking south to Wittenham Clumps

At the minor road (B4105) take great care when crossing as there is a blind corner. Bear half-left onto a track and go to the right of some cottages to continue on the right side of the hedge (N) parallel to the course of the Roman road.

A gentleman from one of the cottages said that the farmers have great difficulty in ploughing the parts of the field where the Roman road crosses due to the amount of stones still on the surface, though on the footpath that leads north-west, we could find no sign of the Roman road in the ploughed field.

Continue on the bridleway to enter a conservation woodland under an enormous field maple tree on the right. It is rare to see such an old specimen.

Immediately, there is a wide variety of species such as ash, blackthorn, wild cherry, elderberry, sycamore, hawthorn, turkey oak and Spanish chestnut. A blackcap was singing in the woodland. We noticed how sandy the soil was.

At the junction of tracks where a footpath crosses, turn left (W) to leave the course of the Roman road to see **Marsh Baldon**. At the edge of the village, where the path forks, go left to follow the footpath bearing left around a thatched house to enter the village green. Here, go left again (SW) following a small perimeter road. Pass a village pond to reach the Seven Stars pub in the south-west corner of the green. Turn right (N), literally across the village cricket pitch, since it is divided by the road with the pavilion on the west side and the pitch crossing the road! When we passed, there were fresh chalk lines across the road, marking the boundary.

Access Point: Marsh Baldon, 4.5 miles. Pub, telephone. GR 562993.

Just beyond the cricket pavilion there is a board that says "Notice is hereby given that members of the public have rights of access to the green for air and exercise" and signed Steward of the Manor of Baldon, The Queen's College, Oxford, August 24th, 1931.

Cricket match across the road, Marsh Baldon

Marsh Baldon village green: a rare survival
This 24-acre green probably owes its survival to winter flooding of the brook that flows across the green, so deterring house-building. From Saxon times, the villagers had taken up their positions around the green. Then, it would have looked very different from the wide, open space of today. Records from the 18th century show that there were 123 oaks, 392 ashes and 3,382 elms sold from the green. From then, the custom was to enclose the green for hay from Lady Day (March 25th) to Whitsun eve, then to turn out the horses to graze; from Lammastide (August 1st) cows could join the horses, and from St. Andrew's Day (November 30th), it became a common for sheep. Disputes were frequent as, for example, when two farmers put 90 pigs on it, thereby causing an upset as the village green was very dirty for the village feast. (*A History of Oxfordshire*, (VCH). Vol V., page 30; 1957).

For most of the time, it is a quiet area: we saw a heron with its lazy flight by the few willow trees still by the brook, and a kestrel hovering over the long grass.

Continue on the road north to turn right after the telephone box and along the edge of the green (E) past the village school. Pass a second pond to turn left (N) through the farm buildings of Parsonage Farm. We have now resumed walking on the course of the Roman road up the slope of Pebble Hill. Just past the summit by the footpath sign, a cottage on the right has some pebbles embedded in its end wall! Continue to where the lane turns right, to go ahead entering a green lane and passing Thurlfield Cottage.

Although this path is officially known as 'Roman Lane', it is known locally as 'Tinny Lane' because large blocks of pressed wreckage from scrap yards were used as the hard-core.

At the end of the lane, turn right along Baldon Row, towards **Toot Baldon** church. At the end of the road by the GR post box and intersection of paths, turn left (NE) to the church on its promontory.

The origin of the name Toot Baldon is a lookout post (OE, Tot = look-out hill), and this churchyard commands a fine view south-east to the Chiltern Hills. Outside the Norman church are the remains of a former preaching cross, and inside is a memorial to the biggest peace-time loss of life in recent RAF history in the UK: 41 servicemen died in an air disaster at Little Baldon on July 6th, 1965.

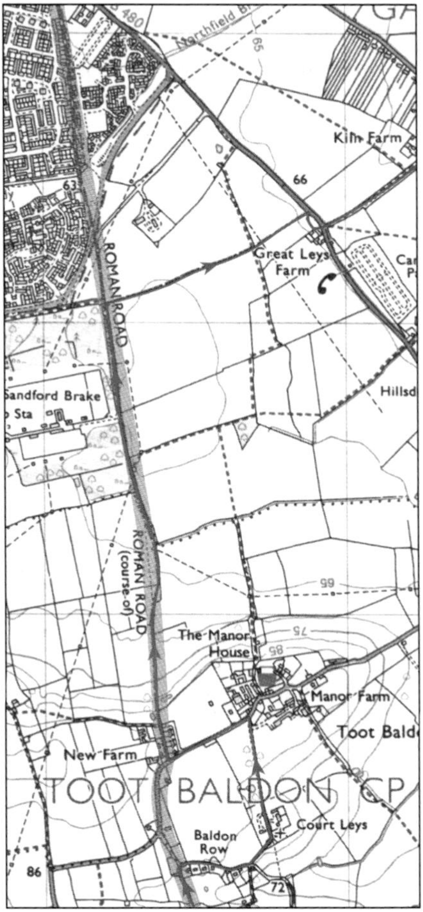

The Green Belt

In June we enjoyed a picnic lunch in this meadow, full of different grasses and literally hundreds of hedge brown butterflies feeding on them. 'Leys' is the former name for meadows, hence the names Cowley and Blackbird Leys. This area is part of the Green Belt and our feeling was that the natural beauty of these meadows south of Grenoble Road should be saved for future generations to enjoy.

In 1945, the Campaign to Protect Rural England (CPRE) wrote "in no case should land already acquired for the Green Belt be diverted to other use, whatever pressure may be brought to bear". In 1955, the government established a national Green Belt policy. The 50-mile walk, part of which we follow later in the day highlights the value of maintaining the rural landscape around cities. With current pressure from the expansion of single occupancy and population growth, these rural belts of countryside around cities need protection just as much as ever.

Outside the church, turn right (N), along the avenue of horse chestnut trees. At the road, the Mole Inn is to the right. Turn left along the narrow road then, just after a side road called 'Wilmots', turn right onto the bridleway (N) on the course of the Roman road at New Farm. Go along the back of the gardens and through a metal gate to follow a path along the right-hand side of a wire fence into a meadow. There is a view of Cowley ahead, with the housing estates of Greater Leys and Blackbird Leys to the north.

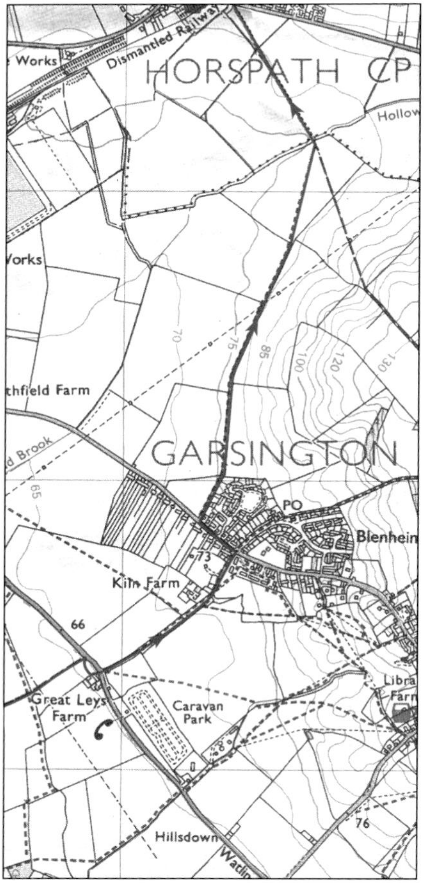

Follow the ancient, thick hedge on the right to pass under an electricity pylon. Go through a small metal gate and into an enclosed path beside a wood as far as a large metal gate before a tarmac track, Blackberry Lane, on the course of the Roman road (N). Subsequent to the closure of the bridleway through the BMW works, now diverted along the busy Oxford ring road, we have chosen a more scenic route going through Garsington and Horspath.

At the large metal gate at GR 564021, turn right to follow the bridleway along the left side of the hedge. Go through a gap in the next hedgerow to continue in the same direction (NE) to leave the field via a small metal gate onto the road. Cross over and turn right to use the footpath to then turn left (NE) onto a bridleway opposite Great Leys Farm.

Follow this path to arrive at Kiln Farm on the left, with its red pantiled roof and continue (NE) along Kiln Lane (the name reflecting the numerous 19th century brickworks in the village).

At **Garsington** turn left for 200 yards, then right onto a footpath (NE) marked 'Horspath 1'. Along this path, there are views of the BMW car works to the left (NW), and we caught glimpses of the shining new minis in the car park.

Further along this path, the radio mast on Shotover can be seen (N). Continue along the left side of the hedge to where the overhead power lines cross. Continue on for another 250 yards to where there is a large gap in the hedge (GR 575038). Bear left (NE) across the field heading towards the left (W) edge of the village of **Horspath**.

BMW Car Works

The BMW succeeded the Morris car works in producing the Mini. This has been highly successful (over 1.5 million have been sold to 75 different countries). Tours of the production line are available.

Tel: 01865 825842 or E-mail: Oxford.Plant-Tours@mini.com

Roman Way, BMW works, Cowley

This sign is at the junction of Gate 8 of the BMW works and the Horspath Road, and can be seen at GR 560032. It is on the northerly route of the Roman road.

Cross the footbridge over a brook and up the left side of a field, through a gate and another field onto the road. Turn left to walk under the railway bridge, ignoring the footpath signs, and walk on past the Chequers Inn and the Taste of India restaurant to a road marked 'Village Only' (NW).

Access Point: Horspath Green, 9 miles. Pub, PO, shop, buses. GR 571048.

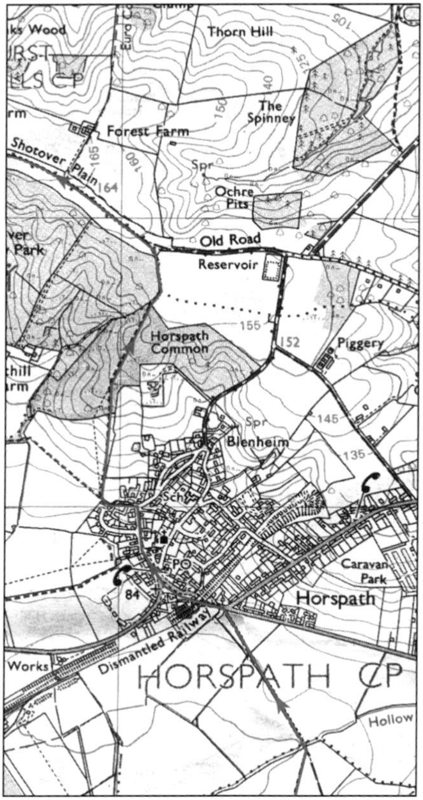

Continue along the village road to Manor Farm, turning left before it to follow a narrow path (the CPRE Green Belt Way) behind the houses to turn right at the field. Climb up the right (E) side of the field, crossing two stiles to arrive at the edge of Shotover Woods. From this point there can be good views of south Oxfordshire. The long ridge of the Berkshire Downs can be seen, the cooling towers of Didcot Power Station, and the twin hills of Mother Dunch's Buttocks near Little Wittenham (see Day 15).

At the woodland edge, turn right uphill then bear left at the next post to follow the Green Belt Way signs.

The soil is an orangey coloured sand that was used to produce the deep red, orange and yellow ochre paints used for the medieval wall paintings at churches such as Ashampstead (see Day 14). Most of the horse-drawn wagons in the 19th century were painted yellow with this local ochre. This sandy slope was also used for practising tank manoeuvres in World War II.

At a crossing path, keep straight ahead uphill, then over another broad track to walk on up to a field ahead. Bear left to walk alongside the woodland edge, and left again onto a wide track (NW). This was the Old Coach Road from London to Oxford, built to take advantage

Horspath Church

This 12th century church is to the right (E) of our route. It has brilliantly-coloured stained glass windows and rare, almost lifesize, carved stone figures on the arch of the bell tower. Its churchyard is designated as a living churchyard and cemetery with 26 different species of wildflowers and plants.

of the drier, high ground. Follow this to the car park. From the car park turn left to go downhill (W) for 200 yards.

Access Point: Shotover Country Park car park, 10.5 miles. GR 564062.

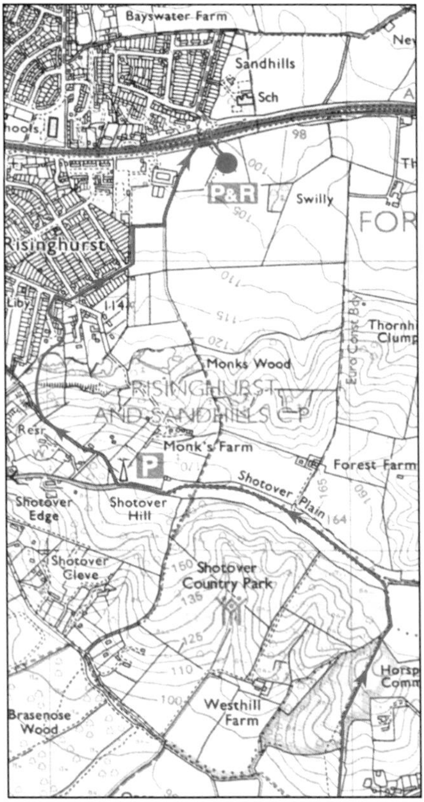

Shotover
An Oxford City Council notice near the car park describes the origin of Shotover as a Saxon forest, which became part of a later Royal hunting forest until the mid-17th century. From a natural history point of view, it is 280 acres of wild countryside with a mixture of wildlife habitats including heathland, woodland and marsh. The sandy soil favours a diversity of species, ranging from a 400-year-old oak tree to rare species of beetles and several hundred varieties of wasps and bees. This makes Shotover Hill a Site of Special Scientific Interest.

150 yards further on, before the descent steepens, turn right (340°) past a telecommunications mast onto a footpath (NW). Go through two metal kissing gates, and past the gateway of a house called 'The Oaks' to continue downhill. Through a gap in the hedge to the right, it is possible to see the TV mast at Beckley. 150 yards beyond the gap, turn right through a metal kissing gate into woodland, now a nature reserve, but formerly the garden of C.S. Lewis' house.

In the wood, bear left at the wooden post marked 'Perimeter Path', walking downhill. At the next kissing gate on the left, keep right on the perimeter path. Bear left on the footpath to descend the slope by a long flight of wooden steps and continue going down hill to a large pool.

Tucked into the bank on the right side is the semi-circular brick 'Narnia' *bench (see box).*

Shotover Hill – a highwaymen's haunt

There is a mounting block (a stepped stone) on the right bank where people remounted their horses or carriages after lightening the load for the horses to climb up the steep slope. This could be risky, as the area on either side of Shotover Plain was a wild and desolate place. In 1739 Charles Wesley's horse went lame near what is now the Crown and Thistle pub, and he was robbed of 30 shillings by highwaymen. In 1760 the Birmingham stagecoach was held up at about 5am by two young fellows in blue close-bodied coats, mounted on black horses. They took about £17 from the passengers, but gave the coachman and postillion a shilling each! In another incident two footpads, disguised in carters' smocked frocks, seized a horse's bridle, clapped a pistol to the rider's chest and took his purse containing over £26. Contented with this sum, they left wishing him a good night. The completion of the Stokenchurch Turnpike in 1775, now the A40, provided a much safer route. (David Steel, *The Natural History of a Royal Forest*, Pisces; 1984.)

Just beyond the pond-dipping platform at the junction of paths, turn left to leave the reserve past a notice board. 'The Kilns' a red-brick house on the left was Lewis' home from 1930–1963. Go to the end of Lewis Close and turn right into Kiln Lane.

Turn left into Grovelands Road and at its end, go through the green park gates, to follow the left-hand (W) perimeter path around two sides of a sports field bordered by a hedge containing big old standard oak trees in it. Go through a metal barrier in the far north-east corner towards the Nielsen buildings. On reaching the main road (A40), turn right (E) and right again into the car park for the Thornhill Park & Ride service.

C.S. Lewis, *Narnia* and *The Lion, the Witch and the Wardrobe*.
'The Kilns', named after the two brick kilns left (S) of the house, is a quiet, private house. For appointments to see round it, telephone 01865 741863. The equally tranquil original clay pits are now part of a nature reserve managed by BBOWT (Berkshire, Buckinghamshire and Oxfordshire Wildlife Trust).
Tel: 01865 775476. www.bbowt.org.uk
By their efforts, it is now possible to sit on the semi-circular brick bench overlooking the pool and imagine *Narnia* as Lewis did. Tolkein, too, visited this woodland which may have provided the inspiration for *Middle Earth*. There may be time to muse here as it is only 0.75 miles to the end of the day's walk. If you wish to visit C.S. Lewis' grave, he is buried at Holy Trinity Church, Headington Quarry, across the bypass 600 yards from our route at GR 555068. The church has a beautiful memorial glass engraved window with *Narnia* as its theme in the church.

'Narnia', C.S. Lewis Nature Reserve, Risinghurst

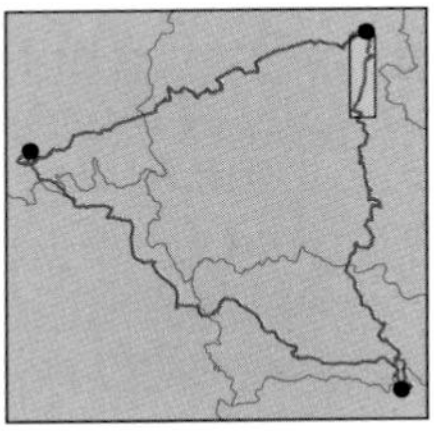

Day 17

Oxford to Alchester

(Wendlebury Gate Stables)

Oxford GR SP 566074 to Wendlebury GR SP 578203

This section goes due north alongside and on the Roman road leading to a major Roman settlement at Alchester. Historians have examined this road; descriptions by Hussey and Margary are vividly detailed. The route crosses Otmoor, well-known for its special beauty as an area of wetland, good for wading birds. The soft mud that the birds like means that, if the water table is high, boots or Wellingtons may be needed. We pass through the small village of Fencott near to the site of a rare surviving example of a Roman timber bridge which crossed the River Ray.

Distance:	10.5 miles (16.8km). N.B. See note about possible increase of 2.5 miles due to diversion on page 203.	
Maps:	Explorer 180 – Oxford, Witney & Woodstock. Explorer 191 – Banbury, Bicester & Chipping Norton. Landranger 164 – Oxford.	
Transport:	Buses	• Thornhill Park & Ride/Oxford city centre. • Beckley/Oxford, 108/118 (limited service). • Gosford/Oddington (200 yards from route)/Fencott/Merton/Bicester, 94 (limited service). Traveline – Tel: 0871 200 2233. www.traveline.org.uk
Taxis:	Oxford	• ABC Taxis. Tel: 01865 770077/775577. • 001 Taxis. Tel: 01865 240000.
	Beckley	• B.R. Cars. Tel: 07742 648900.
	Kidlington	• Sunny Cars. Tel: 01865 373300 or 07900 125321.
	Bicester	• Alpha Cars. Tel: 01869 252552. • Union Cars. Tel: 01869 325325/248248.

Car Parking: Oxford – Thornhill Park & Ride on the east side of the city, south of the A40 (free parking), toilets available.
Wendlebury Gate Stables. (If you use more than three cars for transport, please confirm with staff for a convenient place to park.
Tel: 01869 320665)

Accommodation/Public Houses/Refreshments:

Oxford (Barton) • Underhill Circus shops.
Beckley • Abingdon Arms PH. Tel: 01865 351311.
• Lower Farm B&B. Tel: 01865 358546.
Bicester • Bicester Visitor Centre. Tel: 01869 369055.
www.visit-northoxfordshire.co.uk

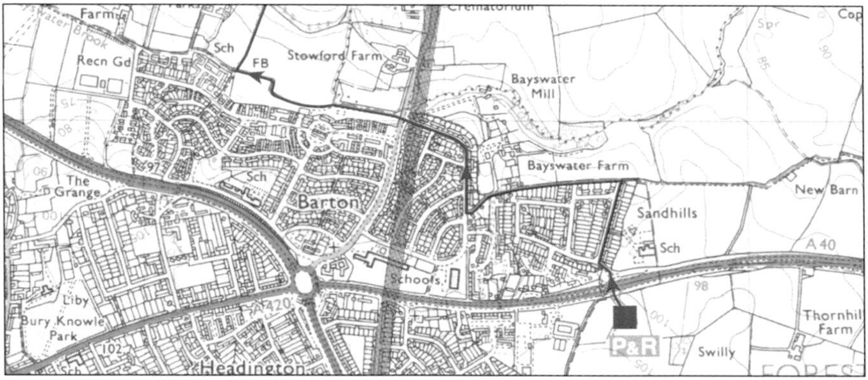

From the car park, walk north to the A40, then immediately turn left and go through the underpass to the other side. Bear left into Merewood Avenue then right into Delbush Avenue to its end, then left (W) along the path separating the city from its rural edge.

There were cows grazing in the field to the north and poplar trees waving in the breeze in the valley of the Bayswater Brook below. A local resident told us that badgers, deer and foxes were seen frequently. This is another area of Green Belt (see Day 16).

In **Barton** (OE bere-tun 'corn farm'), cross the road at Watermill Way (another reminder of this area's history) and continue ahead on the path. Turn right (N) at the next road, Waynflete Road. Cross the main road with care (Bayswater Road) which is the course of the Roman road running north/south. Follow the footpath on the left side of the brook.

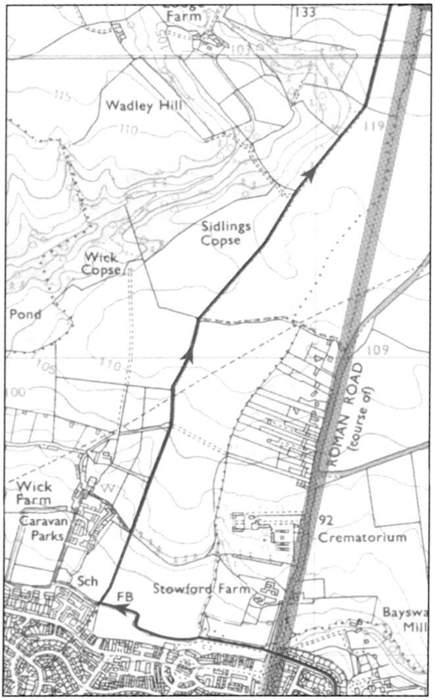

In this part of Barton the houses are prefabricated semi-detached dwellings built from kits provided after World War II, now being painted in a variety of pastel colours. Watercress was growing in the Bayswater Brook, the water of which provided the power to drive the Bayswater Mill nearby; it is a tributary of the River Cherwell. Beside the hedgerow, elderberries, hawthorn and ivy were all in fruit in September.

The footpath passes near the back of Barton Neighbourhood Centre, and nearby there are shops and a post office in Underhill Circus 200 yards from the route. Just after the football pitch, turn right (N) across a footbridge over the brook to begin climbing the hill northwards. The TV mast at Beckley can be seen. At a metal gate into the wood, ignore the path to the left and keep walking north. Wick Farm, to the left (W), is part of the rural landscape.

A great spotted woodpecker flew across our path and a great tit was calling. The soil is very sandy. In the narrow field margin, there is a surprising diversity of plants: mauve dead-nettle, flowering plantain, mare's tail, field scabious, groundsel, yellow hawkbit and agrimony, field pansy, St. John's Wort, white yarrow, columbine, ox-eye daisy, sun spurge and red clover.

At the summit of the hill the soil structure changes and limestone blocks can be seen in the ploughed soil. Just before the end of the field, go past an entrance on the left to Sydlings Copse, a BBOWT nature reserve. On reaching the B4027 road, at the Royal Oak Farm shop, turn right.

The farm is thatched, with a sack-hoist in the gable end. It is a substantial building built of local stone, and was formerly one of four coaching inns on the former London to Worcester road. This was the halfway stage so the Royal Oak, the New Inn, the Red Lion (no longer in existence) and the

White House (further to the east) provided the accommodation and stabling necessary for refreshing passengers and horses.

Walk along the right (S) verge for 100 yards, where, under the hedge opposite the footpath entrance there is a stone marking the boundary of Stow Wood to the north; it is only clearly visible in the winter. Cross the road with care to take a footpath and walk along the east side of Stow Wood beside a woodland bank and ditch. This footpath is on the course of the Roman road.

The hedgerow is old and contains ancient oak trees, hazel, field maple, ash, blackthorn, and hawthorn. In May, we saw a mixture of red campion, white stitchwort and bluebells.

Continue to climb to reach the plateau with good views of Oxford. There was a green woodpecker digging for ants in the sandy soil. On meeting the road, turn left onto New Inn Road (the New Inn was mentioned by Hussey nearly 200 years ago) and cross with care to enter Sand Path (Sand Lane on the OS map, left of a house driveway) to start descending (NE) along this deeply-cut lane.

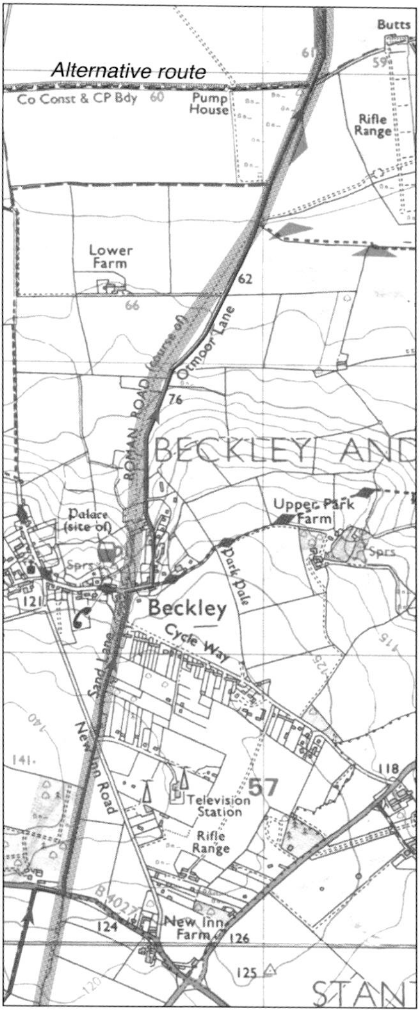

Access Point: Beckley, 3.5 miles. PH, telephone, buses. GR 565112.

At the end of this lane go down the road called 'Roman Way' to meet the village street of **Beckley**. There is an interesting church with medieval wall paintings 350 yards to the left (W).

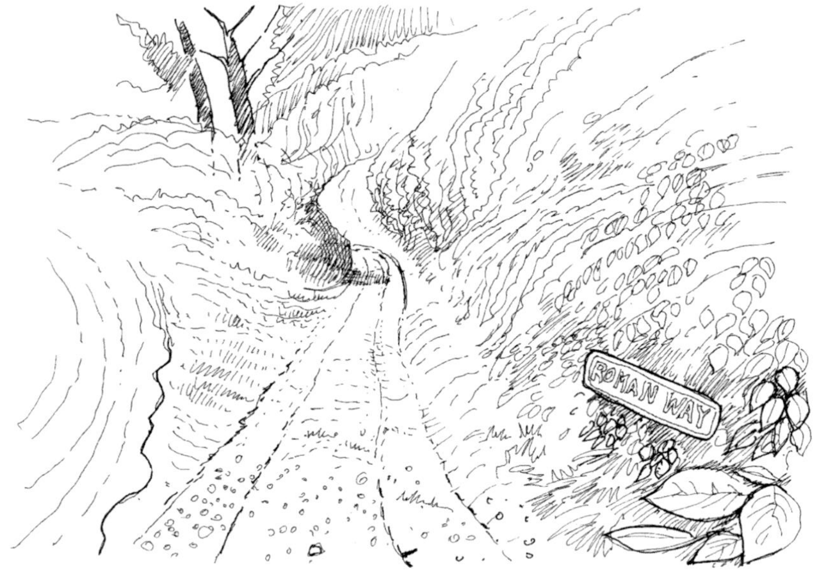

Roman Way, Beckley

Roman roadworks
Both Hussey and Margary comment on this hollow way. It was engineered as a cutting through the highest part of the ridge. They regard it as a remarkable example since it shows first, how the Romans carried a road over a steep hill and second, that it preserves the original dimensions, wide enough for a wagon and wider than some of the streets in Pompeii.

Beckley Palace (see map) was a hunting lodge which was a favourite residence of the Earls of Cornwall in the 13th century. It was probably a wooden building with a smoke hole in the roof as the chimney, not the modern concept of a palace.

Turn right (E) past the pond. Pass the old chapel and Old Manor House. Follow the road as it bends sharp left (N), where it is now Otmoor Lane. At the fork, bear left to keep on the tarmac lane past the 30 mph sign to descend gradually towards Otmoor. Excavations in the garden of the next-to-last house on the left (Middlefield) proved that the

Otmoor as a chessboard

The view north of the small patchwork fields in this low-lying land is reputed to have been the inspiration for Lewis Carroll's chessboard in *Alice Through the Looking-Glass*:

> 'There were a number of tiny little brooks running straight across it from side to side, and the ground between was divided up into squares by a number of little green hedges, that reached from brook to brook.
> "I declare it's marked out just like a large chessboard!" Alice said at last.'

Otmoor Lane

Along the lane in the hedgerow dogwood, hawthorn, sloe and elder were growing, and we saw a robin's pin-cushion (the folk name for bedeguar gall that lives on the briar rose). It is a mossy ball with long thin pink threads where the gall wasp lays eggs in the leaf buds in spring and where, in autumn, small larvae live in cells inside the leaves. Among the flowers were autumnal hawk-weed and common fleabane, a yellow daisy-like flower, which was reputed to repel fleas.

Roman road goes through the garden and is wider there; and it was probably used as a passing place. In the field immediately on the left (W) the line of the Roman road is just visible as a slightly-raised bank. Beyond Otmoor, the square tower of Charlton-on-Otmoor church can be seen to the north.

Where the road goes left into the RSPB car park, leave it to walk north along the green lane. This is once again the course of the 1st century AD Roman road. At its end is a metal gate with Ministry of Defence warning notices. Turn left (W) by the gate for a few yards to see a good view of the Otmoor Nature Reserve. The direct route north across Otmoor is 1.25 miles.

When firing practice is scheduled on the MoD land, a red flag flies or an amber light flashes at the entrance of the rifle range at GR 572129. There is, however, a permissive path that enables walkers to bypass the danger area. For directions, see page 203.

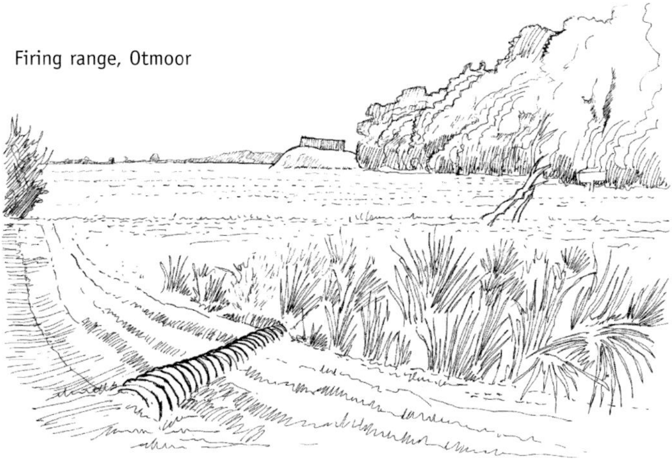

Firing range, Otmoor

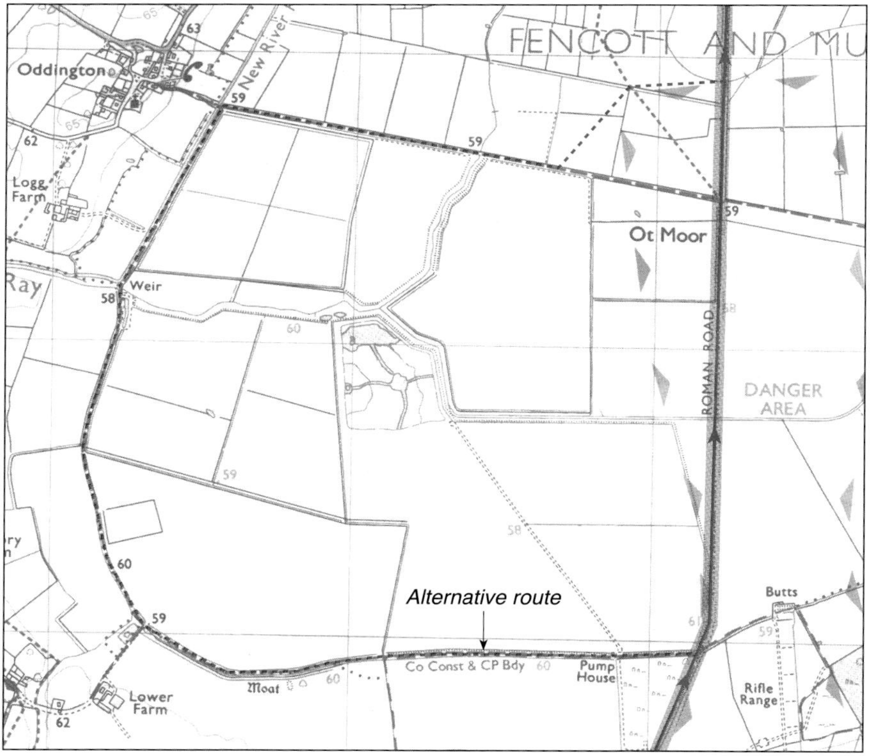

Otmoor: a brief history

In Roman times, the low-lying Otmoor was a large fenland area created by the dendritic (branch-like) river basin of the River Ray. In the 1960s this boggy area was drained for agricultural use, but now, as a result of the RSPB's creation of a nature reserve in 1977 and continued conservation by the MoD, much of the land is reverting to reedbeds, scrapes and wet grassland. In excavations to create scrapes for the wading birds, evidence of both Iron Age smelting and Roman pottery kilns has been found (see Day 16). When the moor was enclosed in 1830, the inhabitants of the seven 'towns' of Otmoor including Beckley, Charlton-on-Otmoor, Fencott, Horton-cum-Studley, Murcott, Noke and Oddington rioted, but all the captive rioters were freed by the crowds attending St. Giles' Fair. The subsequent unease is recorded in part of this old rhyme:

"I went to Noke
But nobody spoke,
I went to Brill
They were silent and still,
But I went to Beckley
They spoke directly."

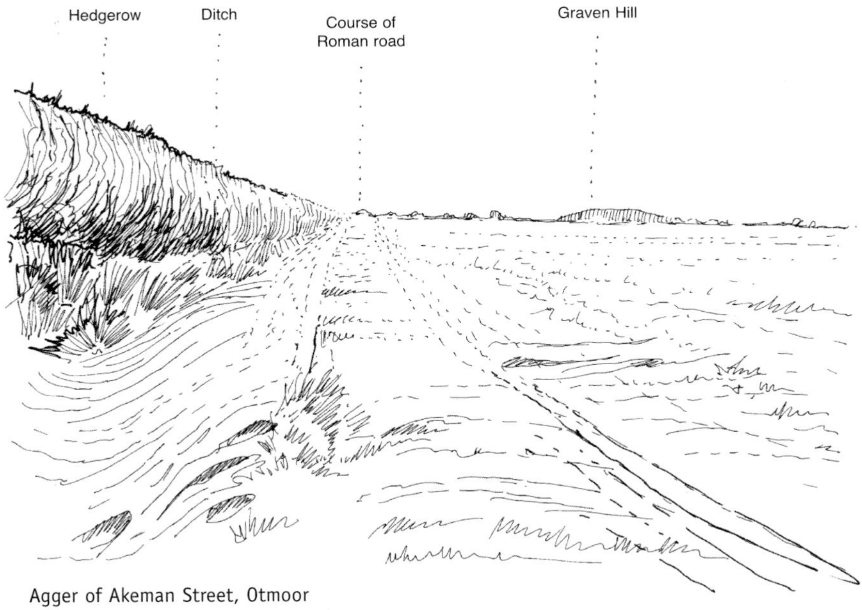

Agger of Akeman Street, Otmoor

The route continues north along the right (E) side of a hedgerow with delicious blackberries in September, to reach a small ditch and pond with reed mace (bulrushes) growing. Cross the concrete bridge over a ditch and into the next field where, although the bridleway is marked beside the fence, it is impossible to follow due to the boggy area. Instead, a path has been cut 200 yards right in a semicircular route (E) around the bog. Aim for a white MoD post on the northern boundary of the field. At the next metal gate and crossing of bridleways (GR 572145), continue north for 300 yards past another MoD post.

Among the tussocky, wet grass we heard the burbling call of curlew, saw lapwing, heron and skylarks and the zig-zag flight of snipe. Further on there is a big hedgerow on the left with wild hops growing in September.

Wild hops

This bridleway is a broad green track bordered by willows and thick hedges with wild hops growing in them. The leaves of wild hops are large and lobed rather like vine leaves, but the part of the plant that is used by brewers to add flavour to bitter beer is the cone or fruit. The cones are clusters of light-brown, papery petals that hang from the twigs.

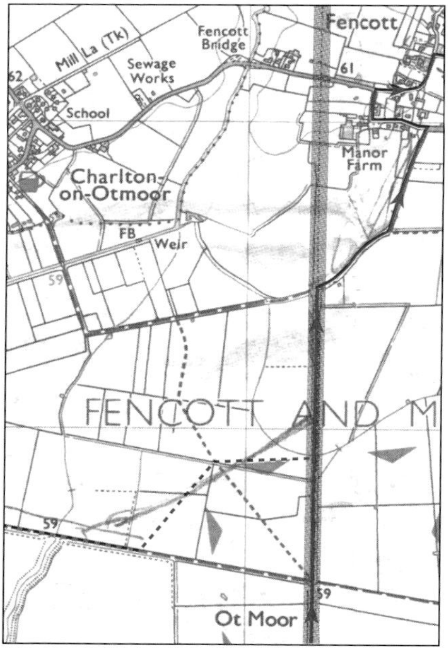

Diversion west and north around Otmoor.

If there is shooting in progress and therefore no access, it is necessary to make a diversion west and north around Otmoor. This diversion adds 2.5 miles to Day 17, making the overall distance 13 miles. Usually the direct path is open on Mondays and Thursdays (to confirm, telephone 01865 358995). The advantages of this diversion are the extensive views of the RSPB reserve with opportunities for watching birds and butterflies and seeing wild flowers along the route.

Directions: at the boundary of the MoD shooting range (GR 572129), turn left (W) on the bridleway following the Visitors' Trail. Ignore the turnings right (N) and left (S) unless wishing to visit the hides by the reed-beds and scrapes. Follow the track (W) for about a mile, to a bridge and concrete pump houses, part of the control system for keeping the water table for the reserve stable.

The bridleway starts to turn right and goes north. The village of Noke can be seen to the left (W). Further on, Islip's square church tower with its pinnacles can be seen (W). After another mile, cross the modern weir over the River Ray. Continue (NE) for 700 yards to a track that goes west to the village of Oddington.

Access point: Oddington, 7.25 miles. On the verge, a few yards north of the telephone box, (200 yards from route). Buses. GR 553148.

If not diverting to Oddington, turn sharp right (SE) and continue for nearly 0.75 miles. The tower of Charlton-on-Otmoor church can be seen to the left (N). Go along a green lane (which can be very waterlogged) to a red and white notice (GR 567146) that states 'When barrier is closed, use alternative route'. Here there is a permissive footpath to the left, avoiding the Danger Area.

Turn left to go through a metal kissing gate and walk diagonally right (NE, 015°) across the field to a white flagpole in the corner. Go through a pair of small metal gates, across the footbridge into another field, to turn sharp right (E, 090°) along the left (N) side of the hedgerow. An MoD notice tells you to keep left of the red and white posts. Go through the kissing gate by a large gate and the tall white pole, to turn left (N) and rejoin the bridleway and the route of the Roman road at GR 572149.

Follow the track for 350 yards to where it turns right (NE) as it turns away from the course of the Roman road, then follow it as it bears left to reach the village of **Fencott**. On reaching the road, turn left past 'The Rickyard' and sharp right around the corner.

The thatched Corner Farm, which was previously 'The Ramping Cat' pub, has a rabbit in thatch over the porch door.

After 100 yards, turn right along Black Bull Lane (so named because it used to lead to the Black Bull pub). Continue on to Black Bull Cottage on the left, then turn right opposite (SE) along Bull's Lane.

A grisly tale

The iron railings of Manor Farm originally had spear-like points. However, an unfortunate cyclist misjudged the tightness of the corner, was thrown off his bicycle and was impaled on the railings. Shortly afterwards, the railings were fitted with rounded hoops!

Manor Farm, Fencott

One of the houses along this lane is still thatched, but further on others (Village Farm House and Ivy Farm) with their steeply-pitched roofs to ensure a quick run-off of rain, show that they also used to be thatched.

Access Point: Fencott, Black Bull Lane, 6.75 miles. Buses. GR 576162.

Continue to the end of this path, then turn sharp left (N) onto a track called Newgate Road. This track leads over a bridge crossing the M40 motorway from where there are good views to **Merton** village (NW), Arncott Hill (NE), Muswell Hill (SE) and the low Street Hill (W), GR 572168, so called because the Roman road goes over it.

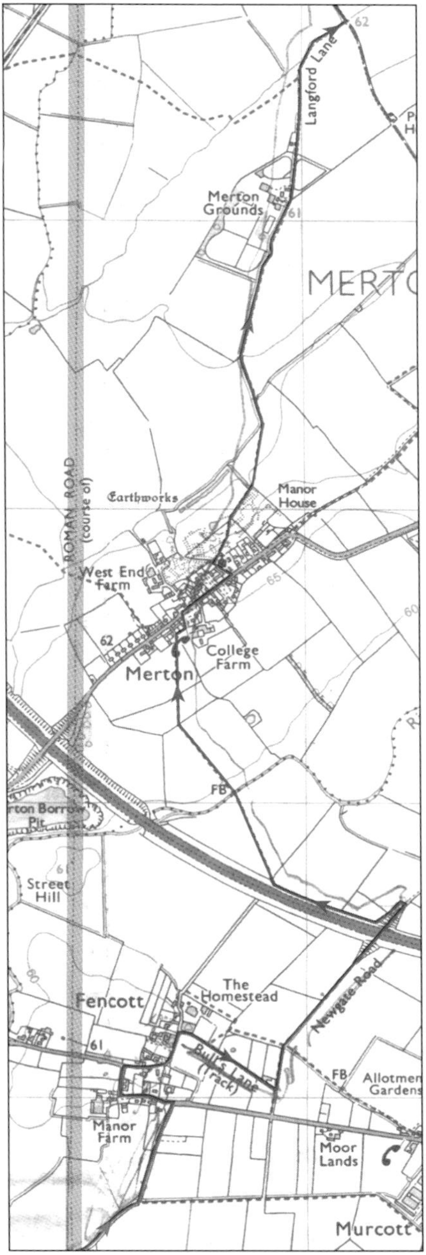

A Roman timber bridge

In 1979, while the River Ray on the north side of Street Hill was being dredged, several oak piles (posts) from a Roman timber bridge were uprooted. An archaeological excavation that followed found a further line of piles which had survived undisturbed. Two of the four timber piles measured 1.3 metres long by 0.4 metres square. Each had been sawn to a point. The overall width of the bridge was about 4.5 metres (15 feet) (*Oxoniensia*, LI; 1986).

Turn left down the steps (NW) and left along a concrete track beside the motorway to a metal field gate and stile. Cross the field diagonally right (NW, 335°) aiming for a white waymark post in the first hedge boundary, and beyond that to the centre of the village buildings. The path leads over a footbridge crossing the River Ray flowing towards Otmoor (SW).

Continue in the same direction but slightly more to the left (320°) to an electricity pole: the two hedge boundaries shown on the map no longer exist. 100 yards after the electricity pole, bear further right (N, 004°) aiming for the field corner near the houses. On reaching this, go over a stile to walk (NW) between houses to the village street. Turn right past the now-closed Plough Inn and the telephone box. Continue along the main street past Forge Close to the church where there is a footpath sign pointing left (NW).

Access Point: Merton church, 8.7 miles. Telephone, buses. GR 577177.

Turn right (NW) out of the churchyard, then almost immediately right through a gap in the wall. After a few yards, go right through a kissing gate in the hedge. Cross a small field (NE). Walk diagonally across the field, to turn right between the hedge and fence behind the large manor house (now a nursing home).

In May, the small field was shoulder high with a white forest of cow parsley, and in August it was filled with thistledown and swifts with their forked tails flying low over the seeds. There is now no trace of the former moat of the Manor House marked 'Earthworks' on the OS map. However, the groups of reeds in the field on the left (N) are all that is left of the medieval 'stew' ponds that provided fish for the manor.

Merton Church

This church is dedicated to St. Swithun (800–862), who was Bishop of Winchester. His body was translated (moved) from his grave outside the cathedral to a tomb inside on July 15th 971 whereupon it rained for 40 days. The saint was said to have disapproved of the move! In the outside walls are pieces of Roman tiles scavenged from Alchester nearby. There has been a church on this site since Saxon times when the village was called 'Mere tun' or 'lake farm', situated on this low ridge of high ground above the floodplain of the River Ray.

At the stile (by a notice about a permissive path) go diagonally left (N, 010°) to the projecting left field corner, so cutting across the left-hand corner of the field. From here follow the right side of the hedgerow (N). Do not turn right along the first hedge, but instead follow the track (NW, 340°) called Langford Lane, to curve right (N, 018°) towards the large, white-roofed barn at Merton Grounds. At the farm buildings of Merton Grounds, continue (N) onto a track beneath an avenue of poplar trees.

Langford Lane has a multi-specied hedge producing delicious wild damsons in September, hawthorn, hazel, field maple and guelder rose.

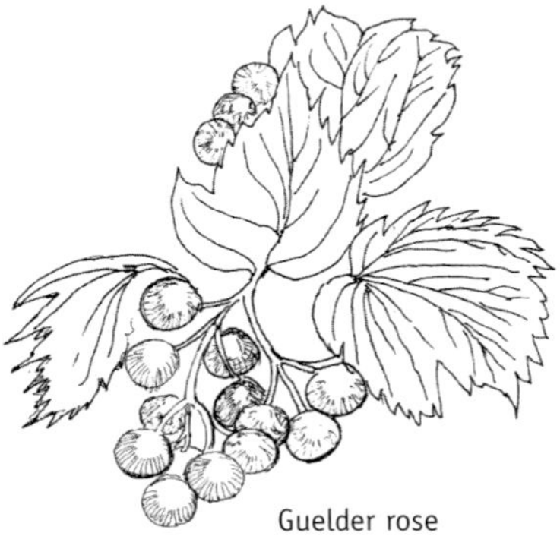

Guelder rose

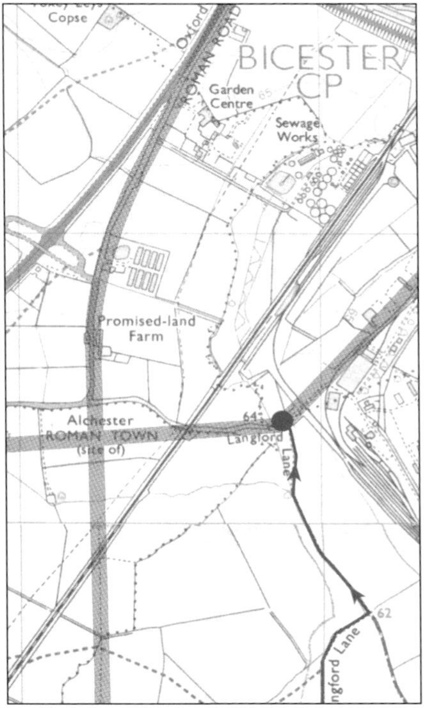

Merton Grounds

The word 'ground' refers to the large-scale enclosures made for sheep farming in the open fields in the late Middle Ages. As the population declined after the Black Death, farmers switched to less labour-intensive sheep farming: another example of farmers needing to diversify. The curious high, angled shape of the original farmhouse is one of only a few remaining examples of its kind in this area.

Keep on the asphalt track for 600 yards to turn left (NW) at the T-junction of tracks. This is a bridleway beside another old hedge bordering a ditch where wild hop, young elm trees and dogwood grow. Continue on the track to the Wendlebury Gate stables where Akeman Street enters Alchester from the east and the end of the Roman Way.

Alchester Roman fort

On looking through the hedge to the left (W), the flat field of the former Roman parade ground of Alchester marching camp (OE Ald-caester, the old camp) can be seen (GR 578202). This area was about 360 square yards, designed for the encampment of a single legion of at least 4,000–5,000 infantry and 200–300 cavalry. The significance of this fortress has been fully described by Eberhard Sauer and others. Although excavations have been completed here and military equipment found, it is now a wildflower meadow, part of the Environmentally Sensitive Areas (ESA) scheme. The owner of this private land told us that birds such as snipe, wheatear, moorhen, skylark and raptors, such as buzzards and kestrels, thrive in this habitat.

Alchester Roman fortress (Reconstruction drawing, after D. Miles-Williams)

We have walked the route four times, each in different seasons.
We hope you enjoy the days as much as we did.